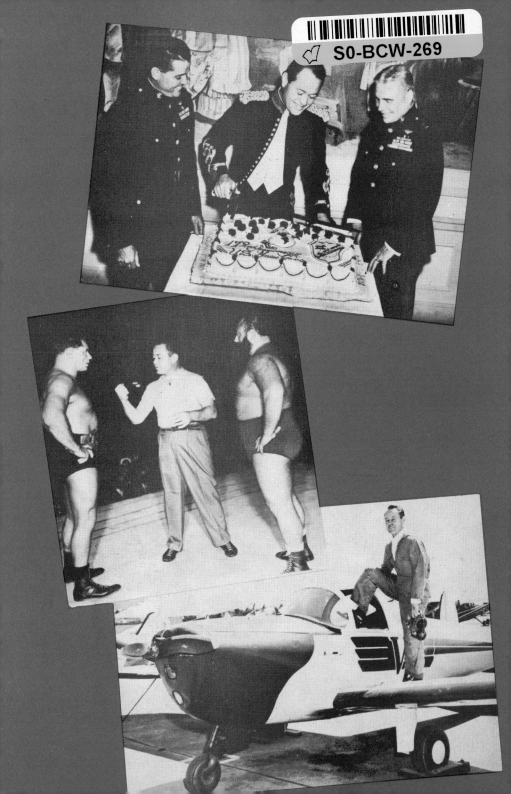

BAA BAA BLACK SHEEP

Frontispiece photo by Douglas Q. White

BAA
BAA
BLACK
SHEEP

By "PAPPY" BOYINGTON

(*Col. Gregory Boyington, USMC, Ret.*)

G. P. PUTNAM'S SONS • NEW YORK

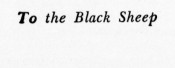

To the Black Sheep

ACKNOWLEDGMENTS

Twelve years ago Max Miller helped me to get started on the manuscript of this book. During the ten years that followed I was in no shape to do much work on it, and it seemed unlikely there would ever be a happy ending of any sort until I met my wife, Frances, whose loyalty and confidence have made all the difference.

I also want to express my appreciation to Eloise O'Brien, who suggested the title.

BAA BAA BLACK SHEEP

CHAPTER 1

Two years ago I got back into flying after an absence of thirteen years. Everyone was very helpful, and many friends put aside their own work to help me get started once again as a pilot.

The flight surgeon who gave me the necessary physical was most obliging, although he didn't know me from a hot rock. A pilot who runs a ground school tutored me for a week, so I was able to pass a written test for an instrument rating, and another pilot who owns a flying school let me fly a few hours for practically nothing. Then I passed a blind-flying check. A local aircraft distributor even paid me a few dollars while I was busy getting some up-to-date flying hours for my ratings.

Two months from the day I discovered I could pass a second-class airman's physical examination, I was all set to go. Multiengine planes, commercial and instrument, were on my flight certificate.

The amazing thing about it all is that the rust wore off in no time at all, as though I had never been away from flying. Getting accustomed to instruments I had never used before didn't give me the slightest bit of trouble. But this is understandable, because, after all, for ten years or more flying was one of the few things to hold my interest for any length of time.

11

In the beginning I was uneasy about the conversation with the control towers and CAA Communications. But this ironed itself out soon, and they gave all the co-operation I needed when I called and told them that I was a "new boy."

At my age it was difficult to get a flying job with an airline, even if you had a good record, but, fortunately, I soon found a flying job. An air-freight company in Burbank permitted me to use their executive five-passenger plane for charter. The airline didn't pay my salary; I was given a commission of part of the charter business I sold. In return for this privilege I piloted for the company officials and their guests at times free of charge. This was okay with me, because it was wonderful to fly again. I was chartered by business people, motion-picture actors, or just about anyone who wanted to go anywhere and was willing to pay sixty dollars per hour.

The airline hangar at the Lockheed Air Terminal is only a matter of five minutes or so from our three-bedroom house, almost in the center of the San Fernando Valley. The direction of the prevailing take-off pattern from Lockheed takes planes directly over us day and night. When friends drop in from other parts of the city, they can't seem to understand how we put up with the racket. They probably don't stop to think that this particular noise is music to me. The take-offs are no bother to anyone in our house, not even our basset hound, Alvin, who has very sensitive ears. But far more important than not being bothered is that I feel close to all those flight crews as they go over.

My flying job led to a sales engineering position with Coast Pro-Seal, a manufacturer of aircraft sealants that supplies the aviation industry all over the country. My flying is limited to weekends and business trips. But whether I fly or do other things, I seem to run across many people I have flown with in the past. Many of the things we joke about today were at one time very serious matters indeed. We do not forget they made the difference between life or death, nor do we forget the hardships and the mental anguish we went through.

At least once each year, sometimes more often, a group of around twenty of us meet here in the valley for dinner. Some are pilots. Others are ex-pilots. And some are men who had a knack for keeping aircraft flying. Most of these people are in their early forties now.

There has always been a great deal of talk about these men since they first became acquainted, but there are very few people who know how they got together in the first place. Few know them by anything but a legendary name—the Flying Tigers.

CHAPTER **2**

THE NAME FLYING TIGERS was unknown to us when we were quartered in an obscure hotel in downtown San Francisco, waiting for a Dutch motorboat that would transport us to the Orient to join the AVG, the American Volunteer Group. The word "volunteer" reminded me of the Marine Corps sergeant who said: "Never volunteer and you will stay out of trouble."

I had answered: "Don't worry, Sarge. I understand, and I'll never forget your advice." Yet, here I was, not only a volunteer, but a member of a volunteer group.

Europe was already embroiled in war, but apparently the United States was in no immediate danger. We knew very little about Franklin Roosevelt's dealings with the rest of the world —and we were not supposed to know, because it was only September 1941. We did know we were to be paid in good old United States dollars, the money to be deposited in a New York bank for us at the end of each month while we were in China. Of course China would owe the American taxpayers for this money, but meanwhile the Nationalist Government could play big shot.

The pilots and ground crews were recruited secretly from the Army Air Corps, Navy, and Marine Corps. Two detachments of pilots and crews were already over in China doing

14

business, I was told. I understood that I was to be in the third detachment to go overseas, but I had no idea that the third was also going to be the last.

A World War I flyer, a retired Army Air Corps captain, breezed around different flying bases here in the United States, recruiting people he counted on having the necessary qualifications. If a pilot or ground crewman signified his intention to go, from there on everything was handled through Washington, D.C.

When I first learned about this deal, I was an instructor at the Naval Air Station at Pensacola, Florida. I was a regular first lieutenant in the Marine Corps with six years of flying experience, most of it in fighters.

The captain never approached me. I got in touch with him. He tried to tell me that any number of the pilots had twenty years of combat experience under their belts. After thumbing back over aviation history in my mind I wondered where in hell these jokers were supposed to have gotten all this experience.

He added: "The Japs are flying antiquated junk over China. Many of your kills will be unarmed transports. I suppose you know that the Japanese are renowned for their inability to fly. And they all wear corrective glasses."

"Captain, it's quite a setup, but how do you know the pilots wear glasses?"

"Our technical staff determines this from the remains after a shoot-down. I haven't mentioned this before because I thought you would be more interested in the flying end, but we have some of the most skilled technicians in the world in the Group. Furthermore, our aircraft will be the latest off the drawing boards. We already have aircraft factories going night and day right there in China. Best of all, there's good money in it—six hundred seventy-five dollars per month. But the sky's the limit, because they pay a bonus of five hundred for each Japanese aircraft you knock down."

And there I sat, taking it all in, mentally calculating how wealthy I would be.

The captain could squeeze me in tentatively as a flight leader

15

—because of all my experience, he said. And with all the ability I told him about he said I would soon be a squadron leader. Somehow, I had the feeling I had to lie in self-defense in order to get along with this Group he was talking about.

The captain tried to impress me with the high character of the men who were to be over me and under me. They were people who drank like gentlemen and paid their gambling debts. Bravery above and beyond the call of duty was dripping all over his suite in the San Carlos Hotel there at Pensacola.

Maybe the dear captain did have all these high ideals, God rest his soul. Maybe he wanted them all for this dream group but had to settle for less. I don't know.

But one thing for certain, I didn't tell him that he was hiring an officer who had a fatal gap between his income and accounts payable. And because of this situation I had to account by mail to Marine Corps Headquarters each month how much money was being paid on each debt. Nor did I tell him that I was a whiz at a cocktail party.

All this spelled but one thing, I would be passed over for the rank of captain in the USMC, as surely as I was sitting there in the San Carlos. I had to convince the captain—and I did.

An unannounced resignation went through the Marine Corps four days later. This resignation was clipped to a lengthy agreement of reinstatement without loss of precedence, if I survived, or if the United States declared war. These papers were to be kept in Admiral Nimitz's secret safe. In short order I was handed a passport with a horrible picture in it, labeled, "member of the clergy."

All this was wrapped up one week after I first met our recruiting captain. The night I started to pack, I thought I'd better go into the bar, which happened to be adjacent to my quarters in B.O.Q. It seemed necessary to make a hero's farewell to some of the student officers I had been guiding through flight school, helping them to get their coveted wings of gold.

Naturally I didn't keep my big mouth shut. The captain's utopian air force was topped as each round of bourbon was being shaken for by a dice cup. I excused myself from this wonderful company only twice during the entire evening. The first time I had to go to my quarters and feed my dog, Fella, a rather large mixture of collie and shepherd. It was against regulations to have dogs or women in your quarters, but that was where I kept Fella when I slept. In the daytime the dog was out at Squadron II, where I instructed and checked students eight flights a day for one hour each, five days a week. He knew what airplane I took off in with each student, because he followed us out to the flight line. These airplanes were all the same color, yellow, and the only difference was the numbers on their sides. So I don't know how the dog could recognize mine, but he did.

I was told that the dog always lay under my desk until our "Yellow Peril," as these trainers were called, came back from a flight and was pulling up to the flight line. Then he would be all wags, standing below our cockpits, while the student and I climbed out. He never had to be cautioned about the propellers. After a few pats on the head the dog would follow us into the ready-room and to my desk. I would explain a number of things to the student and make entries of progress in his flight log.

Many people wondered why the dog and I were so inseparable. As I look back on this, I realize that I was down to my last friend.

During this last week my boss, who was one swell fellow, spoke to me as he walked by my desk, leaning down at the same time to pet Fella. The dog growled, which was unusual, and the hair stood up on the back of his neck.

Commander "Chink" Lee laughed and said: "Why don't you teach your dog the proper respect for your commanding officer? That's no way to get a good fitness report."

"My dog's a hell of a lot smarter than I'll ever be. He probably already knows what you put in my fitness report."

Chink flushed, then added: "You'd better not take that mutt to China, because if you do they'll eat him."

"No, I'm not going to, but I can tell you one thing for sure, he's going to be the only one around here that I'm going to miss."

When I excused myself from my drinking buddies the second time that farewell evening, I took care of my packing. All of

17

my earthly possessions consisted of my uniforms and civilian clothes. There were about three thousand dollars' worth of khaki, blues, whites, mess dress, full dress, and sword. This was not an excess of uniforms prior to World War II. They were required by regulation, but what little I had paid on them in the last five years hadn't made a dent in their original cost. All of the uniforms went on the floor and the back seat of my sedan. Civilian clothes, except those I was wearing, went on top of the heap. This way I knew the dog and I wouldn't be crowded in the front seat.

After packing I returned to the bar and was given the hero's farewell, no doubt the first one since the Marines last fought in Nicaragua. Finally Fella and I were ready to start for the West Coast, but it wasn't until after the Negro bartender said: "Closin' time, gentlemun, that's all for tonight."

My parents came down to San Francisco from their apple ranch near Okanogan, Washington, to say good-by and pick up my car. My mother tried to talk me out of going on such a wild-goose chase. She said: "There are other ways of paying off one's indebtedness."

My answer was: "Oh, don't worry, Mom, I'll get by okay. I haven't got an enemy in the world."

A feeling of remorse came when I saw Fella standing on the clothes and uniforms, looking out the rear window as my mother and father drove off for Okanogan. The dog seemed to be saying: "Why are you leaving me? What have I done wrong?"

Most of the pilots waiting to go overseas were two or three years younger than I was, and they had virtually no flying experience other than what they had received in flight school. Some I recognized as recent graduates from Pensacola. There was only one thing to believe, naturally; all of the vast experience was already in China.

Another thing, these pilots were taking their golf sticks, tennis rackets, and dress clothes. I guessed they were proper in doing this, because the captain had said: "You will be gentlemen in every sense of the word. Wherever you are stationed, you will have an interpreter who will act as a valet."

Of course I didn't know anything about the Orient, other than what little I had learned in school. And I didn't believe that the United States would ever be at war. But I did stop to realize that anyone with twenty years of combat experience, which means something in most businesses, would have been buried for almost eighteen years. Come to think about it, the underwriters were making book on seven years for military pilots at this time. In addition, their actuarial figures didn't have a damn thing to do with getting shot at in the bargain.

And again, I must have been dragging on an opium pipe when Dr. Margaret Chung, of San Francisco, gave each pilot a jade charm on a silver chain to wear about his neck, and said: "You are now one of my many sons. I pronounce you Fair-haired Bastard Number——"

Later the pilots referred to their charms, because they couldn't remember the Chinese words, as "The Jade Balls."

We stayed in the little-known hotel for a very good reason, but conserving money didn't happen to be it. How in hell the press never got the early scoop is beyond me! There must have been a minimum of ten bars in each square block in downtown San Francisco, and each of us was in every one of them during the two weeks, as had been the two detachments that preceded us. There was the captain, too, in uniform, with his prized "La-Fayette Escadrille," extra pair of wings, adorning the lower part of his blouse, which was the proper place to wear such an honor.

Nobody seemed to know who we were, where we were going, or anything else, and apparently didn't give a damn.

CHAPTER **3**

EX-CAPTAIN CURTIS SMITH of the United States Marine
Corps Reserve was in charge of our detachment. Our recruiting
captain had placed him in command, for he himself was remaining in the United States. Smith was thirty-five years old
and had held the highest rank previously.

Smith had plotted the entire trip in minute military fashion,
although we were no longer military men. He had planned
duties, watches, and even disciplinary measures. When Smith
insisted on numerous occasions in gathering us together in
platoon front and calling roll, he would address us in the most
formal military manner. His bluest of blue eyes reflected like
sapphires in the sunlight as he would go into his "Halls of
Montezuma to the Shores of Tripoli" act. The act was delivered
in a strong, clear voice from Georgia. I thought at the time,
and still do, "What a ham—what a ham."

Jesus, how I dreaded Smith's formations. I had counted on
getting away from it all when I resigned, and hoped for something better instead of something worse. How happy I'd be
when the trip was over, and I no longer had to listen to him.

Smith had been at Pensacola, where I instructed. After years
in the business world he had just completed a refresher course,
and he took the AVG job more seriously than any new Annapo-

lis graduate would have. Standing there, trying to fit Smith somewhere into the future picture, I found myself worrying for the first time.

Smith undoubtedly made me a little envious, too. He gave the impression of refinement, a department in which I was lacking, but I gave Smith credit for opening my eyes to the fact that a few, himself included, were not going for the remuneration alone. They were going to free the world for democracy, and were willing to give their lives if necessary. And, funny as it may seem, after a lengthy session in his cabin, one lonely blacked-out night at sea, he damn near had me convinced. Looking back, I think that he might have convinced me at that —if he hadn't run out of whisky.

When we left San Francisco, I knew that I was trying to escape my own common-sense reasoning. If this was strictly a service deal, our mission to further democracy didn't quite gel. And I knew it. Hell's bells, I was twenty-eight years old. I knew that the people I was traveling with couldn't possibly be as different as night and day from those waiting for us to join them. Everything should have been clear to me then, but it wasn't. American citizens were getting so much a head on us. Just the same as cattle. The two ingredients necessary to accomplish this human sale were greedy pilots and a few idealists.

The taxicab stopped at Pier 40. When I arrived, some of my mates were carrying their belongings aboard ship. While Smith was paying the cabdriver, I took an inquisitive glance at the stern of this lady who would lug us halfway around the world. "*Bosch Fontein*, Batavia," was in large letters on the stern. The name meant nothing to me, other than that it was Dutch. I don't recall ever asking what it stood for.

My concern for Smith's formations left me as I walked slowly along the pier from the stern to the bow. Perhaps this came from a habit I had acquired in aviation of always walking completely around an airplane before climbing aboard.

It was midmorning when I boarded the *Bosch Fontein*, home port Batavia, Java, wherever that was. Carl, a three-hundred-pound mess steward, explained to me later that the home port used to read "Amsterdam." They had to change the home

21

port because the Germans had occupied their fatherland. The entire ship's crew had families in occupied territory.

On many an evening I was with these Dutch crewmen sipping Bols Gin, which was their drink, listening to their tales of home and the rest of the world I hadn't yet seen. They were gentle, friendly people. There wasn't enough they could do for us. It was amazing, hearing these Dutch damn England with a far greater hatred than they had for the Germans who occupied their homeland, their loved ones practically in slavery. England was considered the basic cause for all this trouble.

The lunch, with a choice of numerous entrees, was enjoyed by all. We were informed that this Dutch motorboat had a bar but that it didn't open until we passed the three-mile limit. The first meal was not just put on to make an impression, for the quality and quantity continued throughout the lengthy voyage.

The pilots had been having quite a ball in San Francisco, telling anyone interested in listening that they were missionaries. And we were equally loquacious in telling our new shipmates, approximately sixty people we had never seen before. During our first conversations these lovely people listened attentively, refraining from talking about themselves.

At my table were two men and a woman doctor. But what I did not know, not until after I finished shooting my mouth off, was that the other three members of my table were honest-to-goodness missionaries. And furthermore, there were fifty-five of them aboard—men and women. How phony I felt. My orders on what to say, my passport, couldn't possibly cover my feeling of embarrassment. If only I had let them talk first!

Sixteen hundred, the *Bosch Fontein* was ready to pull out. The recruiting captain, immaculate in a fresh uniform, presented Smith with a packet of sealed orders. He shook hands with us, placing an arm around each, telling us how badly he wanted to go overseas with us.

The *Bosch Fontein* was fast for a combination freighter-passenger. She was doing about sixteen knots. As we stood on deck, looking up and back at the Golden Gate Bridge, we knew that we were finally on our way. By 1730 we had progressed beyond the three-mile limit, so the ship's cocktail lounge was opened. Our twenty-seven gathered together in the ship's lounge, which was to become our headquarters. Here we were occupied comparing notes upon our newly found traveling companions.

We were trying to figure out how a clergyman gag would stick with a gang of long-hairs, like we thought these people were. What would we tell them? Or should we merely clam up and be the strong, silent type?

There happened to be three strangers in the bar. One I judged immediately to be a pilot because his eyes had crow's-feet clear back to his ears. And his blue eyes—too blue to be described—peered out under half-closed lids.

I had noticed this same man all day out of the corner of my eye before the ship sailed. He had been always walking by, as if trying to listen in on our conversation. A German spy maybe, because I darn sure didn't know German from Dutch. And over to our table he came, saying: "Mind if I join you? I'm Bob Heising."

"What is the dope, boys?" he asked. "Where are you going? What kind of a deal have they got you on?"

"There isn't any deal," we tried to answer. "We are members of the clergy. Just what it says on our passports."

"Oh, hold on a minute," he laughed. "Let me in on the dope. I know pilots when I see them. I myself am going over to fly for KLM Airlines in Java."

"No, no, we are not pilots," we repeated, remembering our orders.

"Oh, now, come on, give me the dope." He laughed again. "I have drunk myself out of enough jobs around the world to give you all a job."

"But, no, we are not pilots," we tried to say again.

But again Heising laughed: "When I see an Army Air Corps officer with LaFayette Escadrille wings on the bottom of his jacket, and practically kissing you all good-by at San Francisco, you can't tell me you are a bunch of clergymen."

What the hell was the use, trying to kid a guy like Heising and being ridiculous? The answer: we didn't. The idea that if you can't lick them then join them came in handy.

Bob Heising filled us with tall tales from practically all over the world. He told us about nearly getting killed one time in Mexico City when he and a couple other Americans went to see a bullfight, the reason being that they had persisted in shouting: *"Viva el toro"* all through the performance.

Bob enlightened me on the fact that the pay we were getting was inadequate. The Dutch were paying pilots two thousand dollars per month. In defense I threw back: "How about the bonus of five hundred per shoot-down?"

"Man, have you got rocks in your head for brains?" he inquired. "Or did you spend too long in the ring?" He obviously noticed the scar tissue above my eyes. Bob definitely started me thinking when he told me a different side of the equipment we were going up against. He said: "All Japs don't wear thick glasses, if any glasses at all. Hell, they wear clear goggles, the same as you do, dope." Right then I commenced dividing my financial future by denominators of varying size.

At this time German submarines were knocking off shipping, but the *Bosch Fontein's* crew was thoroughly trained in evasive maneuvers. Our pilots, too, stood watches in the crow's-nest to help make the situation safer if possible. The voyage had its scares. Several times we spotted smoke on the horizon. One time I thought the *Bosch Fontein* was going completely over because her skipper turned the ship so sharply.

From sundown to sunset all ports were closed. No lighting of matches on deck was permitted. All garbage was saved until sunset, then tossed overboard, so that the ship would be a whole night's run away from any submarine spotting the debris the following morning.

Of course it took very little time before these genuine missionaries realized that we were traveling under false colors and weren't missionaries at all. But the manner by which they let us know that they knew was done rather cleverly—not in the Heising manner.

One day one of the real missionaries came up and asked if I would give the sermon for next Sunday's services, explaining that the duty was rotated. I had to decline the invitation to lead the services. But I wish now that I had gone ahead and given it

24

anyway, because then—today—I could say: "Well, I've done everything now."

As it was, the same missionary invited me to the next Sunday service aboard ship. He was one of the younger missionaries, and he himself gave the sermon. But as he did so (I was seated in one of the first rows) he seemed to direct the entire sermon at me and at the group I represented. His point was how horrible it was for people to fight for money.

This sermon did leave an impression on my soul, lasting for a couple of hours, at least. Then I went back into the old routine of boredom and practical jokes with the other pilots: Three weeks at sea with ex-Captain Smith's unnecessary regimentation, as I recall, had commenced getting on others' nerves as well as my own, and one evening a couple of the pilots were putting up a mock fight in the dimly lighted ship's corridor next to the bar. The fight sounded authentic enough. But I knew that it was a sham when Dick Rossi ran into the bar, pleading for help. Dick winked at me when I offered assistance, so I nodded, and then deliberately lagged behind. Smith officiously stomped from the well-lighted bar and into the corridor where the action was taking place. He held the two ruffians apart by the scruffs of their necks. A third party, unknown to me, planted a well-timed right on Smith's eye.

Poor Smith would have held a general court-martial right then and there, and said so, if there had been sufficient military-court experience among us. But unfortunately none of us had ever sat on a court-martial of any type. And again, the dear captain couldn't possibly try twenty-six pilots. No one seemed to know who had committed the dastardly act.

Four weeks out the tension mounted still higher, as we were unescorted and zigzagging all over the Pacific Ocean, it seemed. The pilots had begun to snarl at each other in earnest. A few had lost too much in card games. As for the others, I never knew what went on in their heads.

One day when I was in the ship's doctor's office having a bothersome wart removed from my elbow, two pilots brought in the bloody and unconscious form of Bob Prescott. The doctor was in the middle of his cutting on my elbow when Bob

25

came to and realized where he was. Bob reeled and started out of the door, saying: "Just hold everything, Doc."

"Vait vun minute. I fix you next," the Dutch doctor called to Bob.

But Bob left, saying: "Just wait here, Doc. I'm going out and bring you another customer."

At that particular moment I didn't know what he meant by that, but I didn't have to wait long. The doctor had just completed my simple operation and was bandaging my elbow when Prescott came back, being steadied by the same two pilots. Upon inquiring I was informed that Bob's intended customer was six-foot-two-inch, two-hundred-twenty-pound Gunverdal, who wouldn't have harmed a fly unless in self-defense.

And I can never forget stopping by one of the poker games Gunverdal was seated in. He was apparently losing a large sum of money, and was laughing so hard that tears were running down his cheeks. Observing all this, I asked: "Gunny, if you're so far behind, how come you're laughing?"

Gunverdal, amid bursts of convulsive laughter, said: "I'm not laughing, believe me, fellows. I'm crying."

What a long time without sighting land! The first visible land in about a month came one morning when I awakened to discover islands passing alongside. We were heading west in the Java Sea, north of the Sunda Isle. It was a tremendous relief to see land, even small patches of it.

About a month out of Honolulu, where we had stayed only long enough to take aboard water, the *Bosch Fontein* had put into Soerabaja, Java, then into Batavia, then back to Soerabaja again, then finally to Singapore.

It was not that we were completely disinterested in the sights of Soerabaja. Nor were we completely disinterested in the sights of Bali, which some of us got to visit while our vessel was laid up at Soerabaja. But I got a little sick at one of the sights I saw on Bali. Maybe it was sort of religious ceremony of some kind, or maybe it wasn't. But a beautiful Balinese girl was being held down on the ground while a priest was filing off her teeth. And even now, today, I can still hear the sound of that file. I had to hurry away. The rest of the scenery, though, I highly approved of. No brassieres and so forth.

At Soerabaja I said good-by to Bob Heising, never to see him again. But I did hear about him. Three years ago I read in the newspapers that he had flown into the top of Mount Fugi in Japan.

It would appear—though I don't really know—that fate had turned off the switch on a great guy for the last time.

CHAPTER 4

LEAVING JAVA FOR GOOD brought no regrets, brought
little feeling for that matter, as I was anxious to be on my way.
My feelings seemed to parallel my life of travel. I was forever
going somewhere but never getting anywhere. For the most
part I was always leaving some geographical location just prior
to my being asked to leave. By uncanny foresight throughout
my life I have been able to sense these critical departure points.
Anyhow, I spent a lifetime priding myself that I had never been
fired.

Our course held us in almost constant contact with the northern coast of Sumatra, winding in and out of the smaller islands
off its coast. For hours we appeared to be barely moving, as we
wound our way into Singapore's harbor, which gave the impression of great security. It was surrounded in its entirety by high
landscape. Then I realized what the British meant by saying
that Singapore was impregnable. Of course they were speaking
about bygone history and meant that this stronghold was completely safe from invasion by sea. They were under the supposition that this was the only manner in which an enemy would
attempt to attack Singapore.

But after leaving Soerabaja and reaching Singapore, where
we were to remain three days and three nights, we found our-

28

selves sitting in Raffles Hotel. Here one of our flyers happened to recognize a distinguished-looking elderly man, sitting at one of the tables. Dick Rossi, the flyer—thank God for guys like him —was always arranging things of genuine interest for us to do. Dick had also planned that little sojourn to Bali. And to this day I'm positive that many of our yearly get-togethers would have been just good ideas if Dick Rossi hadn't taken time to plan these and write each one of us a personal reminder.

Anyway, Dick went over and introduced himself to this elderly gentleman, then returned saying that this man was the Sultan of Johore—the most powerful of all the Malay States sultans. When we inquired of Rossi what the Sultan was showing him in a leather case, he informed us that he was carrying bourbon in it. Actually it gave the outward appearance of a large pair of binoculars.

I was to learn a lot more about him during the subsequent days, of course. I was to learn how the British Government paid him tremendous sums a year just to keep his good will, although the Sultan was very wealthy in his own right.

For some reason he must have had a liking for us or been bored by his own surroundings, because he sent us a note written half in Malay and half in some other language. It was his own manner of writing code, we were to learn later, and the only people who could understand the writing were the officers of his guard at the border station of his realm. And the note turned out to be an invitation for all of us flyers to visit his palace, the codelike note itself being a permit to pass his gates.

The palace was on the other side of Singapore, across and beyond the famous causeway the Japanese later were to storm to get into Singapore.

On reaching the palace grounds and showing our strange permit we were escorted through the Sultan's old castle. We were not invited into the new castle because his family resided there, and one had to be a Mohammedan to get into this new one.

But the old one was beautiful enough, containing showcase after showcase of solid-gold statues. Some of them were almost waist high and so heavy I doubted that one man could have tipped them over.

The banquet hall was so large it could seat four hundred people, and the service sets were of solid gold and sterling silver. It took little imagination to place visions of bygone nobility in their colorful costumes seated, bowing, or strolling elegantly about this palace.

The Sultan had his own private golf course, and some Englishman (I can't recall his name) was managing it; he kept it as groomed as any golf course in the world. It was too hot for us to play, however. Besides, not expecting this, those of us who had golf sticks had left them stowed aboard ship. So instead we were entertained in the bar of his clubhouse, a truly up-to-date affair, a thoroughly modern building, especially for that end of the world.

Occasionally from the bar, as so often happens, we would have to make trips into the bathroom. And here we would stare and stare again at the pictures on the walls, hardly believing what we were seeing. For we were looking at exceptionally large photographs of some of Hollywood's most prominent actresses, all standing around in various poses, and all of them nude.

How the Sultan had gotten such pictures we never were to know. Maybe he had had other nude bodies cleverly dubbed to the faces. But if so, the dubbing had been so cleverly done we couldn't tell the difference.

But the Sultan of Johore certainly was a jovial old gentleman, so jovial that he was not allowed in the city limits of Singapore after dark. He was treated like some schoolboy in having to return to his own domain after curfew. One of the reasons for this, as the story went, was that the Sultan had, as one might say, "contributed to the delinquency of minors" there in Singapore.

The Sultan had had many a white wife. I don't know which one he is working on now, or even if he is still alive, but we saw one of his wives there, an attractive English girl, or she could have been an Australian. He was also a big-game hunter. Even the Englishmen, who are hard to impress, had classified him at the time as one of the most skilled big-game hunters in the world.

I mentioned once before his binocular case, which he always

BAA BAA BLACK SHEEP

carried on his rides across the causeway into Singapore, and how the case contained, instead of binoculars, a couple bottles of bourbon. This was because he didn't like the kind of stuff (he called it "stuff") they served at Raffles Hotel or in any of the other high-class places in Singapore.

So with his binocular case he would come into Singapore, and then, just before dark, would have to go away again—back to his fabulous palaces. During one of our visits he told us that he was getting darned sick and tired of living over there and running the Malay States. He wanted to go back to Hollywood. Apparently Hollywood impressed him much more than it did me.

"I want to go back to Hollywood and live," he repeated, almost longingly. "I like that better than I do over here; but unfortunately, I am the Sultan."

It was here in Singapore that I became acquainted with the ricksha and their coolie runners that are so plentiful in the Far East. What a way to make a living! It might be terrific exercise, I thought, admiring some of the well-muscled legs of the coolie runners, but I let any thought of trying it out go by, when I was informed that the average coolie runner is worn out by the age of twenty-one.

Few rides were taken in rickshas after the novelty wore off. There were taxicabs and we used them for our travels. One trip took us out in the jungle to visit a rubber plantation. The plantation was much the same as I imagined it would be, how the trees were tapped, and the manner in which rubber originates.

The interesting part, to me, was the factory where rubber was dried, processed, and formed into huge bales of raw product. "Oh, the sweltering heat of this place! How could any human work for long?" I recall saying to some pilot. But they did, for they knew no other way.

The bulk of the work within the plant was done by women, under the direction of a smattering of male overseers. These were Chinese women, and the tiniest women I had ever seen before. Most of them I judged as weighing around eighty pounds or so. Talking about conveyor belts, the human con-

31

veyor belt they had in use here was most amazing. Two muscular Malay men would strain to lift a bundle of this raw rubber onto the turbaned head of one of these tiny women. And these women would walk slowly, one after the other, through the factory, some places appearing to be nothing but catwalks to me.

When I asked the weight of one of the bundles, one of the English-speaking overseers laughed and said: "Why don't you pick one up and see for yourself?" Several of us pilots tried to pick up a raw-rubber bundle and couldn't budge it. Some of us even took off our shirts because we were getting hot and sticky with the physical effort, and gave it a second try. We couldn't lift a single one.

Yet these little women walked along, smiling at our futile efforts, without a bead of perspiration on their faces. We were told that when one of these women slipped, which wasn't often, the weight broke her neck.

I learned two things from this exhibition. It is all in knowing how. And secondly, life is cheap in the Orient. Furthermore, I was to learn later just how much cheaper an Oriental life was in comparison to our value of it.

Another full day, arranged again by Dick Rossi, was to be most enjoyable in our exploration of a world new to us. Not being an art critic, I can't possibly tell you anything but how I was impressed with it all. I am speaking about the residences of the famous Tiger Baum magnate, the Salve Man, the Chinese who made a multimillionaire out of himself by putting out a prepared salve that cures all illnesses. He had two such places, the old one in downtown Singapore, and a new residence in the suburbs, each filled with the finest of jade statues, guarded by tall Sikhs who must have been around six foot seven or eight.

Tiger Baum's old residence had been converted into a museum, open to the public or tourists, anyhow, as no one appeared to live there but the tall, turbaned Sikhs. The masses of nearly perfect jade of various shades were worth a few fortunes within themselves, let alone the increased value of the exquisite sculptoring. It was here at Singapore that I confirmed whatever impressions I may have had about the Far East or what I had read and learned from various sources in the past.

At the Baum estate in the country, where we were allowed to visit this afternoon, we were everywhere except within the quarters where the family lived. Again we saw equally beautiful jade statues, but something here of a completely different nature held me spellbound.

As we strolled slowly through this vast estate, looking in wonder at its treasures, we had to touch and smell them in order to determine that some were not real.

There were trees and plants I was familiar with, from virtually all over the world, and they had been laboriously and tediously manufactured to almost complete perfection from non-perishable materials. In and about the vegetation were animals placed in natural poses, and to all outward appearances were superbly mounted. But when we gave them a closer inspection, we saw that they were made of materials similar to those of the scenery.

Today, though, whenever I take a charter flight at night over to Las Vegas and observe the various names of places in brilliant lights there, I can't help recall those few nights in Singapore.

In comparison to the wild or odd names over doors in Las Vegas the larger dance halls in Singapore had worked their names down to the simplest of detail. The names went like this: one was called The Old World, another The New World, and still another The Great World.

We pilots got into all three of them in time, naturally, but first of all, and being so new from the United States, we wanted real Chinese chow. Four or five of us went up to a roof garden on a building in Singapore where there were no other white people, the patrons being all Chinese. There was a Chinese orchestra consisting of six one-string instruments upon which every so often the players would grab a string, give it a twang, while a pair of girl vocalists would give a lengthy "Ai-oo-oo-oo."

This was totally different from our bands and accompanists, for not a trace of a smile came from any of the entertainers. The

33

dignified, better-class Chinese, I gathered, seated about the other tables, were equally somber.

This seemed to be about all there was to it, excepting that we had been drinking a little too much, and finally the manager asked us to leave. We couldn't appreciate his decision at this point.

But it turned out just as well, since in time during the subsequent nights we moved to all three worlds, The Old, The New, and The Great. These were tremendous taxi-dance affairs, the girls being of mixed breeds, either English with Chinese, or Indian with English, and so forth, all half-caste or quarter-breeds. The combinations impressed us as becoming, even beautiful—the whiteness of the whites blended into the symmetrical features of that part of the world.

We went by taxicab to their flats. They are quite different from our girls in the same business in the United States. These girls didn't mention the word "money" either. But we found out, in the beginning, what every American finds out away from home: the United States dollar was readily exchangeable to the native currency wherever we traveled. Damn few of us had any native money left when we pulled out of any country, possibly enough for a souvenir, but those who did sometimes experienced difficulty in exchanging back.

These young women were very congenial. They would ask you if you cared for a drink. And you would say, "Yes, scotch and soda," which was the drink in that part of the world. So then she would take a large brass key and unlock a carved teak cabinet and pour you a glass of good scotch and fill it with chilled soda. No ice. She doesn't join you in a scotch and soda. She doesn't care to drink, she says, because drinking in a hot climate like Singapore is not good for one. And before the evening is over, you begin to realize the same thing. After each effort of physical exertion throughout the night the young thing goes to the bathroom and compresses hot steaming towels and mops the young man down from head to foot. It is very refreshing.

To this day, and I'm not trying to be naïve, either, I don't know how to describe the status of these lovely creatures. In

34

some cases I am sure that it is not what one would ordinarily assume. However, in the critique that followed our visit in Singapore we found that our fellow pilots usually left ten Straits dollars, five dollars in our money, upon the girl's dresser when he departed.

When the *Bosch Fontein* pulled out of Singapore, it was with some regrets, although we were all anxious to get to Rangoon, Burma. Intrigue had gotten into all of us, I believe. It would be just a very short haul from Singapore to Rangoon, then our adventures would commence in earnest.

My comrades had settled down. There were no quarrels for a change aboard ship. And the last thing I remember about Singapore is that a member of the crew threw a piece of meat over the side after inviting us to watch, and a huge shark came from the depths to snatch the meat. Then the shark disappeared into the darkness of the water, as did Singapore, too.

CHAPTER **5**

OUR DESTINATION AT LAST . . . Rangoon, Burma. It was somewhere in the middle of November of 1941. We were happy to land, for we were airmen, not seamen.

Here at Rangoon the missionaries and the volunteer pilots' trails parted, though I was to meet several of our shipboard friends later. The Dutch crew sent us ashore amid hugs and fond farewells, for the pilots had really hit it off well with the *Bosch Fontein's* crew. Even her captain was no longer the stern, retiring person he appeared throughout the long voyage, for he was all smiles as he helped his crew members bid us good-by. He vowed that they would be back to pick us up after our year-long contracts had expired, the same as that of any construction worker.

Excitedly we attempted to obtain information concerning the goings-on of the AVG, everybody talking at once, from the handful of representatives who were in Rangoon at the time. We got little from these few. About all the dope we could get was that we were not going to be based in Rangoon. Instead, our training center, or whatever they called it, where we were to depart for by train that afternoon, was somewhere in central Burma, about halfway to Mandalay.

But our spirits were not dampened. Mandalay had a mystic

ring to us. And the Burma Road had become a famous back-door inlet to the interior of China.

What usually was neglected in our school geography books about the Orient was the smells. Rangoon, for instance, one of our first stops, was hot, dirty, and sticky and with many residents limping around with elephantiasis. I'll swear, one Indian we saw had this disease so badly, his privates were so enlarged, that we suggested to each other he should have a wheelbarrow to lug them in.

Until becoming used to it all I wandered about in a daze, my lips remaining clamped tightly together for fear that the stench that hung in the air would get into my mouth. But, as with everything else, one gets accustomed to Oriental odors after a while. Even today, after spending those four years in the Far East, bad odors don't seem to bother me as they did at one time.

Rangoon was probably the city in which most writers stayed while working on their books about Burma, because in no other city in Burma were there any permanent buildings as we know them here. Probably those writers stayed at the Grand Hotel, which is really quite modern, and it could have been there that they turned out their mysteries.

What I first noticed about Rangoon was that the paved side-walks were covered with blotches of red, indicating that many murders had been committed the previous nights. But I later found that this red was merely the spit from the people who chew betel nut.

Our little detachment was under orders to stick closely to-gether until we departed that afternoon on the train. So I hadn't gotten rid of ex-Captain Smith quite yet, as I had imag-ined I would.

Anyhow, I thought that I could stand his formations a little while longer. And there in the AVG I was to run into two more Smiths, as Smith is a common name. Both of these new Smiths were wonderful guys, much younger than the one that got my nanny. And the differentiation between the two new Smiths had already been handled before I arrived, one was called Bob, and the other R.T.

All the time we waited for our train, with the exception of

a shopping trip for tropical clothing, bush jackets and shorts, was spent at the Silver Grill, which was taken over by the pilots. It was a restaurant, or the only so-called night club in this large city. And it turned out to be a nightly hangout of the AVG later, when we were finally stationed back in Rangoon.

Here in the Silver Grill, where everyone wasn't talking at one time, we were able to inquire further about the AVG. As the story was told to us, the group had been stationed in the big city when the first arrivals had shown up, but recently they had been moved northward in order to pacify the British longhairs running this fair city.

And as it went, the Rangoon newspapers had printed articles about the American ruffians who call themselves the American Volunteer Group, and had said in no uncertain words what they were going to do about these roughnecks. They were capable of defending their own land as they always had before. After all, hadn't they an adequate supply of Brewster fighters (lend-lease from the United States) the same as Singapore? Who are we to let trash defend us? If we should need more aid, England will gladly supply us with an ample supply of Hurricane and Spitfire aircraft.

Another illusion the English had been under for some time was the potential of the water buffalo, a semi-domestic beast that tilled the rice-paddies; they thought that these beasts would become ferocious killers if a white man came near them. And, come to think of it, it must have been aggravating when some playful, drunken Texans shot their myth full of holes, for they rode these buffalo down the streets of Rangoon while they yelled: "Yee, ho-oo-oo." Actually, the only reason I could see that this superstition had been carried on for so long was that the English in those colonies had stayed away from any physical labor for so many generations.

But the English weren't the only ones who were talking about the AVG, even if the Americans didn't know about us at this time. The Japanese were talking about us. We hadn't fooled them for one minute, and they stated that our being over there had to be considered another warlike act. The Japanese gave the United States an ultimatum of quite some length, and in it was: Get your flying missionaries and laborers out of the Far East.

Our stateside belongings, plus our new purchases and ourselves, were herded aboard a small train that ran on a narrow-gauge track. Doors opened both sides of its cars completely, not unlike some of the European trains I had seen in motion pictures. So the tiny cars could be opened up for complete ventilation, or closed for the monsoon season. So by this conveyance we moved on up to the AVG training center, shooting our sidearms at the telegraph poles as we traveled along.

This place in central Burma, where we finally arrived in the middle of November 1941, was a small village named Toungoo. We found nothing in Toungoo but grass shacks and the airstrip the RAF had constructed. But our airplanes were there, and we were met by other members of the group who had preceded us to the Orient, arriving in May or June of 1941.

These older members assigned us to grass-thatched barracks with wooden floors, and windows with no glass. Breeze was more important than anything else. There were nightly attacks of millions of squadrons of mosquitoes, though. These little devils would start blitzing us at dusk. Their work was serious until sunup the next morning.

The heat was so fatiguing that, as one example, I couldn't get enough energy to jump out of my net-covered bunk while some of the other pilots were busy in the grass barracks near my bunk killing a cobra.

A scorpion sting is not fatal, but it can be damned painful. One morning I forgot to shake out my shirt while getting dressed, and for two days after that I wore on my back a lump the size of a cantaloupe.

Little wonder some of the earlier arrivals to the group went home in disgust. Six months of waiting. No action. The monsoons had to play themselves out before the pilots could fly.

We were informed that our detachment made one hundred pilots and about two hundred ground crew who had come over to date. But we were also informed that forty of the pilots who had preceded us had become fed up and returned home again. And we were to be informed a few days later that no more personnel of any kind would be coming, or any supplies of any nature. This came straight from Franklin Roosevelt, as this was one of his secret babies.

Toungoo was where I first set eyes upon our leader, who was to become famous, Claire Chennault, and I was genuinely impressed. In fact, seeing Chennault, and listening to him talk, was the only thing about this deal I had seen so far that did impress me.

Chennault was in his fifties, a stern-appearing military man, and looked as though he had been chiseled out of granite. This character had furrows and crow's-feet on his granitelike face that I thought bottomless.

Everyone addressed him as Colonel, I gathered right off, and with genuine respect as far as I could see. Chennault seemed to be a person who commanded respect. Colonel wasn't his real rank, because we had no ranks, for Claire had been shanghaied out of the Army Air Corps and told to retire as a captain. I was told that he was one of those who had backed Billy Mitchell to the hilt, and a premature retirement was the result.

Lack of hearing was the diagnosis, so I was informed, for his being retired from the Air Corps, but I noticed that the old man could hear everything he wasn't supposed to hear. Physically I admired him tremendously, for it was something to see a man of his age so trim. When we played baseball occasionally, Chennault was always a part of it. I never saw him hit a ball out of the infield, but he never stopped running, either, although it was obvious that he was a sure out at first base.

The admiration that was shown the old man by the three female members of the AVG—this was a setup wallflowers dream about—didn't impress me as completely military. As a matter of fact, my wife said that she had been attracted by Chennault ten years later, when she met him at a banquet at the Roosevelt Hotel in Hollywood. No use, I told her, for he is now married to a beautiful young Chinese woman, and they have at least two children that I know of.

Two of these women were American nurses. The redheaded gal married one of the pilots, Petack, who was killed later. And the other nurse was holding hands steady with some other pilot.

Then there was Olga, wife of the executive officer of the AVG, Harvey Greenlaw. They said that Chennault had found Harvey and Olga, his Mexican-Russian mate, stranded in the Orient and had employed them both. I never did know exactly what her job was supposed to be.

Here at Toungoo, the first week of December 1941, our airplanes were finally ready for action. They were P-40s that had been equipped here in the field in far-off Burma with machine guns, self-sealing gasoline tanks, and armor plate added to make them war planes. Actually, these P-40s had been borrowed (lend-lease to Britain) back from our English ally. One hundred of them. Furthermore, that was all the AVG was able to borrow.

Shark faces were painted in brilliant color combinations on the natural silhouettes of the P-40 engine cowlings, an idea appropriated from a magazine picture of a P-40 in North Africa.

Having never flown before in an aircraft with a liquid-cooled engine, I knew nothing about their manipulation, least of all this airplane doctored up with armor plate behind the pilot's seat, with guns and ammunition, none of them taken into consideration when it was designed. The pilots who had flown them said these "Shark Fins," the name the British hung on us, had an unorthodox manner of spinning end over end with its unengineered modifications, and that unless one had sufficient altitude to get them out of a spin it was impossible. They had several tombstones to prove their point.

One day, after I had been given a cockpit checkout by a qualified pilot, I had my first ride. The revised P-40 didn't feel too strange, considering that I had never flown one before and had been inactive for three months. I didn't spin it, however, for I believed their story even though I didn't think it possible.

Everything went okay until I came in to touch down for a landing. Having been accustomed to three-point landings in my Marine Corps flying, I tried to set this P-40 down the same way, even though I had been instructed to land this plane on its main gear only. I bounced to high heaven as a result of my stubbornness, and I started to swerve off the runway. So I

41

slammed the throttle on, making a go-around. In my nervousness I had put on so many inches of mercury so quickly that the glass covering the manifold pressure gauge cracked into a thousand pieces. After I had landed in the proper manner on the second try, I was informed in no uncertain words: "You can't slam the throttle around like you did in those God-damned Navy air-cooled engines."

Jim Cross took the same P-40 up after lunch and the engine blew up. When this happened, Jim was lucky to make a wheels-up landing in a nearby rice paddy. Even though Jim wasn't hurt, I felt very bad about it, as they were forced to use this P-40 for spare parts.

This feeling left me shortly when I discovered that I wasn't the only one, and that even my squadron commander had arranged for spare parts in three P-40s. One pilot had five American flags painted on his plane, for he had wrecked five P-40s, which made him a Japanese ace. This became the only way of getting spare parts, as there was to be none shipped from the United States. I suppose it was only human to want somebody besides oneself to supply these parts.

There were three squadrons of nearly twenty each. Approximately sixty pilots and sixty P-40s remained intact by the end of the first week in December. These squadrons were called the First, the Second, and Third Pursuit on what little paper work the group had to contend with. But to us pilots they were the Adam and Eve, the Panda Bears, and Hell's Angels.

Our detachment of twenty-seven was split up, nine of us being placed in each of the three squadrons. My squadron was the Adam and Eve, the First Pursuit, which is the first pursuit man knows of, incidentally.

Shortly after I had arrived in Toungoo, I began to cause consternation in some of the so-called staff of the group, although Chennault never said anything to me. In my way of thinking most of the men in this non-flying staff Chennault was stuck with were Asiatic bums of the first order. Chennault later had to call us pilots together when he realized we wouldn't take orders from the staff, telling us his sad story. He said: "I was to have a competent military staff for this group. However,

everyone of staff rank is frozen in the United States. I have to
do the best I can with what little staff I've been able to pick
up out here. And all I ask of you is—please understand—and
bear with me."

His talk touched me deeply, but I couldn't get over the fact
that his staff damned nearly outnumbered his combat pilots.
Maybe, I reasoned, he had to have many because, in more or
less his words, it took about ten of them to do one ordinary
man's work. At this time I hadn't been able to discover exactly
what each did do, except to show up at mealtime.

Harvey Greenlaw, the self-made executive officer, called himself Lieutenant Colonel Greenlaw, although no one else would.
The manner in which Harvey was forever talking courts-martial
to threaten a group of civilians gave me the impression that he
must have been at least one jump ahead of a few himself in
his military days. The poor guy gave the impression that he
hated everybody. Maybe Harvey had his reasons. Who knows?

Harvey was even going to court-martial Frankie Croft and
me for unofficer-like conduct when we came back from the
native village of Toungoo, pulling two grinning Burmese in
their own rickshas. We had to pay them plenty to do this. If
only Harvey had known how much trouble it had been, with
a language barrier, to get these two ricksha runners to let us
pull them in a race.

Of course this was all prior to our going into action, and I
guess Harvey had to be important. However, there were a heck
of a number of times later on when he should have gotten
disciplinary. But I always managed to change Harvey's mind,
when these times came, with one of my appropriate expressions.
One I used was: "Get lost, Greenlaw, or I'll bend your teeth,"
and while trying to figure this one out he would forget all about
the court-martial.

Japanese planes flew overhead at considerable height on more
than a few occasions, probably taking aerial photographs. They
never got close enough for us to get a decent look at them. I
imagined that they were laughing and thinking what damage
can a few little planes like this cause us. As we never flew out
of this Toungoo area, how were we to know what was going on

in Japanese-occupied territory in next-door Thailand or French Indo-China.

And then it started—or at least action of some kind—and war for the United States. Everyone had been sound asleep in our grass-covered barracks. Now lanterns were moving about in the darkness. Then I heard Harvey's excited shouting, and he said: "Pearl Harbor has been attacked! Pearl Harbor has been blown up! Get everybody up. Hurry. Take off as soon as possible."

"Harvey has finally flipped his wicket," I thought, and so did the others. But we were awake, and might just as well get up, and I suppose I was curious to see where they were going to confine poor Harvey. But this was no gag. This was real. This was war. It was coming in over the radio.

We were instructed to take off as soon as possible. Good God, what could we do? It was pitch black. There weren't even any lighting facilities on this field. Later I found out that the idea was to have our planes flying in case the Japanese had planned a simultaneous attack (the reason for darkness was the time difference between Pearl Harbor and Toungoo).

Some of the pilots had gotten air-borne as their Allison engines coughed and sputtered, owing to the fact that they had not been sufficiently warmed up. Some others refused to take to the air, and came to a grinding and clattering halt just beyond the airstrip, having their landing gear torn off and bending the propeller blades.

About this point in the wild confusion the rest of us who hadn't started to take off were instructed to cut our engines, and the planes in the air were called down. They figured it was better to take a chance on the Nips' bombing accuracy in the dark than to lose our entire air force to the black night. And a wise decision it was, too, for in that unlighted country, on a night like that, it would have been a miracle if anyone had found his way back and sat down in one piece.

There was no such thing as sleep the rest of this black night of confusion. The following morning found us still in a state of bewilderment. But the realization finally dawned: what we had come over to do—our plans—everything had been changed for us—by the Japanese.

44

In facing fact this meant the finish of our training program before it had even started. We were now standing by for alerts. In place of the gloriously planned offensive we were completely on the defensive.

CHAPTER **6**

WE WAITED FOR the Japanese to attack us at Toungoo. There was no such thing as a warning system, no spotters, no radar, so the wait was cut short.

Chennault bundled up his little air force and sent them on their way to Kunming, China, a much safer place to be stationed. Kunming had been originally chosen as the main base of operations, and our original job was to work for the Chinese, not the Burmese.

Besides our P-40s the group had three Curtis interceptors, high-powered, air-cooled craft, led by Eric Schilling, and they took off first. Their very capable pilots gave us an air show before they disappeared to the north, which helped boost our morale considerably. These three lads took my thoughts back to the Miami Air Races, where I myself had done stunts in formation for the spectators' thrill.

The rest of us in our P-40s took off, one by one, joining up in our respective positions after we were air-borne. "Sandy" Sandell was in charge of the group, responsible for taking us a little over six hundred miles of unfamiliar terrain to the north and east of Toungoo. The weather, as far as cloud formations, was definitely against him. Neither Sandy nor any of the others had ever flown into inland China.

46

As we continued to fly northward, the mountains became higher, and the terrain was by far the most rugged I had ever witnessed. At that time the maps of this territory we were forced to use, for lack of anything better, happened to be very inaccurate indeed. We found that points of reference, in some cases, were off a hundred miles or so.

But I had to give Sandy all the credit in the world. He found the six-thousand-foot-high valley, and the three lakes nestled within, amid the surrounding high mountains and the layers of stratus that covered them. A reminder of the complete lack of weather stations or radio navigational equipment I do not believe is necessary.

Sighting the lakes near Kunming—verification of the proper position long after passing the point of no return on fuel—was indeed welcome. The P-40s had all made it. Landing on the main strip we found to be impossible because it was under construction, so we landed beside the strip on the dirt.

This seven-thousand-foot runway at Kunming had been under construction for over five years, we were told. And it never was completed until the United States forces came in to complete the work long after we were gone. An all-coolie project was this large airstrip. Men and women alike broke the rock by hand, forming the foundation for the strip. Any time one glanced over in the direction of the new strip, he would see in the neighborhood of some two hundred coolies pulling a huge roller by ropes. This roller was tamping the crushed rock into a firm foundation in the claylike soil, so it would be capable of supporting heavy aircraft.

Our Curtis interceptors were not as fortunate as the P-40s. For all three had crashed into the side of a mountain, lacking about a thousand feet of having a name like Mount Everest, or some of the other mountains people climb. All three interceptors were lost, as well as two of their pilots, Eric Schilling being the lone survivor. And he had to bury these two friends up on the mountain.

The living quarters assigned to the group were in two places in this centuries-old city. Over half of the working personnel plus the entire staff were in an old stone schoolhouse on the

47

other side of Kunming. This was headquarters, Hostel Number One, and probably about as modern as any building in the city.

Hostel Number Two, as it was called, was where the rest of us ended up. It was situated not far from the flying field, a series of ancient adobe quarters with well-worn wooden floors. If one dropped anything smaller than his sidearm on the floor of his quarters, he would have no way of retrieving it through the spacious cracks between the boards.

The name of our quarters, and everything else, seemed to stand for second-best. In fact I gathered that the entire attitude was one of first come first served. As far as I could determine, this applied to squadron commanders, staff, and to women. It didn't take long for my new friends to teach me that I was all mixed up and everything in China ran a different direction. Come to find out, I had even been wrong in my definition for Semper Fidelis; it meant, instead, Every Man for Himself. I only hoped that this didn't apply to fighting as well.

Of course everyone is entitled to his own opinion, but I had the feeling that the organization dealt us just enough to keep us around prior to the action. Much the same way I feel about politicians. And the lads who were controlling this were politicians.

We couldn't wait to get downtown that first night for a tourist's tour. Japanese bombers had come over that very morning and dropped bombs upon this defenseless city. We viewed the destruction in various parts of the downtown area. Several hundred Chinese had been maimed or killed outright.

In walking along these narrow cobblestone streets it was educational to me to realize that people had existed in such filth for so many generations. How many generations? I do not really know, but the surrounding hillsides, where the city had buried her dead for centuries in peculiar little mounds, covered areas many times the size of this large city.

Somehow I had a feeling that, if this kept up, in time they would be forced to plant a little rice on top of some of the older graves in order to be able to make new children.

It was bitter cold in Kunming in December. Perhaps the change of climate had something to do with it, though. I was

48

amazed to see tiny tots running about these streets in pants that resembled a cowboy's chaps. Their little round bare buttocks, which stuck out of these pants in this cold weather, gave me the impression of a well-ripened peach back home.

One day I saw a little fellow doing his daily elimination upon the sidewalk, without the obvious necessity of having to take down his trousers. A Chinese woman, apparently the child's mother, came out of a doorway and spanked this tot severely. At first I imagined the discipline was for adding to the accumulated filth of centuries. But no. Even though I wasn't able to understand the language, it was obvious the mother was instructing her child to use one of the wooden buckets beside the stone building.

Human excretion was a commodity of value here, for it was the only means of fertilizing the land. Many years later I found that persons I had referred to as though they were completely formed of this raw product have a very definite purpose on this earth of ours.

God, what a place! Many mongrel dogs seemed to infest the outskirts of Kunming. They had chowlike heads, and these dogs would slink off with their tails between their legs, even when you offered them food. These dogs trusted no one. They preferred to feast upon the unclaimed bodies that lay in the cemeteries, people who could do them no harm.

Our generation, to say the least, certainly learned a lot of geography fast. And in a manner to make it stick. So I pity the poor geography teachers unless, by chance, they may have been around in the war too. For my ideas about the world had been confined to what schoolteachers had told me, or to books.

The Chinese were supposed to have stopped binding tiny girls' feet before I started to grade school. It wasn't quite that way. I witnessed many women in inland China, when I was nearly thirty years old, whose feet had been bound long after I had been instructed in school that no longer was there any such binding.

Getting back to flying and shooting down enemy aircraft, the reason I personally had gone over to China, I believe that

49

I had better predict the future. Which is easy in this case, for I'm only relating the past.

The definition of flying is: hours and hours of dull monotony sprinkled with a few moments of stark horror.

Maybe it is better this way. Or you might get the same impression I got when I read the *Black Ace of Germany*. After getting along to the monotonous, repetitious twenty-fourth kill or so I became so bored and confused that I hoped to God someone would shoot him down and get it over with.

Flying then was, and still is, a problem of having your aircraft in flying condition. Flying is a strain. So we worked out a day-on, day-off schedule for the pilots, which happened to fit in perfectly with the P-40s our small ground crew labored day and night to keep in readiness.

Here in China was a unique air-warning system for our Japanese invaders. It was as good, if not better, than radar was at that time. It consisted of countless country telephones, spread over this rugged interior of China. How any human could understand several hundred people on the same party line was beyond me, but it worked wonders.

Gingbow was the Chinese expression for air raid. And when they came, the Chinese in the plotting room in operations, from the maze of sounds over the telephone system, would work out the courses, the speeds, and the number of enemy aircraft. Even if the Japanese were unidentified, we knew they had to be enemy, because our P-40s were either on flight plan or on the ground. This system worked better than radar inland, but it wasn't worth a damn on border territory, we found.

In December there occurred several *gingbows,* which I tried desperately to run down. Each turned out to be a lone aircraft that streaked for home long before I was able to intercept it. No doubt these were observation planes, as fate would have it, and were looking for no fight. On the twenty-first of December I was having my day-off routine, not having a P-40 naturally, when the real McCoy came. In hopes that there might be a spare P-40 I ran like a madman to each one, checking to see if it had a pilot. I found that the only planes that didn't have pilots were out of commission.

So some of us had to just listen while we heard Sandell, over the radio in operations, making contact with the enemy. No doubts, they were pouring it to some twenty unescorted Japanese bombers, judging from the high-pitched and excited conversations. No Nip fighters had accompanied their bombers, or we would have heard.

The action lasted for an eternity, it felt, before Sandell called for a return to base. Sandy realized that they could chase the remaining bombers no farther and still have enough fuel for the return trip.

How eagerly I listened to the accounts of this first AVG action. How two of these bombers had burned in the air. How one of the twin engines of a bomber had torn out of its mountting, leaving the wing to disintegrate before their eyes. How one pilot was close enough to see the limp form of a tail gunner slumped over his gun.

Micky Mickelson's eyes were like saucers as he told of the horror of the terrific blast that rocked his P-40 when he followed an injured bomber to the terrain below. Jim Cross returned with a P-40 full of bullet holes. And this pattern seemed to follow Jim, and his plane always seemed to collect bullets, apparently motivated only by to-whom-it-may-concern. "Cokey" Hoffman, former aviation pilot in the Navy, the most ancient of all active pilots by far, was asked why he had persisted in making passes, after he had informed us upon returning that his guns were jammed.

Cokey said: "I figured I'd better keep scarin' 'em to draw fire from them who could shoot."

About this time we were receiving the radio broadcasts of Nippon progress, spreading like a cancer beyond control. I had received one lone letter from home before the action started, then there was no more mail for anyone.

The Philippines, Wake Island, Hong Kong, as well as other places, were on the broadcasts. Important, yes, but too far away to be realistic.

Close by, but definitely. The Malay Peninsula and Singapore, which we had just left, were what concerned us most. The Brewster fighters had been wiped out at Singapore. The famous

51

Spitfire was no competition for the Japanese Zero. Even the Spitfire had been shot full of holes in trying to turn in dogfights with the Japanese fighters. What a grim picture.

The English at Rangoon radioed for Chennault's AVG, ruffians or not. There was much bickering going on. But the windup was that Chennault, through kindheartedness or pressure, sent one of his squadrons, the Third Pursuit, to help reinforce the RAF's Brewsters at Rangoon.

The Third Pursuit, Hell's Angels, was commanded by a former Air Corps lieutenant, Orvid Olsen. And I'll always remember Olsen best for his remark that came later, upon his return from Rangoon. The remark had been prompted by Madame Chiang at one of the banquets we had in the royal couple's honor in Kunming.

One of the things that Madame Chiang, a brilliant speaker, had elaborated upon was the Chinese expression of "losing face." Later, when the pilots were referring to some action, they would twist this around and say: "I figured it was about time to get to hell away, because I'd much prefer losing face to losing ass."

Anyway, Olsen had just flown into Kunming from Rangoon by himself, and had told about spotting twenty-odd Zeros near Lashio, Burma, on his way back. We had inquired: "Did you fire at any? Did the Zeros fire at you? What happened to you? You didn't get hit."

Olsen had thrown up his hands and said: "Pa—lease, wait one minute, fellows, let me explain. Madame Chiang's immortal words seemed to run through my mind about the time I saw them. Remember? She said: 'One AVG member has proven he is equal to ten Japanese.' Well, I didn't want to make a liar out of the Madame. But if there had been *less* than eleven—I would have felt *free* to attack them."

Olsen's Hell's Angels were in Rangoon on Christmas Day, 1941. The Japanese didn't observe Christmas as a holiday. Or maybe they just wanted to be nasty. In any event, the Japs choose this day to plaster Rangoon.

Again we got radio reports, reports involving our group personally this time. Things had begun to happen fast. The self-sufficient high command at Rangoon had changed its tune completely now, for it was calling Chennault for more aid, even before the last of the planes had crashed on that first attack on Christmas Day.

Then Olsen's report was radioed: "Two AVG pilots killed. Rangoon bombed. Able to stave off concentrated attack. Only two Brewsters left. Most of RAF destroyed on ground. Disregarded RAF orders and took all airworthy P-40s off on first alert. This is only reason AVG was spared . . ."

If my memory serves me correctly, the Hell's Angels knocked down twenty-six Japanese planes out of some one hundred twenty that had come over. Duke Hedman, a quiet, unassuming young man, was the first American in World War II to become an ace (five planes downed).

Report after report came through until, in the first week in January, Chennault decided he had better augment Hell's Angels with his Second Pursuit, Jack Newkirk's Panda Bears. How I envied the Panda Bears as they too left to join the battle at Rangoon, or take on where the Hell's Angels had left off.

Newkirk's Panda Bears did exactly that, as most of the Japanese bombers were not able to get any closer than the outskirts of Rangoon at that time.

In the meantime our Adam and Evers might just as well have been back in the United States blowing bubbles in the bathtub, for nothing came over Kunming or even near it. Damn it to hell. Stuck here. Our First Pursuit seemed to be worse than second-best, maybe third-best.

Many of the Hell's Angels were back by this time, telling us of the scares, the thrills, and their victories. And while we were listening to these boys, we got all the glowing reports from Jack Newkirk to top it off.

But these feelings didn't last for long. Two weeks, perhaps, at the outside. Then Sandell was called to send our old Adam and Eve pilots to help Newkirk. What a moment! I couldn't seem to swallow, now that the time was here. A hard lump stuck in my throat, lasting until the following morning, until after I started my P-40 rolling down the dirt runway.

CHAPTER 7

RANGOON-BOUND AT LAST. It exhilarated me. My poise
had returned once again, and the hard lump that had been
lodged in my throat was gone. Perhaps the relief I possessed
when flying came from feeling inadequate while on the ground.
I don't know.

Our First Pursuit had been divided into two groups of ten,
because our P-40s would be low on gas when we arrived at
Rangoon, and we weren't putting all our eggs in one basket.
Our two groups were spaced twenty minutes apart, for we had
planned to have the last off to arrive on the button at dusk.
Getting the other half of our squadron there fell upon my back,
as Sandell was miles ahead out of sight. Thoughts of seeing the
ground crew, and the few of the staff who had waved farewell
as we had taken off, came through my mind. On most of them
I had interpreted this wave to mean: "I hope you get back
alive." I assumed that a few were thinking: "I hope you never
get back." But to hell with them. To hell with them all.

However, my only purpose, after delaying twenty minutes,
was to get the other half of the squadron to Rangoon. I was
fully aware that I had to plan to the minute my navigation and
the amount of time refueling in Lashio, in order to arrive at
Rangoon just before dusk. Not after dusk. In the lower lati-

BAA BAA BLACK SHEEP

tudes there is no such thing as twilight. As the sun sets, you get the impression that someone has suddenly put a bucket over it.

One factor is definitely in the favor of inexperienced navigators out there, same as on the east coast of the United States, where I had done most of my flying. The magnetic-compass variation is zero degrees, thank God. Anyway, we eased up on Mingaladon Field, Rangoon, just before dusk, February 2, 1942.

After landing we refueled and dispersed our aircraft as usual. It was too dark after landing to do much sight-seeing about the field; until retiring we spent most of the night in the RAF officers' mess, there on the field. We drank with them, RAF and AVG alike. We coaxed all the information we could out of the pilots who had seen action, anything pertaining to the performances of Japanese aircraft we would be up against. As we talked and drank, this information became all the more important, for the ceilings and walls around us in this mess bore mute evidence that this was no game. The Nips were playing for keeps. Although this mess had been spared by the bombs, it was perforated by machine-gun fire. One even had to watch his elbows upon the bar, or he was apt to pick up splinters.

When I inquired as to how the alerts were announced, some AVG pilot facetiously said: "Long before the RAF gets around to announcing the alert, you will see two Brewsters take off in a westerly direction, regardless of the wind sock. That's the signal."

The Japanese were flying in from the east. And deep down in my heart I couldn't blame the two English pilots of the Brewsters that remained, considering that this craft had already proved its inadequacy. The Brewster fighter was a United States product that had been lend-leased to England, and it turned out to be a perfect dud in combat. It is not unusual for one aircraft to perform better than design while another is unsuccessful. This happens all the time.

Furthermore, I even felt more sympathetic later when I found out that a Brewster squadron of my old Marine Corps buddies at Midway had only one survivor out of an entire squadron. And but for the grace of God I could have been in that squadron and not here. This lone survivor was my old friend Slim Erwin. And he had said: "The Japs had diddled my Brewster with so many bursts they gave me up for dead, or I'd never gotten back either."

Another AVG pilot, apparently feeling no pain from good scotch, added: "The Japs can outturn you. But no one, no one, can follow a P-40 when it dives."

This statement turned out to be very true, for it was not until the Messerschmit 109E came along that a P-40 pilot couldn't dive away when he so chose. The slow-climbing P-40 used this evasive maneuver until an ME-109E pilot sportingly displayed what his new plane could do, in North Africa when they first came out with the 109. As the firsthand story was told to me, the South African pilot had dived out, pointing his P-40 straight down, but, much to his amazement, an ME-109E German pilot slowly passed him in his dive, rolling back his hood, and holding up the first two fingers of his left hand in a "V" for victory.

Again, here was big Gunverdal, with a smile on his lovable face, which had all the appearance of a hog looking at a slop trough. And Gunny said something I'll never forget: "I didn't believe it would be humanly possible to get all two hundred twenty pounds of me under one of these tin helmets. But by God, I did, when the Japs bombed the field Christmas."

I learned later that Gunverdal had acquired a position as a test pilot after he left the AVG, and was killed while testing a new airplane back in the States.

After drinking all the scotch I dared I was shown to the RAF barracks, where I was to sleep for the next few nights. Surely, if the mess looked like no man's land, the barracks were worse. In addition to the machine-gun ventilation an unexploded bomb had gone through the roof, down through the two-story wooden building, and finally come to rest in the earth beneath the ground floor. We slept there even though a sign said: "BE-WARE UNEXPLODED BOMB."

There were many roped-off areas, I discovered the following day, in which the RAF demolition crew hadn't had time to disarm the bombs as yet. Skeletons of burned aircraft were strewn about Mingaladon Field in a haphazard manner. Former hangars were blackened heaps about the field.

The AVG had attempted upon several occasions to track down Japanese bombers at night, afterwards avoiding night flying altogether. One of these nights several pilots were sitting in the front seat of an automobile waiting for a P-40 to land, after one attempt. Another pilot had dozed off in the back seat of the same car. One of the pilots, realizing in the nick of time that the P-40 making a landing was off the runway, had screamed: "Get to hell out, quick." And later, as these pilots were dusting off their clothes, they were laughing and complimenting one another upon their narrow escape, because the propeller of the P-40 had chewed the car to pieces when it crashed into it.

A few minutes later these same pilots checked with an RAF cleanup crew to determine if the car they had recently jumped out of had been removed from beside the strip. And to their amazement the Englishman in charge had answered: "Sir, we are attending to that. But what shall we do with the body in the car?"

The name of the pilot who was dozing off on the back seat seems to have slipped my memory.

The first few days at Rangoon passed by without too much consequence. The formality of getting our RAF passes, with the usual photographs and fingerprints, took us to the guardhouse at the gates of Mingaladon Field. There we saw a native lying grotesquely in death, because he had become confused or had misunderstood one of the sentries at the gate. Tensions were running high around here.

Then one morning around ten o'clock, after a relatively peaceful three days, I saw the two Brewsters take off to the west. A few minutes later came "scramble," an unidentified "bogey" had been picked up upon RAF control radar.

Boy, oh boy, this was what I'd been waiting for. Ten of us climbed out of Mingaladon in our P-40s. Eight in close formation, supposedly with one of Jack Newkirk's seasoned veterans leading us, with Cokey Hoffman and another pilot flying high cover a thousand feet above us.

The eyes of any formation had to be the leader's, for the rest are busy watching the aircraft they are flying close to. None of us flying close formation had been in combat before, just following blindly and trusting to luck that our leader would know where to take us. Over my earphones came a garbled "forty to sixty bandits" and their approximate location. This information changed from time to time. Our formation leader came in with: "I've got them spotted. Between forty and fifty I-97s."

The Japanese I-97 was a single-seater, highly maneuverable, fixed gear airplane. Finally I spotted the Japs in the haze above us, occasionally losing them, as we were climbing into the sun, which was quite high at that hour. It wasn't my business to question, but I couldn't figure why we were always climbing under these babies with the sun in our eyes. I had hoped that the guy who was leading knew what he was doing.

Another few minutes, and we were directly under these Jap fighters, about two thousand feet, I imagined. What an uncomfortable position to be in, I thought. Couldn't that jerk see where he was taking us? But I found later that this was also his first fight. The leader wasn't one of Newkirk's old hands, he was one of us.

My thoughts were soon interrupted as I witnessed each of these Japs slowly half-roll onto their backs, glittering momentarily above. And then all I could see was their flat-plate areas and smoke and tracers from the Jap machine guns. Cokey's P-40 above us gave all the appearance of a fish writhing in agony out of water.

As I glanced out of the corner of my eye, the entire formation I had been sitting in a second before had disappeared completely. They were headed straight down for old mother earth. So I pulled off and down to one side to get out from underneath the diving Japs. And what a relief to have free air above me for a change.

Soon I spotted a pair of Japs off to the side of me, so I added throttle and started to close in behind them. One of these two pulled almost straight up, going into a loop above my P-40 about the same instant I started my tracers toward the other. I knew that I had to break off firing and commence turning, or the Jap who was then above my P-40 would have me bore-sighted.

Recollection of how I had been able to outturn the best of the United States Fleet pilots in peacetime practices probably gave me self-assurance. I really am not sure. The fact that I had learned to tighten my neck muscles in my intercollegiate wres-tling days, retarding the blood from rushing out of my head, I had found extremely useful in simulated combat in the past. In those earlier days pilots had no squeeze suits, which were designed and worn later on for the same purpose I had been accomplishing with my neck muscles.

But I soon found that little asset wouldn't solve my problems against this much lighter Japanese aircraft. I discovered that even hauling back on my stick and turning with all my might, my neck muscles and breath locked, gave me no advantage whatsoever. As a matter of fact, I was sufficiently blacked out not to be able to see whether my bursts had gotten the I-97 I had been firing on. I had pulled myself plumb woozy. All the time I was pulling this terrific "g" load, tracers were getting closer to my plane, until finally I was looking back down some-one's gun barrels. "Frig this racket," I thought, and dove away.

So true, it was, that nobody could follow you if you dove with sufficient altitude in a P-40. I should have realized, then and there, that the tactics and close formation I had been so thoroughly trained in weren't worth a damn with the Japanese, and I imagine that nothing but pride and ego led me to try once again, even though I hadn't the faintest idea where my mates were by then.

In trying once again I gave myself a much better break, making a faster pass from a thousand feet above. As I ap-proached this Nip fighter, he also permitted me to get close enough to where my tracers were sailing about him. Then I witnessed this little plane perform one of the most delightful split S's I had ever seen, and then I discovered that I was turn-ing again with some of his playmates.

"Who in the hell said: 'These little bastards can't fly'? To hell with this routine!" I thought, and dove out. Bonus money of the fantastic variety fluttered to the ground like so many handbills, and with them the last of my illusions.

It probably isn't worth mentioning now, because I hadn't even felt it at the time it occurred, but while flying back to Mingaladon Field I became conscious of something sticking me like a pin, somewhere on the underside of my upper left arm. In rolling back my short-sleeved bush jacket I found the cause, a 7.7-millimeter had evidently struck my P-40 and its jacket was imbedded in my arm.

As I went back to base, I pulled the metal delicately out of my flesh, intending at the time to keep the bullet for a souvenir. This I soon forgot about, though, for there was hardly any blood. Besides, our outfit didn't give out Purple Hearts. It happened to be an incendiary round, and the chemicals attached to it left a large vaccination-like scar—which is souvenir enough.

A complete picture of dejection and disillusion flew back to the field. Vaguely I recall people telling me how sorry they were about the mistakes they committed, and how happy they were when I had returned after being considered shot down. As if from another world, I recall Bob Prescott standing up on my plane's wing just after I taxied up to the flight shack. Bob told me years later that by my glancing up out of the cockpit and saying: "We didn't do so hot. Did we, podner?" I had helped him tremendously.

I didn't recall these exact words, but this was about my attitude then. I hated myself so badly I didn't even bother to write up my first combat report, for this could have happened to others—but not to me. Self-pity had always been one of my greatest indulgences anyhow. And how I could feel sorry for my injured pride, when we had to lay poor old "Cokey" Hoffman to rest the following day, I don't know.

I don't intend any sacrilege, but I became nervous and perspiring, looking into the open grave with Cokey's coffin beside it. We stood there, listening to an English minister drone on in the hot sun, and he seemed to be stretching the ceremony out far too long. For after all, he hadn't known the old chief A.P. as we had. As we started to lower Cokey to his final resting place, the grave turned out to be too narrow about halfway down, and the coffin jammed there. By this time the minister sensed the strain as we struggled with this impossible situation and he quietly said: "You may all leave now. We will take care of the rest."

As we walked away and lighted cigarettes, leaving the old chief aviation pilot, I imagined I could hear Cokey reprimanding: "You bastards. You were doing great. Why did you have to leave me fouled up—halfway down?"

The old attitude had left our English friends by then. They seemed to see us in a completely different light, for, outside of an occasional lone bomber coming over at night, they were beginning to feel comparatively secure. During the hours of daylight not one single bomber ever even tried to hit that city again, after the First Pursuit arrived in February. Nothing but fighter sweeps were sent over by the Japanese, to try to neutralize our air defense.

Rangoon's residents then sat in their patios and watched "a bloody good show," because aircraft were crashing at a more comfortable distance from their fair city. I too was compelled to witness some of these "shows" from the ground, because it was impossible to have an airplane every day. During one of these battles the air above would become so full of vapor trails the sky gave the appearance of some giant bird leaving chicken tracks in barnyard mud.

It was rare, but occasionally we would have to duck for cover, when a single Jap fighter would come down and strafe too near.

The Nips' aircraft were no match for ours in many ways, after we learned how to fight them. We had two .50-caliber and four .30-caliber machine guns against the Nips' two 7.7-millimeter machine guns. Also, we had armor plate behind the pilot and self-sealing gas tanks, of which the Nips had none. Our P-40s were faster than the I-97s, and after we had spread out the enemy, we learned to whack them off one by one. Our P-40 proved to be capable of taking a beating from gunfire and yet go on flying. No longer did we turn with the Nips when we didn't have to; we made them play our game.

The ground viewers could see the Nips come down in flames

or disintegrating parts. Or if they were not completely burned out, a loud explosion was heard, and a column of smoke would rise off the edge of Rangoon.

During the middle of one fight Sandell landed a P-40 that was literally bathed in oil. As Sandy braked his P-40 to a halt, he vaulted out of the cockpit and ran across the field like a jack rabbit. And immediately we saw the reason for his actions, for a Nip was bearing down upon his vacated P-40 with machine guns wide open. This I-97 barely clipped the P-40's tail surfaces, crashing into smithereens a few yards beyond.

A few of us ran over to see if we could assist Sandy in any way. He said he had gotten three Nips that day, prior to being forced down with holes in his cooling and oil systems. We also wanted to get a good look at a Japanese fighter, but it was in too many pieces to tell very much. And so was its pilot, too. The largest part of the pilot I could recognize was a tiny left hand with the severed tendons sticking out. No doubt subconscious reflex had thrown up his arm in a futile attempt to protect his face.

Another Nip fighter, knowing that he could never reach home, deliberately dove at one of our planes parked in a revetment, and, so help me, he couldn't have done better, for us at least, because it was the same as if he had put the last piece into a jigsaw puzzle. This Nip had committed hara-kiri in that revetment without placing so much as a scratch on the parked aircraft. It was unbelievable that this I-97 could have fitted into the unused space at any angle except the one it did—straight down.

As luck would have it, a "bogey" came at the same time of day, two days after my first flubdub. The Japanese always appeared to come over like clockwork. These folks certainly believed in monotony, if nothing else. On this occasion I got to lead the scramble, and I personally didn't give one damn whether these bandits got over Rangoon or not. All I was going to make certain was that, when we made contact, I was going to be on top of the heap and remain there.

And on top we were. With the exception of Cokey our ten pilots were the identical formation in which I had my first fight. As I lowered the formation down over the neat-looking Jap fighter formation, they loosened up, spreading in depth and width below us. Their idea was to suck the P-40s inside this beehive, in hopes that we would turn with them. I became so familiar with this change in the Jap formation when about to be attacked that it made them look like a flock of vultures as they hover over a single spot.

There had been no turning this time. We worked methodically from the top down. I caught my first Jap just right, and he blazed into an inferno. Shortly afterwards I heard someone scream over his radio: "This is for Cokey, you son of a bitch." My sentiments were the same.

Pulling off to one side, I saw another safe shot. As I continued a steady burst into the fighter, pieces of his fuselage ripped off at point-blank range. In a second or so this plane also went on its way earth-bound, twisting crazily and burning like a torch.

Because of the first sad encounter, or maybe because we merely desired to leave well enough alone, the remaining Nips were free to go home alone. We did not give chase. On this second fight we flew back to Mingaladon with an entirely different feeling, however, because we had knocked down sixteen enemy, while we lost no one.

Although my own spirits were bucked up considerably, I didn't permit myself much enthusiasm, for I knew only too well that this was going to be a struggle for survival—not for money.

CHAPTER **8**

HERE AT RANGOON I was to meet two of the most genuine friends I ever hope to have. For two semi-portly gentlemen
in their fifties, showing the signs of years of good living, came
across my path. I didn't realize then that, no matter where a
person goes or what kinds of problems he may have, he always
has friends.

Jim Adam and Bill Tweedy did everything a little differently
from the way other wealthy colonials acted there in Rangoon.
They came out to Mingaladon in person and picked up six of
us AVG pilots. It was very cute, I thought, the way the inseparable pair worked together. Later, I learned, they had
continued this relationship, which started when they served together in World War I. As two young men, they had realized
the lack of opportunity in Scotland and had struck out to the
colonies to better themselves, remaining there ever since.

Jim and Bill were in the oil-refining business in Burma. Both
were bachelors and always had been. And both of them had
selected picturesque knolls in the suburbs of Rangoon, where
they had constructed their dream estates, approximately a half
mile from one home to the other. The construction, the land-
scaping, the servants, everything appeared to blend in peaceful
harmony.

64

Jim Adam came directly to the point when they picked us up at the field, and asked us to come live with them. He said: "Bill and I have spent most of our lives in comparative comfort. But we know what the other side is like. And we decided it was awfully selfish of us, not sharing our homes with you fellows, who are the only reason we are able to live in them."

By this time all of the pilots had been billeted with different colonials in their homes. However, the six of us, living with Jim Adam and Bill Tweedy, were the only pilots whose hosts had insisted that no room and board be paid. Furthermore, they dropped everything of importance to make us feel at home, and we became inseparable.

That the best things in life are free certainly was applicable within the Adam-Tweedy homes, for at no time previously had I lived with a feeling of complete comfort. And to think of the misery of the countries we were in, with a war going on full blast. The enjoyable routine still lingers in my memory, or I wouldn't bother to talk about it. And after a day's stand-by or work at the field, we would park our P-40s for the night in close-by rice paddies that had no water, just before sunset. We did this so there would be nothing but an occasional bomb crater to be filled on Mingaladon the following morning. Even lightning cannot strike something that is not there.

After our P-40s were bedded down, I would drive home to Jim Adam's lavish abode. Always, without exception, I found one, or sometimes both, of the kindly Scots with the pilots, seated about the patio next to one of the hilltop estates.

"Chota Peg" or "Burra Peg," came the friendly invitation just after darkness had set in. These were names for scotch and soda out there. The "Chota" was a single. The "Burra" was a double. Bill Tweedy laughed one night and said: "You chaps even caused us to change the name of one of our drinks. We have had to change the name of our 'Burra Peg' to 'the American Drink.'"

These evenings out of doors were augmented by typical Southern California weather that February of 1942. After we briefly accounted for the day, we downed our Burra Pegs and excused ourselves, then retired to our quarters to freshen up before continuing the enjoyable evening with our hosts. For these two Scots were the same as foster parents.

Each pilot had his own spacious bedroom with the customary large paddle-blade fan hanging from the ceiling and a large, soft four-poster bed, covered with a roomy mosquito netting. Even Angus, Jim's black dog, a great Dane, had his own bedroom and his own mosquito net.

Each household had approximately ten domestics, Indians and Burmese, ranging from gardener, chauffeur, and number-one boy to first, second, and third cooks. The Indian servants lived in quarters separate from the main house, while the Burmese commuted from Rangoon.

Every bedroom adjoined a good-sized bath that was serviced from an outside door. It was baffling that with so many servants and all the attention to make your living so smooth you rarely saw more than one at a time, almost as if these servants were accomplishing the job with mirrors, as they moved soundlessly about on their bare feet.

Usually I entered my bedroom relieving myself of my dirty, sticky clothing as I walked. And by the time I entered the bathroom there was always a hot tub waiting, and the proper temperature for me. Perfect co-ordination, regardless of the hour I arrived. And Anto, a husky Burmese, the number-one boy, had already left unseen through the outside bathroom entrance. Nor do I remember ever calling for Anto to serve me; he must have had telepathy in addition to all his other fine attributes. If not before, I soon discovered, after I had eased myself into this refreshing tub, that cigarettes, matches, and a cool, fresh "Burra Peg" were within easy reach.

It was a kinglike feeling when, in fresh linen, I rejoined my associates and host out on the tastefully shrubberied patio. As we sat around, delightfully passing the time of day, I was almost positive at times that my glass had been empty when I last set it down. But each time I picked up my glass, shaking it to be positive, I discovered that Anto or some other servant had replenished it unobserved.

Some of the evenings before dinner, which was never served before ten o'clock, Jim would ring next door on the telephone.

And the conversation would go like this: "I say. Hurumph. Hurumph. Are you there, old boy?" Blank "Sir Archibald Wavell speaking." Another blank "Would you do me the honor of cocktails and dinner this evening?"

We would alternate back and forth sometimes, with all eight of the two households at either one home or the other. Jim's Indian cook, tall and thin, was a true artist, and he served the most tasty meals I have ever experienced. This was the number-one cook, who did all of the marketing, also.

Jim explained that, owing to the higher wages in Burma, an Indian could work three years away from India, then return back home and live a year without working. Several of the Indian servants had been going back and forth for a couple generations.

The mornings, even though I was awakened before sunrise, were equally pleasant—no clanging alarm clock, no bugler, merely the delightful aroma of freshly brewed tea. This came from a teapot and a poured cup upon a table beside my pillow. And for once in my life I was able to get out of bed by degrees and enjoy myself. The cup of tea was very nearly consumed by the time I had finished a cigarette and had gotten my other slipper on my foot. Then into the bathroom for a shave and a toothbrush I went. Upon returning to my bedroom I found fruit, ham and eggs, marmalade and toast, and more tea, placed upon the little table beside my bed. What a way to live! How could I ever forget this part?

The only occasion I recall for ever having a great deal of conversation with any of the natives must be considered as a justifiable bawling out by an Indian. It had been accomplished in an orderly manner, though, and I got his point, realizing my mistake. We were there at a time when these people had been getting along without us for so many generations and before the land was infested with G.I.s who so wantonly tossed their money about.

The incident occurred when I had given an Indian youth three rupees, equivalent to a United States dollar at the time, for spending a whole day cleaning and polishing my dirty field boots. The boy's eyes expressed supreme delight when I paid him for his troubles, so, when the father confronted me in anger afterwards, I got a chip on my shoulder immediately, for I imagined that I had been accused of something I hadn't done —cheating his son.

The father simmered down quickly, as did I, and he explained the situation I had unintentionally created. The point being that I had given his son far too much money, as much as his father made in a week. Not that he didn't appreciate generosity, he explained, but through my actions he would lose the privilege of disciplining his son. He would be lowered in the son's estimation, upon the boy's discovery that he could make more money than his parent.

For causing this trouble I apologized to the Indian father. And today there is little doubt in my mind concerning world attitudes about the U.S. dollar and the manner in which we toss the God Almighty Buck around.

With all this excellent living nothing but craving for excitement and women could tear us away occasionally to the Greek's Silver Grill in downtown Rangoon. There were enough members of the AVG, by each of us going on occasion, to make the Greek an excellent living in his moth-eaten night club night after night.

One night when I had a terrific load aboard, an air raid sounded while we were busy whooping it up at the Silver Grill. I guess that the Greek had about enough of our money for one day. Anyhow, he was wringing his hands and telling us *we* had enough for one evening—to go home. That part was okay. But the Greek went too far; he couldn't get us out quietly, so he ordered us out.

Automatics and revolvers were part of the dress for these nights out. But on this occasion they should have suggested that all firearms be left with the hat-check girl, like in the movies of the old wild West. We answered the demanding proprietor of the Silver Grill, carrying out our threats by shooting down the chandeliers. God knows what the Anglo-Indian prostitutes upstairs thought, if there were any of them left up above at the time.

Americans had a rather crude way of getting what they

wanted under these circumstances. Later I learned that P. Green, as we always refer to Paul, almost had some difficulty in obtaining service in another colony, when several pilots were ferrying planes back from the Gold Coast.

P. Green, the handsome Jim Clinton of Kunming, as we call him, was wearing two holsters for this Gold Coast trip. Hot and thirsty, the pilots had stopped in a British colonial bar, where apparently liquor was rationed, and ordered a round of drinks. The bilious English bartender informed these pilots that there was sufficient whisky for Englishmen only.

As the story went—and who am I to doubt it?—P. Green saw red. He tossed both of his heavy West Texas pistols, crashing down upon the bar top, and screamed: "Whisky me, boy. Whisky me, boy."

P. Green and his buddies were served. Served with smiles, too, all they wanted. So, it wasn't all our fault, like one might have believed, the cause of the grating feelings that existed. I have to admit, personally, that I didn't help the situation much.

During an early moon one evening we were seated on the Adam lawn, quietly sipping our scotch and sodas and listening to the drone of a Japanese bomber. Occasional bursts of anti-aircraft fire, blending in with the searchlights, were rather pretty, I thought. No worry concerning our P-40s, for they were off the field. The whistling and the cla-umph cla-umph of the bombs in the distance were normal sounds by then.

But the next night was a complete surprise. First we saw a more or less horizontal burst of tracers at some altitude. We saw another, Roman-candle-like burst, which appeared as if it had been fired straight down. Then came the ever-increasing howl of a pair of twin engines, winding up as though they were about to tear themselves out of their mounts. The crescendo increased gradually until it terminated in silence, after a blinding flash of light, which preceded a terrific explosion.

After this little show we realized that the tracer bursts had to be from a fighter, but had no idea who it could have been. The following morning we were to learn that Wing Commander Schaffer, survivor of the Battle of Britain, had been doing a bit of night flying in his RAF Hurricane.

It was an honor to meet this handle-bar-mustachioed gentleman in the RAF mess a few days later. That is the way I felt. I couldn't blame the commander if he felt differently.

It is odd, indeed, what things we do in an emergency. This thing I did paralleled the actions of a towheaded youngster I was to meet in a Japanese prison camp in Japan. This sailor had filled his pockets with canned goods before he was released to the surface in an air bubble from the *Tang*, an American submarine, resting upon the bottom of the Sea of Japan, unable to rise.

While talking to Wing Commander Schaffer I became so engrossed I failed to recognize a certain sound. But he did. He yelled: "Strawf. Strawf," and out of the RAF mess door his lean frame went, his mustache streamlined out along his thin cheeks. What caused my actions, or how I did them, I don't know. But I had followed the rangy Schaffer, hurdling a high porch railing that should have taken me three jumps, followed him into a slit trench, landing with both feet in the middle of his back, poor fellow. And, as I gathered my senses, lying there on some rocks, I discovered that I was clutching an unbroken bottle of scotch in each hand.

One morning in the middle of February our squadron received a sad blow. An extremely quiet morning, as I recall it. Sandell had been out early, testing his repaired P-40, and was killed. I was on duty this day, but I hadn't seen the accident. But some of the RAF had seen it and told me about it.

They said that it appeared as though Sandy had spun his airplane deliberately, at fairly high altitude, and then appeared to be having difficulty in recovering. But eventually the plane recovered completely and was in a steep dive. At fairly low altitude Sandy apparently hauled back on the stick too rapidly when pulling out of the dive, and his P-40 half rolled slowly, going into the ground in an inverted attitude.

The following day only half of us could attend Sandy's funeral, and I was on duty at the field for an alert. There was no direct contact in mass this day. We had taken off twice, during the same alert, and couldn't make contact with any bandits the first time, although the reports were coming in from RAF Radar Control. A hazy day made a will-o'-the-wisp game out of it. Here they are. No, they aren't. Finally, after about two hours of this, I saw one lone Jap fighter, almost across the bay leading into the Settang River. Apparently he was heading for Moulmein, about out of fuel.

It was simple to ease up behind this I-97, and I had all time in the world to set my sights for a no-deflection shot. He never saw me, at least not before I fired. Fear that I had missed him was soon over. The I-97 slowly half rolled and plowed out of sight under the water. Realization that I was seventy miles from Rangoon hit me suddenly, so I scooted back to base while I still had fuel left.

There were a few Hurricane pilots around the city by this time. After I had gotten back, a couple of their pilots told of sighting the main body of the I-97s. The two of them had been sitting above approximately fifty Japs, sensibly waiting for some of the AVG to reinforce them before making an attack.

They asked me who was in a certain numbered P-40. I remember saying that I didn't know offhand but could find out—and why do you ask?

One Hurricane pilot said: "While the two of us were waiting, we saw Number —— climbing up, and counted on his joining us." He added: "But to our complete surprise Number —— plowed into the whole bloody bunch alone. And the next thing we knew he was in a bloody spin with Japs all over his Shark Fin. They damn nearly got us both when we decided to give him a bit of help. Here's a little friend I found imbedded in my parachute pack," he said, dropping a 7.7 slug into my palm.

This may all seem pointless. But this lone character turned out to be Big Jim Howard, Newkirk's second-in-command, to whom we fellows always gave a horrible ribbing, for he acted so gullible.

After Big Jim's AVG days he went on, and they gave him the Medal of Honor for his work over Germany. I can imagine how he baffled the German pilots, thinking they were up against an automatic pilot, or something out of the ordinary, at least. Jim

71

who didn't give a damn about the odds Madame Chiang had made book on. Though I considered Big Jim one of the better boys, I somehow had a feeling that I was as close to him as I was to a cigar-store Indian.

The pleasant company of Jim Adam and Bill Tweedy was too good to last, and I knew it. The Japanese ground forces had steadily marched on west, with poor old General "Vinegar Joe" Stilwell one jump ahead of them.

I first met the general at Mingaladon Field. Even now I can still see him as he was during those days. Of course nobody would have recognized him as a general in the clothes he was wearing at the time. Stilwell informed me at Mingaladon that he was without American troops, and the few Chinese and Burmese with him were forced to move back all the time. But I believe Stilwell knew that if he had so much as stopped to tie his shoelaces, let alone fire a round, the Japs would have surrounded them.

Well, whenever we stopped at an airfield, along the road would come General Stilwell with a group of refugees. I'll never forget the time at Magwe, Burma, a west-coast town, where they evacuated refugees to India. One of our mechanics was opening a can of tomatoes and he turned around to the general and said: "Hey, bub, do you want some of these too?"

The general answered: "Sure thing."

They ate out of the can and slept practically beside each other on the ground all night, and it wasn't until the next morning that the young mechanic learned the identity of the man he had called "bub."

Getting back to our genial hosts who were saying good-by, for Rangoon was in the process of being almost flanked from the north, the only way out. Jim called me in one day in early March and told me of the plan to evacuate Rangoon. He said he had talked to the servants, and they were willing to remain with us pilots. So I was instructed briefly in how to manage these servants. Jim suggested that we double their wages because of the uncertainty of things. You could have knocked me over with a breath of cool air when I found that by doubling the help's wages it was still only thirty-some dollars a week.

Whether this included the supplies the cook bought I can't remember offhand. Anyhow, it would be little more.

Then I was the head of the household, a position I have never been able to manage very well at best, but I pretended to carry on the routine, the same as Jim Adam had, if for nothing other than to keep this excellent help around.

The Indian cook would bring in his ledger before dinner, every other night or so, and I would pretend to study his ledger with care, as I had observed Jim do so often. It was impossible for me to tell up from down about the damned thing, for I couldn't even pronounce the few words I knew in Hindustani. Anyhow, I would point at some item at random on the page, and pretend I was angry, like a wrestler does in exhibition. Then the cook would be all explanation and apology. I never will know how much he fooled me, or I him. Much the same as a game of darts in the dark.

The most pitiful sight I ever saw was when these two old Scots were leaving Rangoon. They had said farewell, and were to travel by foot with light bundles over their shoulders. As they walked down the road, they looked much like two of our own Knights of the Road back home. Before they started, I asked: "Anything I can do for either of you after you go?"

And Jim had said: "Set a match to it. It's too good for the Japs."

Angus, the great Dane, was left behind also, for Jim had made me promise to shoot Angus before the Japanese arrived. Little did Jim realize that I would have less trouble shooting one of the pilots than I would slugging old Angus.

Another thought ran through my mind, watching the two balding gents go their way with my pity, about how relative everything is. Only a couple weeks ago we had been complimenting our hosts on what a great way to live, and bachelors, too. And Bill Tweedy, the spitting image of the actor Charlie Ruggles, had said: "I'll have you know it was much more exciting than this, for once upon a time, these hallowed halls were occasionally blessed with beautiful Anglo-Burmese girls who came to dinner." And he had said this with a delightful chuckle.

Since February there had been South African crews in twin-

engined Blenheim bombers, carrying bombs into next door
Thailand. And from our old training base, Toungoo, a squadron of Kashmir Indians was flying ancient, single-engine Ly-
sanders loaded with bombs. Neither the South Africans nor
the Kashmir Indians needed or accepted fighter cover, and they
never appeared to get much higher than the jungle terrain they
flew over, either. How I admired them both!

Though the Japanese ground forces came steadily onward,
averaging roughly ten miles per day, about as fast as they could
walk in a day, the air was commanded by a handful of RAF
and AVG. We were getting few alerts by then. One of the last
alerts of any size came around the middle of February, but I
never saw any bombers personally. Some of the pilots spotted a
few, and knocked a couple down, far away from Rangoon. All
I could see were fighters that apparently had been up for some
time. By then I had learned where to find some easy shooting,
when the enemy is going home low on gas with his guard down.
If one wanted to run into anything going home after a raid, he
had to get down low, or he would never see an enemy. The Nips
would be taking a free power glide, their attention being taken
up somewhat by the gas gauges and the anxiety to get back
whole, getting closer to the terrain as they approached home
base. So it was extremely difficult to pick them up, but there
were some fairly easy pickings if you did and had a lot of gas
left.

As an aid safely to searching down low I found something,
quite accidentally, I was to use to good advantage thereafter.
Pilots had been coming out of the sun since World War I, and
so did we. But to make certain that no one sucked me in for a
sun approach, or if he did and I couldn't avoid it, I used a
trick to keep track of him: I closed one eye, holding the tip of
my little finger up in front of the open orb, blocking out just
the fiery ball of the sun in front of my opened eye. I found that
it was impossible for an enemy to come down from out of the
sun on a moving target without showing up somewhere outside
of my fingertip if I continuously kept the fiery part from my
vision. This is mentioned only because I assumed that others

74

were doing the same thing, but the war was over before I knew that most of the pilots I talked to didn't.

Anyway, with this little bit of knowledge, I felt comparatively safe this day, chasing some homeward-bound Nips. And it paid off, too, for I was able to get two Nip fighters with short bursts, one after the other, only seconds apart. There were no flames from either one, both were perfect no-deflection shots. As a matter of fact, this was the only shot I ever had complete faith in, regardless of all my practice back in the States—a no-deflection shot.

The third fighter didn't go down quite so easily, it seemed, and something made me feel squeamish. Air fighting had become impersonal, for there was no personal contact—except on this one occasion.

As a boy I remember reading the air stories of World War I, and how the opposing pilots at that time, in their rickety machines, did everything except fire revolvers at each other. And, on remembering some of these stories, I think that at times the pilots did even this.

On this occasion I had sent a burst into this little fellow. He had an open-cockpit fighter. The plane didn't burst into flames, and it didn't fall apart, but was definitely going down, out of control. As I flew right beside him, I could see his arm dangling out of the cockpit, flapping in the slip-stream like the arm of a rag doll, and I knew definitely he was dead. For no other reason, or maybe because we were supposed to bring a claim back in our teeth to get credit, I sent another long burst into his plane and literally tore it up. That was the only time I ever felt squeamish about the entire affair.

From this time on the AVG pilots knew that unless they came down practically within the city limits of Rangoon they would stand little chance of getting back at all. The Burmese members of our help disappeared without notice one day. Their action frightened so badly our Indian servants, who were definitely not pro-Japanese, that they announced they would be on their way to India on foot.

Ed Liebolt, one of our pilots, forced down with engine trouble on the outskirts of Rangoon, was expected back, surely, for some other pilot had seen Ed get out of his wheels-up landing in a rice paddy and commence running. However, Ed Liebolt never got back, so we can only assume the Burmese had killed him.

We discovered that the Burmese had turned pro-Japanese in a hurry, and for safety we moved back out to Mingaladon Field, where we could fly out on a minute's notice and set explosives to anything we had to leave behind. Our ground crew had been sent on to the next base of operations in trucks, Magwe, Burma.

Remembering my promise to Jim Adam, I had to think fast, so I talked Bob Smith into going back to set the fire and kill Angus. I was flying out of Rangoon with seven P-40s in need of complete overhaul, before the last of the AVG was to leave, so I told Bob that I didn't have time to do this unpleasant task.

The next time I saw Bob Smith I didn't even bother to ask him if he had set fire to Jim's house. My only concern was whether he had found Angus, and Bob answered meekly: "Yes."

"Did you shoot Angus?" I asked, not daring to look Bob in the eyes.

"I shot at him. But I missed him. He got away," was Bob's rather weak answer to my inquiry.

No further inquiries were necessary.

CHAPTER 9

SEVEN TIRED P-40S left Rangoon in early March 1942 for the last time. These same planes made brief halts on their way north, such as Magwe, Mandalay, and Lashio, Burma. We remained about three days in each of these places to provide cover for the trucks and refugees coming along by road.

The last members of the AVG to leave Rangoon were making a good account of themselves, we heard, as they too were stationed briefly in the same places we seven had recently moved out of, these same cities I had stood by to defend when no Japs came over. It was probably just as well this way, for our seven P-40s were in the saddest condition of the lot.

All seven pilots were happy to get back to old Hostel Number Two, as bad as we thought it was. We had timed our arrival to the day with our ground crew, who had come in by truck. When they unpacked, we found that they had brought back a few unexpected purchases. One mechanic had bought a tame female leopard. The lad kept her for a mascot on the end of a leash and collar, tied to a truck bed out in front of our hostel, with a mattress for her to sleep on. The mechanic had said that this leopard was tame, but I had my doubts. Especially so after witnessing the big cat awaken from a pretended sleep and then pounce upon a mongrel that was about to steal a meal from some of her leftover food. And again, when I had been informed that this large puddycat wouldn't harm humans, I didn't know what to think. In any event, I followed the instructions of the cat's master and played with her like the others. This leopard would permit rolling back her huge pads, where one could see long claws tucked underneath the pads. When the cat playfully cuffed one, it felt the same as soft boxing gloves, as she never extended a single claw. And her natural instincts were playfully displayed when she rolled one over, placing the two bottom fangs underneath the base of one's skull below the ear, and the upper fangs somewhere over one's opposite temple. And then the cat would gently twist the head, but never roughly, I'm happy to say. The leopard's tongue, which felt much like a number-ten-grade sandpaper, would lovingly lick the back of your neck after she released the hold upon your head.

We found that there had been no action around Kunming all the while we were south, but I couldn't help wondering why none of our staff ever seemed to leave China. I could only assume one thing: Our glorious staff had patted themselves on the back for running events by remote control, in the meantime living as ladies and gentlemen should live. Work was for the coolies. Fighting was for the troops.

At this particular period the AVG, as small as it was, happened to represent the only citizens of the United States who had not only held their own but had gone on to create a most enviable record. Their success, not defeat, was by far the greatest in the war to date. So, a high-ranking general in the Air Corps recognized personal glory to be within easy grasp if he could but annex this group of civilians to his command.

One other minor little detail had to occur to make this proposed annexation complete before this general would be able to boost his stock and yet give a legal appearance. All of the AVG pilots had to be inducted, as it was so aptly worded for lack of better words, into the Air Corps. I personally considered this to be the rottenest kind of a farce, for, though Chennault himself was a dyed-in-the-wool Air Corps man, he had earned his reputation with a crew of pilots of which better than 50 per cent had come from Uncle Sam's Navy and Marine Corps.

There was another puzzling factor about this that I could not understand at all. I realized that Chennault had experienced hunger after his forced retirement, and had to roll his own cigarettes for a while, and I appreciated that he would welcome any opportunity to be retired as a general after the war. However, he appeared to fight this much more at the time than he pretended to resist the inducting of Navy and Marine Corps pilots later on.

Furthermore, this induction was to take place even though the Air Corps could not supply the group with so much as a toothbrush (cost $5.00), let alone any airplanes or other supplies. Without post exchanges a person couldn't even exist upon a service salary with the sky-high inflation that existed in China at the time.

I momentarily left our ungreeted arrival back in Kunming to explain why our esteemed staff was too preoccupied with ticker tape to bother with us. We had to welcome ourselves back, out at good old Hostel Number Two.

At the time we had figured that we were back where a bit of relaxation was in order, safe in Kunming. Our faithful ground crew had brought back an ample supply of whisky besides the leopard, and some refugees, Anglo-Burmese girls, as well. Some of the fellows were interested in making love, while others were occupied with target practice on the adobe walls of our hostel with their sidearms. But everyone seemed interested in getting drunk.

The soirée we put on for ourselves would have probably gone unnoticed but for the fact that an ancient Allison-engine representative happened in on it. And we apparently frightened the poor old devil to death when one of our bullets ricocheted near him. This representative then went to the trouble of driving across Kunming to headquarters and spilling a story to Chennault, who was forced to look into the matter then, and as a result I was chewed out for not controlling my troops and for my part in the drinking festivities. My punishment was—a limit of two drinks per evening. He hadn't said how large, however. So I assumed this to mean two full water glasses.

After our arrival things settled back to normal for a few days, with nothing much going on at the field but to think of other ways to bore oneself. Nothing ever seemed permanent in my life.

Indeed, because of a series of incidents occurring fast in March 1942, six of us Flying Tigers (as we were called by now) were fortunate that we did not become guests of Japan right then and there. This was almost two years before I finally was shot down and did become such a guest. But the first time we literally came within thirty miles of landing plumb into Japanese-held territory, and without knowing at all where we were.

The whole thing started one March morning when word came into our pilots' ready room at Kunming that eight fighters were needed to escort the transport plane carrying China's first man and lady. There was no hesitation for volunteers, for this was the same as being asked to escort Franklin and Eleanor Roosevelt. But the catch was that no one told us where we were going. Each thought the other might know, or at least that the leader might know, so we did not bother to find out. I look back on the whole thing as some experienced old man might at some of the damned-fool things of his childhood.

As we scrambled into our P-40s, with their hideous shark-faces painted on their noses, we could see a farewell reception gathering next to the DC-2 transport waiting for the famed couple.

A jeep messenger came up to us at the last minute with some instructions from good old Harvey, but not enough of them. The instructions were merely that we were to circle in sections of two at three thousand feet and then put on a demonstration, and "make it good." It was this last phrase in the order that helped cause the havoc, for when pilots are told in addition to "make it good," then believe me, they usually will take up the stinging sort of challenge and everybody else had better watch out.

Off we went in the shark-faces, and as we circled the field, climbing, we could see the official cars stop and let out Madame and the Generalissimo. Much bowing and handshaking could be detected in the tiny forms down on the field, the official party next to the transport.

At a signal from the leader the shark-faces moved into a Lufbery column. In turn each of us dove at the far side of the field at full throttle. Each pilot leveled out just off the ground. As the planes approached the official party, they started to roll, so that by the time they arrived over the transport each plane was on its back.

And this is where we overdid it. The lead planes were so low that all the figures on the ground—and this included the famous pair and our own boss—threw themselves flat on their faces, and stayed that way. And we knew then what Chennault and his dignified guests must be thinking about us, or saying about us, as they lay there. But it was too late.

One pilot with very limited flying experience told us afterwards that he had rolled quite naturally to the upside-down position by merely following the P-40 in front of him, but when the time came to roll right side up again, he was at a total loss because the P-40 in front of him had left his vision by pulling up. He said the only thing that saved him was remembering: center the needle and then the ball, which was taught him in instrument-flying school.

With this novice, and another pilot whose baggage door flew open, the distinguished pair had only a Higher Power protecting them from their own airplanes. Yet all this was but the beginning of a long series in what could be termed a "comedy of errors"—except that the comedy was lacking, at least at the time.

No sooner had we finished "making it good" in regard to the demonstration, and were back up in formation, than the formation leader saw that he couldn't continue with his open baggage door and motioned for me to take over the lead for the escort mission.

As I recall, one other plane dropped out of formation too, leaving only six of us. The tired old P-40s were weak from lack of spare parts and from other ailments.

Finally the DC-2 transport was loaded with the dignitaries and took off. And now it was my turn, as leader of the escorts,

81

to wish that I had been informed of where we were going. I just simply did not know, and neither did the other escorts. It had all happened so fast. But on top of all this my compass was not working, and I couldn't hear anything on my radio. As the trip progressed, I divided my time between scanning the sky for Nip fighters and trying to pick out some landmark, any landmark at all, on this unfamiliar, rugged terrain of interior China. We had, for all practical purposes, just arrived in this interior country, it must be remembered, and had not had a chance to fly around much. What few charts any of us had were virtually worse than useless.

We had flown for about two hours when it finally dawned on me that the precious load in the transport might be bound for Chungking. Thick, billowy clouds were forming rapidly, and no longer were the rugged mountain peaks visible at all. We were flying through a windstorm, and this would never do, for our little fighter planes did not carry enough gas for much of this. And what a storm it was we were to learn later, when told that the wind in this particular locality often reached the velocity of a hundred miles per hour. And we were in such a storm now, with cross winds.

Knowing that no Japs could possibly find a DC-2 in that cloudy weather, I wobbled my wings good-by to the transport pilot and started my own fighters back for home or some landing place. But with my compass not working, and my radio not working, and no familiar landmark anywhere, all I could do was to try to guide our way back out of the thick clouds and be able to see something. The whole thing became a race between the clouds and our remaining gas.

The gas finally won, but only by ten minutes. This is all the supply of gas I had left when at last we broke out of the heavier clouds and I spotted what appeared to be a tiny field in a valley between rugged peaks.

On flying by for quick inspection the field turned out to be not a field at all but a hill with the top flattened off. In reality it turned out later to be a Chinese cemetery way up there in the mountains. But it would have to do, even though it was much too small to land anything as fast as a P-40, and especially at

that distance above sea level, six thousand feet. Yet this cemetery was our last and only chance.

So one by one we dropped over the edge of this tiny clearing,
and each landing was disastrous to the plane, for all around
this little plateau of a cemetery was a couple hundred feet of
drop-off, and we had to set our planes down with the gears retracted. A couple pilots tried it the conventional way but were
far worse off than those who didn't.

Each plane, on being stopped in this manner, would skid
along on its belly, damaging the landing gear even though it
was retracted, and either one or the other wing tip in some
cases. But what surprised us after that was the speed with which
we immediately became surrounded by a horde of Chinese. All
of us had not yet had a chance to drag ourselves from the damaged planes before the Chinese began pouring in around us. We
did not know at the time where so many could be coming from,
but it turned out that they were coming from a neighboring
village, and there were hundreds and hundreds of them. None
of them seemed to understand English, but they stood there and
stared at us, and we stared back at them.

Finally a young Chinese came up to me and in very broken
English explained that he was the only man who could speak
our language. Among other things he tried to tell us, while all
that horde stood around jabbering, was that the nearby village
was Wenshan and no white man had been there for more than
ten years. This man had learned English from missionaries
when he was a boy.

The village, we further found out, was only a few miles from
the Japanese-occupied border. In other words, I had barely
missed becoming a captive of the Emperor of Japan two years
before I finally did become one.

On one of the plane radios that still happened to be working
we finally managed to contact the home base. We informed the
base where we were. The answer, from our very good friend
Harvey, had this to say to us: "Happy to hear from you fellows.
We have made arrangements for you to stay in the bridal suite
of the Grand Hotel, and God damn it, don't ever come back."

We did, though, live for a week with the mayor of Wenshan.

During this time we learned about ten words from our genial host. The only one I can remember now is *"gombay."* At each meal the mayor would propose a series of toasts, first to the United States, then in turn to each one of us. Each time he would fill his cup with rice wine, drink the entire contents, turn the empty cup upside down, and say: *"Gombay."*

We did the same, first drinking a toast to China, and then to the mayor. Fortunately we had two meals a day or we could not have stood up under it.

The mayor, through the English-speaking interpreter, wanted to know when we were going to fly away. But with our planes strewn in heaps all over the cemetery we had no answer to that one. Instead, we politely explained that we were out of gasoline or we would not have dropped in on him.

The mayor came out with the classical remark that he had five gallons in a can at his home, and that he would lend these five gallons to us. We hardly could keep straight faces because obviously this would not be enough to make our planes even cough.

During this stay at Wenshan we took daily hikes about this ancient city up in the mountains, to see if we could find a means of getting out. Wenshan was surrounded in its entirety by a huge rock wall of the approximate vintage of the Great Wall of China. We were told that for centuries the present populace had been supplied by convicts, in much the same manner that Australia had gotten its beginning. We climbed nearby hilltops so that we could see what lay beyond. In doing this we scaled stone fortifications that were former lookout towers in various forms of dilapidation. We found that excellent construction had battled time, and quite possibly repeated attacks, in a remarkable fashion. But we found nothing to help us.

After a week of all this we were becoming desperate. In our wandering about the village we discovered a camouflaged U.S.-manufactured truck hidden in the brush. After much double talk we finally managed to locate the driver. Because he was the only one among them who could drive a truck, or at least who thought he could, he had been made a colonel in their army.

We dickered with him to take us back home, and he finally agreed to do so. But we no sooner had gotten under way over that rugged terrain than we observed that he hardly could drive at all. The mountains were so steep, the trail was so rough, and his driving was so terrible that after four days of moving we had gone only a little more than a hundred miles.

We were so afraid that he was going to run us off one of these thousand-foot drops that we begged him to let one of us take over the wheel. But the colonel would have no part of it. So then we tried to take over the wheel through force or trickery, but he was on to this, also, and each time we tried to grab the ignition key, he would jump out of the truck, running up the mountainside with the key in his hand. He would sit on his heels in the brush, and wait at a distance, until we convinced him that we would not try again.

Not only was there room for only one beside the driver in the truck cab, but he insisted that it be that way after the first key-stealing attempt was made. We alternated for this choice position, because trying to be comfortable in any position in that truck bed was impossible.

Even at comparatively slow speed, on this rocky, gutted roadway, the constant jarring had us physically sore from head to foot, not to mention our mental attitudes. At times the up-and-down jarring became so rapid it would leave the loose chaff and dust that had been lying upon the wooden flooring of this canvas-covered truck suspended about two inches above the floor like a false bottom.

Along the way our driver ran across four Chinese soldiers, and got the idea over to us that they would ride in the back too. We said okay, and the soldiers gave us toothy grins, climbing aboard the truck. After but a few miles of this careening and constant jarring, it became evident that Oriental boys were unaccustomed to vehicular motion, and then these Chinese soldiers commenced to vomit. Now the truck bed became covered with slimy rice as well as unbearable thumps.

I'll never forget to my dying day the words of one of our pilots whose feelings had gone beyond their breaking point. This pilot lunged over, grabbing one of these deathly-ill Chinese by the throat with both hands, and started screaming at him: "I warned you, you slope-headed son of a bitch, if you puked once more, I was going to kill you." The rest of us had to drag him away from the poor Chinese.

I was learning about Chinese now, and very fast, but I was still to learn a lot more. Finally we came to a swift river up in these mountains where the only means of crossing was by primitive barge pulled by ropes. On the banks of this river, and apparently in control of the barge, were mountain people who did not seem to care much for us. These mountain boys all had on Fu Manchu mustaches, indicating that their wearers were bandits in their spare time and did not give a damn about the Generalissimo.

We tried for half a day to get the "colonel" to coax these mountain boys to pull us across, but, he explained in sign language at various times, for some reason or other they would not do it. My own cursing and shouting at these mountain boys were about as effective as shoveling straw into a strong wind. So at last in desperation I stormed down on the barge and tied together each line I could find. Then I removed all my clothes and tied one end of the line around my waist. My idea was to swim across these swift waters and secure the line to the other shore so that we could pull across the barge ourselves. Otherwise it would have been about as easy to convince the Japs as this crowd, and we did have to get going. But as I started to get into the water, with the line around my waist, there was much shouting and brandishing of rifles.

The "colonel" stepped in then and had another parley with the mountain boys. What he said to them, or what they said to him, I do not know. But after a while they condescended to take the barge across.

Some days later we managed to reach our home base, Kunming, looking like forgotten men. Our reception was very cool, and rightly so. Because of my apparent blunder, in getting lost and so on, I volunteered to fly these planes out of the cemetery at Wenshan if they could be put in running order.

This was agreed, and I was flown to Wenshan in a light training plane. A small ground crew of our own, working with hammers, went to work straightening the propellers and wings. And the men managed to fix up four of the six planes sufficiently to take to the air—maybe. It was up to me to find out.

From these four planes all surplus weight, such as guns and the like, was removed, and only thirty gallons of gas were put in each. And now I was confronted with the toughest flying job I ever had up to this time.

These thirty gallons would have to be enough to warm up the engine, taxi me down to one end of the tiny cemetery, and then—if I could get off before plunging over the plateau—these same thirty gallons would still have to be enough to carry me over the twelve-thousand-foot mountains and land me at the closest field, Mengtsz, sixty miles away.

I selected the first of my four planes, got in, strapped myself, and then began using every bit of knowledge I had to carry me through. After testing my vibrating engine I stood on the brakes and pushed the throttle slowly forward until the manifold pressure was well into the red.

The tail of my plane raised off the ground into a horizontal position. The ground crew waved a solemn farewell of good luck, and down the tiny strip I went for better or for worse. There was no turning back at the end of that strip. There was only that drop of a couple hundred feet, and I could not have changed my mind even if I had wanted to. Also there were the cemetery mounds and gravestones to remember.

When I reached the very last footage of the runway, and just before the drop, my plane either would or it would not. All I could do was hold the stick all the way back in my lap and then pray. The craft dropped nearly fifty feet, nose high, and I sluggishly wobbled about a mile at full throttle before getting my plane under complete control. Then I managed to turn for my climb over the mountains, something that had to be done fast, for I could not waste any gas.

As it was, when my plane did get over the mountains, and was within easy reach of the Mengtsz field, the engine gasped its last, out of gas, and I glided in with a dead-stick landing. It was up to me to do the same thing all over again. The second trip I retracted my landing gear after take-off, even though in its

87

damaged condition it might not have come back down again, so that my gas consumption would be less.

Two down and two to go, and I was ready to go again. Our training plane and pilot and I were just in the process of taking off at Kunming to go fetch the third, when my friend Harvey came tearing out in his jeep in his usual excited manner.

Harvey was truly Asiatic, I thought, after all the time he had spent in the Orient—expressions, the works, for that matter. He motioned for the pilot to cut his engine by dragging his fingers across his throat. I jumped out of the back seat of the training plane and said: "What's up now, Greenlaw?"

"You are not to return after any more planes," he said in the most authoritative voice he could muster.

"What's the matter? Don't you like the way I'm bringin' 'em back?" I snarled back at him.

Harvey smirked back at me and said: "That's not it. But I'm afraid you'll save too much face, if you do."

CHAPTER **10**

ONE MORNING IN KUNMING I was awakened by a series of rifle blasts that sounded close by. At first I thought our own boys were having a bit of target practice upon the hostel walls again, and I was debating with myself whether to tell them to knock it off. The noise had awakened me sufficiently for me to realize that it was fairly late in the morning, so I stretched and walked out of my quarters to see just what the lads were doing.

It didn't turn out to be our boys at all. Then I saw what I thought was some kind of war game or something going on about the cemetery next door, because there were any number of Chinese soldiers firing rifles. My thoughts were: "Gosh, but these Chinese certainly make this look a hell of a lot more realistic than our soldiers back home."

This affair lasted for an hour at the outside. But it didn't take me more than a few minutes after I started to watch them to see that these Chinese weren't playing, weren't shooting blanks; they were firing for real. With this realization I continued to observe throughout the remainder of their battle, but not as nonchalantly as when I first walked out, for I was prepared at any moment to get better cover if the action spread any closer to where I happened to be standing. Closer, did I say? It was as close as it could be, without having some of the soldiers enter my quarters and commence firing.

One side had won over the other, because it was over almost as soon as it started, the Chinese with rifles rounding up more Chinese who had dropped their firearms. They all looked so much alike I couldn't tell which side any of them were on.

After this was over we ran for our interpreters and started asking questions in order to get some plausible explanation for this gunplay. These interpreters of our always appeared to play it cagey. I didn't know for sure, but I got the idea that they told us very little more than what they were instructed to tell us.

The lowdown on this most recent affair was that one of the feudal lords, of which there were many in China, had been plotting a little revolution. We had just witnessed the squashing of an outbreak. I didn't care to find out who was right or wrong as long as it wasn't endangering my life, but I realized that there had to be opposite feelings if people were killing each other. I gathered that political differences were settled à la Nicaragua fashion.

One of the interpreters explained that our most recent rebellion had been interrupted in its early stages through an informer. The informer method, which I found so prevalent out in China, one person getting ahead of another by turning his compatriots in for gold or favor, made me become more and more anti-social as the years went by. Even in a minor way this method was used in our squadrons. For years I thought that my imagination on this score might possibly have played tricks, but I was to learn that it had not. I know now that an informer just can't help himself.

Many times in recent years I have wished that I had majored in history instead of engineering, for I could have had a great deal more out of life, and maybe I would not have expected so much of people—myself included. And if I had been a history major, I would have been satisfied that I was involved in making part of history, only in a minor way. And that grade-school history books for children's protection present everybody as a noble character, except the bad bad enemy. The actual people these books are talking about had every rotten habit and foul idea known to man, because they were human beings also. History has its Napoleons, Cardinal Richelieus and Milady DeWinters.

Lest some might gather an impression that this story is an exposé, I wish to say I have no intention of such. If I had chosen to write an exposé, I could have taken fiendish delight in doing a dilly fifteen years ago, when even our government was not too certain about things that went on. But to make one man's story interesting to others he must run into good and bad situations.

I have long since discovered that there is no such thing as bad people. There are just two kinds of people, because people are people. There are those who know and those who don't know. And I don't wish you to think I have any intention of shoving onto a few the entire blame for China becoming communistic instead of something else. In a way, even though I didn't make a fortune like some of the others, and my main motives were not greed and power, I honestly feel that I am guilty along with them. And even though my main crime was ignorance, which is a by-product of emotional immaturity, I deserve to be included with the China gang.

My only hope is that we didn't louse up the future generations too greatly, so that they may have a chance in the years to come.

Another one of my off-duty days in March my interpreter got around to telling me, in a rather awkward manner, about some Chinese wanting to enter my quarters and talk to me. I don't know why, but I always thought my interpreter wouldn't know what side he was on if one asked him real quick.

The best way I am able to describe my visitor is that there was a sort of knowing, pimp-like wiseness about his manner. By my pretending to go along with him, merely trying to draw him out, I learned a good deal more about China. Though the purpose of the call appeared to be something else, my visitor was offering me five hundred American dollars for my .38-caliber revolver and a certain number of rounds of ammunition. In pretending to dicker Oriental style, knowing also that they had no respect for anyone who settled for the first offer, I was able to find the real purpose behind this intended purchase. Thinking that I was a right guy by then, my visitor smiled slyly and

91

said: "You don't have to worry. I represent a province some distance from Yunan."

Something else became clear. These yellow-skinned bums weren't with the United States against the Japanese. They were all fighting for power within China, standing by for an opportunity to take over. And they went for the guy they counted on giving them the most in the end.

Being one of the few ex-career officers on the setup besides Chennault, I had studied ground warfare in the Marine Corps schools. So this Chinese unknowingly explained why the Chinese accounts of valiant defenses and actions didn't add up to the few I personally knew about. It was so obvious by then that the Chinese weren't fighting with the supplies that were given to them.

I cannot tell you that I was clever enough to figure out the complete picture, for I doubt if but few could have done that. But I had more than a sneaking hunch that someone was making bigger suckers out of the pilots than any of them realized.

Chennault had made a speech about this time, concerning the great harm that could be done with smuggling, because a few of our ground crew had been involved in smuggling arms in an amateurish sort of way. The full meaning of this came to me during my conversation with my visitor from another province. It was a pure case of mistaken identity as far as I was concerned, for he thought I was a big shot and had access to a lot of arms smuggled in from Burma—not merely my own personal revolver and a few rounds.

I was only bothered thinking about myself at this time. But as the years went slowly by, the patient Orientals waited to unload our Allied supplies upon us in Korea, and by rough analysis I figure that only about 5 per cent of the arms and munitions, medical supplies, and the like from the Allies ended up for their intended purpose. Then, too, it was beginning to dawn that they didn't appreciate amateurs messing up a deal that was making a few of combined nationalities multimillionaires.

By April, Burma was almost completely gone, and I had something other than China's interior troubles to contend with.

Chennault was ready to go hog wild with what remained of his little volunteer group of civilians. Joe Stilwell and another general, who both outranked our boss but were still without combat troops of their own, came into the picture for keeps. Prior to this I had always imagined that for some reason we were more or less putting on a show of some kind.

The manner in which these three argued over control of this handful of pilots impressed me much the same as three whores would have—arguing over their virginity. The combined stars upon their own shoulders were as numerous as the combat pilots they happened to be arguing about. And apparently we pilots weren't to be consulted.

The Third Pursuit squadron, which was based in Loiwing near the Burma border, was getting the works at this time. Under the combined-command scramble the Third was being sent out on every conceivable kind of strafing mission. Jungles were strafed, mountaintops and river beds were strafed in that rugged wilderness, resulting in a few pilots being killed for nothing. All the boys seemed to be ordered to strafe some locality where the combined three might possibly dream there was a concentration of Japs, or anything, for that matter, to keep combat reports rolling back to the United States.

The Third Pursuit were not dummies, to begin with; furthermore, they were not in any air force and it wasn't in their contracts, so they politely said nuts to this corny racket. So Chennault bundled himself up, flying down to Loiwing, saying that he was going to give a dishonorable discharge to any pilot who refused to strafe as ordered.

This expression, dishonorable discharge, became so monotonous. It was used whenever anyone wanted anything done in the group. From the manner in which our glorious staff took this expression up, I ventured a guess that many of them had suffered the real McCoy from various services. Actually, I thought one guy had gone mad, because he was talking about giving civilians dishonorable discharges.

Maybe he was going to put General George Custer of the Little Big Horn fame to shame, for he apparently wanted to fight to the last pilot, but ours was unlike Custer's situation in a couple of ways. One, he wasn't with his troops, and secondly, because the Japs couldn't surround us, we were supposed to put ourselves in that position individually by strafing between jungle trees.

Perhaps this was more than a parallel in my case, because of my Sioux blood. I know a few who didn't share the historical accounting of Custer. The guys who kicked hell out of Custer took him for an egotistical sucker.

The outcome of Chennault's parley with the Third Pursuit was—they didn't scare. So he flew back to Kunming—and what a talk he put on—the world's best. And he ended up talking parts of the First and Second Pursuits into a strafing mission on Chiengmai, Thailand.

By then he had backed up a wee bit, for at least there was logic to what he proposed to us. For my money, his purpose was to show up the boys in the Third Pursuit. And indeed, I felt much the same as I imagine a scab would going through a picket line, for there was money offered to us in our strafing mission.

I volunteered for this venture, a habit I couldn't seem to break, not because of bravery, for only my Chinese laundryman and I held the secret of mortal fear. I don't believe that I would have refused even had I known that Madame Chiang was threatening a separate peace with Japan at this time. Her threat was given to force more aid from America for the Kuomintang Government.

Come to think of it, a couple of spectacles I witnessed undoubtedly led me to volunteer, just to get away from the horrible place and the people in Kunming.

The first of these spectacles was a rather queer procession going by in front of our hostel. A ragged Chinese with feathers tied to his matted hair was being pushed along in front of this procession, which included an officer on horseback, a few soldiers, and some Chinese in rickshas. There were about a hundred in all, and most of these were on foot.

The procession stopped in the cemetery in front of our hostel, while the officer got down from his mount and the people climbed out of the rickshas. The ragged man with the feathers was forced to kneel on the ground. These soldiers turned out to be a firing squad and in a few minutes sent a volley into the back of the poor devil kneeling on the ground. As he fell forward onto his face after the shots, the accompanying crowd broke into excited shouting, running up to kick and stab at the crushed form.

Soon the officer walked up, motioning the crowd back and leaning over as if to examine the bleeding form. He slowly unbuckled his automatic, pointing it at the back of the victim's head, then fired.

This apparently ended the affair as the procession quietly left the cemetery the way they had entered; the Oriental faces had a look that appeared as emotionless as time.

Yes, this was all, except that a body is left four days, and if no relatives claim it for burial the state takes over. But if there are no claimants, and the state is not prompt, then the starved, chowlike dogs get a free meal.

Upon inquiring into what traitorous deed or murder this unfortunate had committed, we found to our surprise that he had been caught stealing. Let me remind you that stealing was legal in the Orient; we had visited the thieves' market in Kunming, which covered several square blocks. The only thing that was illegal was getting caught before the articles were in the market.

The second revolting spectacle was when we ran into a parade downtown one night. This seemingly endless procession had the paper dragons and disguises of all natures in brilliant colors, moving along in centipede fashion like a long worm through the narrow, crooked streets.

The part in particular that got me was when two men, naked excepting for loincloths, were brought along in this parade. These two almost nude men had their hands tied and were jerked along by collar-and-leash affairs. They were emaciated and dirty, and their faces were expressionless.

Upon getting someone to explain this I found that these two men, poor souls, were Japanese prisoners who had survived in captivity for some time.

So it might be small wonder that I left Kunming for Loiwing, again with no regrets, even if it meant endangering my life.

We arrived in Loiwing preparing for our strafing mission on Chiengmai, Thailand. The pilots who were stationed there were the Third Pursuit Chennault had just gotten back from talking to in regard to all the strafing at random. They were anything but warm to us when they found we were going. In fact one pilot said: "I knew somebody would strafe. But I don't think it's for free, like us."

Our Chiengmai strafers didn't have to watch the Third Pursuit and their glares that night, because we got to stay in the beautiful American hostel on the hilltop. This hostel had been built for the staff of the Central Aircraft Manufacturing Company, who were supposedly running that farce called a lend-lease factory.

The hostel where they lived was a gorgeous layout, but the so-called factory didn't impress me at all, even though I am B.S. in A.E. I never found out whether the factory ever completed aircraft one, but that was not important, I believe. The main idea was that they lived like kings in this hostel, which, for but few differences, might have been a swanky country club back home. The view was ideal, also, as large plate-glass windows overlooked the mountainous valley and winding river below.

The defending Third didn't live in the hostel, for they were a little different class than these lend-lease friends. They had been housed in far less pretentious quarters down near a crummy Chinese village. In fact the only reason I can figure out why we were spending the night was that we were going along with Chennault's program and the Third had refused.

Whether the phrase "getting the word" is a general one here I do not know. But I do know that in a private sort of informal way the phrase was rather general with us out there in China, and referred to people having a feeling they are not going to live through something.

Maybe I imagined it this night in the American hostel, but Jack Newkirk was not the same smiling Jack I had attended a few shore leaves with off the U.S.S. *Yorktown* prior to the war.

Nor was he the same as he was when I had flown with him in Rangoon. Previously always an affable gent, but this night he just didn't want to talk at all—about anything.

There was another, "Black Mac" McGerry, who was an unusually quiet sort ordinarily, and I truly enjoyed spending this night in Black Mac's company at the hostel. Mac and I had pooled our resources and purchased a couple bottles of scotch from our hosts, and settled down in front of the spacious windows to enjoy ourselves. We were very much alone, and as the evening wore on Mac became loquacious for a change. He reminisced, at the time, about how his family would be shocked if it were possible for them to see him enjoying a bottle of whisky.

Little did I know, while we were drinking, that I would run into Mac's brother upon my return to the United States and have to leave out part of this enjoyable evening with Mac. For I thought Mac dead, and wanted to give him the part of Mac that I thought he would cherish in his memory.

Morning came and I skipped breakfast, as I recall. We were briefed by Newkirk and some pilot from my own squadron. We were to leave that afternoon in order to arrive at a lonesome base somewhere in a Burma outpost near sundown to keep the Nips from getting wise.

The lot of us were to remain in this practically vacated RAF emergency field overnight. On the following morning we were to take off in two groups, Newkirk's Second Pursuit, and our own First Pursuit, and the take-off was to be in the dark.

The plan was to arrive over the Chiengmai airstrip in the morning at the exact instant—and it lasts for only a minute or so—when one can see the ground from the air and they cannot see you. Therefore, we had split ourselves into two groups because we wanted to make certain one group hit at the exact time. After strafing the airport and its aircraft we were to return immediately to this RAF outpost, gas, and be gone in a hurry.

We flew into this base just before dark because the only air-raid warning they had there was a bugler on a hilltop some two miles from the base, meaning that our people were given just

97

sufficient time to flop on their faces in a trench if the Japanese were to come over. So we went into this field of ours at dusk so that the Nips might not see us and come over and strafe our planes when they lay on the ground.

After we had gassed up our planes late that evening in the dark, we finally went to wash off the caked dust and get a bite to eat before turning in. We were going to have to take off at four o'clock, in the dark, the following morning.

I was standing beside Jack Newkirk in this RAF washroom, which consisted of a bamboo hut. A little RAF sergeant came up to us and said in cockney: "Hi, fellows. It's all right to use that water to wash your face and hands in, but don't drink it or brush your teeth with it because it's polluted."

Both Jack and I said: "Thanks," and the sergeant walked away.

But the first thing I noticed Jack do was to dip his toothbrush into this polluted water and start to brush his teeth.

I looked at Jack and said: "Jack, didn't you hear what that guy said?"

Jack grinned at me and smiled, then he said: "Well, after tomorrow, I don't think it'll make any difference."

They awakened us all the next morning. Morning, hell, it was pitch dark, with no moon. It seemed like the middle of the night to me.

All we had for bearing on take-off from the rolling dirt strip were a couple of trucks parked on the field with their headlights turned on dim. Everybody got off, all eight in each group. And we joined on our respective leaders, who were to navigate us over the mountains and jungle in the darkness. No running lights. Merely the reddish-blue glare from our own exhaust stacks to fly formation on.

What was passing by in the jungle below us, or how close we came to any mountains, was in my imagination only. Finally light started to appear in the sky above us. And then I could begin to see dim outlines below me.

At about this same time our lead planes turned sharp left like they were going to run into a mountain. They started to dive. I wheeled my plane and dove after them, although I couldn't make out any target as yet. Even before I saw the field I saw tracers from the guns of my mates preceding me. Then the field seemed to take shape in the semi-darkness. I sighted in on the same place where the previous tracers had gone, some of these tracers were visible ricocheting as if being fired from the opposite direction.

The first pass got three transports ablaze, which, owing to their size, were the easiest to pick out that time of the morning. In turn the burning transports helped to light up our target area as we wheeled around for a pass in the opposite direction. I don't see how any of us knew which one of us was which.

The second pass was made under much better visibility, even in those few seconds it took to turn around. It was evident our attack had come as a complete surprise, for I strafed down a line of planes that were parked as I remembered before the war at old Squadron II at the Navy training center in Pensacola, Florida.

I could see blurred forms jumping off wings, out of cockpits, and scurrying all over the field like ants. I made two more passes, witnessing fires all over the Chiengmai airfield.

By the time we made the last couple of passes the air was so full of black puffs of anti-aircraft fire it was difficult to determine whether the Japs had launched any aircraft, or even to see our other P-40s.

Radio silence was broken finally when someone yelled: "Let's get to hell out of here."

And as we pulled away individually, I saw a P-40 throwing smoke. This was just a little while after we had left Chiengmai and were over the jungle. The pilot's engine apparently stopped and he rolled his plane over on its back. In a second or so I could see his parachute open, and see him swing back and forth on the ends of his strings, settle down, and disappear into the jungle below.

When we got back to our base, I found out that chute had belonged to Black Mac. I knew that he had landed alive. I only prayed that he would be able to find his way through the jungle without running into any Jap patrols.

Mac was never heard from until after the war, for the natives had turned him in to the Japs, and he was held in Thailand for the duration. I saw him after the war, but if I thought he had been quiet before, it was nothing compared to when I met him after the war. Though I have inquired about him many times since, he appears to have drifted out of circulation on his own this time. I can only imagine that he had it pretty rough, although he did not say.

Later, when we talked to the Second Pursuit, we found that Jack Newkirk would not be back either. He had not found the Chiengmai field, but had found a line of trucks instead, which his outfit had strafed thoroughly. One of his pilots said that the last he saw of Jack was a ball of flames as his plane plowed into the ground, rolling end over end in a crumpled mass.

My thoughts couldn't help go back to the two previous evenings. Jack had gotten the word.

CHAPTER **11**

BY APRIL I became so anxious to get out of Kunming, and all that it meant to me, that I damn nearly would have volunteered to walk back to the United States.

Chennault had again called us together after more recent developments, and he gave us the lowdown concerning the group's future. He talked about the imminent "induction," and said that he had been able to stall it off so far. He said that he had told the top Air Corps general in Far Eastern Command that he could not permit the "induction" until the time came when the Air Corps was in a position to supply aircraft, personnel, and matériel.

There had been a deadline set for "induction"—July 1, 1942. Chennault claimed that he had fudged a bit on this agreed deadline date, that already the Air Corps was in a position to let us have a few P-40s ferried into Kunming, and that it would not be long before personnel and matériel would be coming.

I had a regular commission waiting for me in the Marine Corps, as I happened to be the only regular who had gone on the mission; the others were all reserves. I asked: "What can be done in a case like mine?"

Chennault's answer to this was concise and positive as he said: "I have my orders. Everybody is to be commissioned in the Air Corps not later than July 1, 1942."

101

I wasn't satisfied and said: "But how about the written agreement back in Washington? I understand it is legal."

"I thought I made myself clear." He turned, ending the conversation for good. It appeared impossible for Chennault to register any emotion on his deep-lined, leathery face at any time. I gathered the impression that he thought his face was a piece of Ming-dynasty chinaware he was afraid might break if he were to show emotion of any kind.

My thoughts were really tangled up by this time, beyond belief. Apparently those secret papers lying in Admiral Nimitz's safe in Washington were to be no help for me in far-off China. I already had plenty to worry about without adding concern for the current predicament I found myself in. The one and only letter I received prior to the mail being cut off by the war had been a bitter one from my mother. I never got completely out of one situation before I was in another.

My mother hadn't gone into much detail, but she said that the juvenile court had taken our three children away from my ex-wife in Seattle, but not to worry because they had gone down and picked up the children, and they were on the ranch with her. My arrangement with my parents and a lawyer was being carried out, to pay off my indebtedness, for I had allotted practically my entire salary for this purpose.

Actually, I had a great deal to be thankful for, and I didn't realize it. I was an emotionally immature person of the first order, which does not help peace of mind or make happiness. Frankly, this is what makes screwballs, and I'm afraid that I was one.

Regardless of any of my self-manufactured troubles, or any troubles a mature person may have that he solves by himself, there was one thing that dwelled in my mind. If I were forced to continue my occupation for any length of time, I might not survive, for this war had all the earmarks of being a lengthy affair. And if I didn't survive, there was going to be a slab of marble with Gregory Boyington, USMC, inscribed thereon in Arlington National Cemetery.

For I had discovered that there are some United States Government-connected careers that pay off handsomely, and I hadn't chosen one of these. Not that I wasn't a government worker of sorts. But my chosen field, sitting behind a single engine killing people with six machine guns, was no way to get rich—or, for that matter, even live to a ripe old age.

Apparently, at this time, I was suffering from something I like to call "mental diarrhea." This state occurs when a person devotes so much time to working out things that might happen —and they usually do—that he isn't capable of taking care of his daily thinking worth a damn. So, in desperation from thinking, he usually winds up getting stinking.

Although this is fairly clear to me now, there were very few who felt free to discuss the subject with me in the past, unless they happened to be affected the same as I was—and were feeling much braver than usual. Occasions of this nature did happen, however, altogether too often to suit me, especially when I was in places where I didn't try to conceal my emotions at all.

One night I had held up a Chinese driver for quite a lengthy time outside our hostel bar, while I carried on an endless conversation with some pilot seated in the bar. The driver didn't seem to mind, but one of our mechanics most certainly did, and said so.

In answer to a great amount of swearing, finally, I left my bar stool and went outside to get into a waiting station wagon. The mechanic, seated in the back of the vehicle, had apparently been drinking, and shouted: "You God-damned ex-officers think you can hold anybody up. Don't you? You're nothing but a bunch of drunken bastards."

I must say that "bastard" was accepted as a word of endearment, but the word "drunken" cut me deeply.

Then he threatened: "I'm going to teach you a lesson you'll never forget," and out of the station wagon he started.

I have no idea why my Supreme Power blessed a lug like myself with strength and co-ordination both, but he did. And as my adversary threw open the car door and started to lunge out, my co-ordination came into full play, for I believed that he was going to try to do just exactly as he had threatened to do. He had one hand occupied pushing the door completely open, one foot on the ground, and the other foot on the way down to

103

propel himself in my direction, and that was my time to counter, not after he had swung a punch. So without hesitating I stepped into him and my right crossed automatically.

One blow and he crumpled to the ground, but he hadn't been knocked out even though my blow had struck him flush on the button, I thought. But his leg was broken. On this occasion I felt truly sorry the next day, and went across town to the hospital near Hostel Number One to tell the poor fellow so. He happened to be a good sport, for he held no grudge, and had informed the staff that he had slipped and broken his leg when they inquired.

We AVG Flying Tigers were invited one night to another banquet in the famous couple's honor once again at the large dining hall in Hostel Number One. I had gotten dressed up and I had driven over to the hostel with the others, but I didn't go into the banquet hall, so I spared myself the last of the corny after-dinner speeches that Madame Chiang was so famous for. An ex-Navy flyer, Bartell, and I had decided to remain in the bar while the Madame was blowing smoke like she always had before, so we didn't go to dinner at all.

We couldn't see the dining hall from where we sat, but we could hear hands clapping down the long corridor to the bar. Each time we heard clapping we would re-enact, from past performances, a part of her speech.

As I recall, Bartell's and my conversation went like this:

"I wish to thank General Chennault and his glorious staff, who are seated at my table, for instructing you in tactics."

"What tactics, lady? I've seen better-looking men in line-ups than you got at your head table."

"The Generalissimo and I would be willing to give our own lives, if we could, along with those who have so gallantly given theirs."

"I would like to get close enough to the mummy she calls the Generalissimo, just once, to see if he is really breathing."

The dinner and speech were finally over and Chennault was taking the famous couple through the hostel on a Cook's tour, when the party ran into Bartell and myself in the bar. Apparently my friend had had so much to drink by this time he had to remain seated, but I jumped to attention. Chennault later complimented me for at least having the courtesy to stand at attention.

Personally I couldn't see how Chennault figured them. It was so obvious that the Generalissimo was nothing but a front who never said anything on his own or even thought for himself. The Madame did everything. Chiang Kai-shek just seemed to be led around where she wanted him to be led, and, right or wrong, I was positive that the Madame was a number-one con artist if I had ever seen one.

I had doped out that the male's having to be the power for Oriental prestige was the only reason for Chiang being around at all. It was to take a long time, but I was finally satisfied, for even the Democrats got wise to this setup. The last trip to Washington for both Chennault and the Madame proved fruitless, according to the newspapers.

Of course the newspapers hadn't mentioned why, but I doubt whether they really knew. Even provided that everything was on the level, how in hell did we think Chiang could clean up twenty-six different-speaking provinces when it took us nearly a hundred years to clean up the Tong wars in San Francisco?

Shortly after the dinner episode I got a welcome brief trip away from Kunming. We got an opportunity to escort some twin-engine Russian bombers flown by Chinese pilots. And our fighters had to gas up at my familiar old mountain village, Mengtzu. During the confusion of rolling many gasoline drums about the strip there I thought back upon my two previous visits alone.

Mengtzu was handled by one lone AVG radioman. I recalled his inviting me into his tattered quarters and explaining how he had overcome the months of loneliness. He had told me of making a purchase in the little village.

This radioman had bought a Chinese woman from her father, and she lived with him as a wife, cooking his meals and helping him while away the lonely nights. I had seen his woman, a typical native, and she spoke only Chinese. I recalled turning down everything in the nature of hospitality that the radioman offered me, except a couple of drinks before I flew back to Kunming.

Our P-40s escorted this group of Russian bombers flown by Chinese on a bombing mission over Hanoi and Haiphong, French Indo-China. The reason for meeting them over Mengtsz was the difference in range between their bombers and our fighters.

This mission I remembered as ungodly long, for we flew above the stratus that covered the high mountains with the exception of a few high peaks. These peaks looked like tiny islands in a large ocean of snow-white water, all over Japanese-held terrain underneath us, we knew. Thoughts of my engine quitting and letting down into enemy territory in the soup weren't exactly morale builders either.

I never did see Hanoi, or Haiphong, for that matter, but it was easy enough to determine when we arrived over each of these cities. As we flew above the stratus, in between the bomb-ers and our fighters came the familiar black puffs of exploding anti-aircraft shells. I'm not going to tell you that the black puffs were so thick you could walk on them, but the fact that the Japs had our altitude and direction was sufficient to make me uncomfortable.

Smoke and debris flew from one bomber, and as we watched it slowly turned back for home unescorted. I had hoped that these bombers would decide to guide us back before we were out of fuel. On our own, this would not have been an easy task, for we were not navigating and didn't know much other than the names of the cities we were supposed to strike.

Finally the last of the bombs had gone out of sight into the vast whiteness below us. And no Jap fighters came up. Not being able to see where the bombs had landed left me only to wonder how successful the mission had been. Later in Kun-ming I read where we had practically demolished both targets. But I automatically cut this down to a few vacated, rural out-houses, since I had discovered long before that a large denomi-nator was necessary to decode Chinese claims. To get back to Mengtsz had been success enough as far as I was concerned.

Back in Kunming again, but not for long, as I had held up

my hand when someone had asked: "Who wants to go down and help the Third Pursuit." When I flew to Loiwing on this trip, I figured that I was going to stay for a while. This time I was nothing special in Loiwing, and I wasn't invited to bunk in the American hostel, either.

I remember the fellows joking with someone in the Third Pursuit they had nicknamed "Fearless Freddie," and how they had accidentally run into his father-in-law. Fearless Freddie had become engaged to a gorgeous Anglo-Indian girl while stationed at Rangoon, and her father was quite naturally very dark complexioned, for after all he was an Indian.

The girl and her father were with some other refugees who had come out of Burma with Stilwell. But the outcome of the entire thing was that Fearless and this girl wanted to get married in the worst way, so we said we would help him solve his problems. We did this in a manner so that we could have a little fun too. So Loiwing was incorporated in true pilot fashion and we nominated the manager of the CAMCO factory as honorable mayor, so he could perform the wedding ceremony, as there was no minister.

Our gag was arranged so as to make certain that we had the American hostel at our disposal—by making the manager mayor. We planned for flowers and all the flourishes for this occasion. When Fearless became worried about the legality of our plans, we passed it off with first one vague explanation then another. But we didn't tell him that we had arranged for a minister, who would appear at the last minute and make their marriage legal in every land.

The wedding was scheduled to be held at night, and I happened to be on duty at the field while the off-duty pilots were making the final arrangements that day. An air raid sounded about noontime, and I warmed my engine briefly before take-off because I wasn't expecting any extra time before the Nips were upon us. I don't believe I gave a second thought that the attack might louse up the wedding, because my P-40 felt like it was dragging as my engine was sputtering down the runway on take-off. This sputtering wasn't too bad and it had become an

107

everyday occurrence by then, but with this dragging all I hoped was that at least it kept on sputtering.

But not this time. My plane was little more than in the air —and I had used up the entire length of the runway—when my engine coughed its last. I didn't even have the opportunity of getting the wheels retracted before my plane slammed into the ground, wheels and all. The impact was so great that my safety belt had broken and I was flung forward in the cockpit. My instrument panel tore into my knees and I damn nearly gargled the gun sight. Fortunately it didn't get my teeth, but the gun sight split my head open near my temple.

As I crawled out of the cockpit, the hood, which I had locked open for take-off, looked like an accordion when it shot forward under force of impact after shearing its lock. I was completely dazed as I struggled out of the cockpit, but I knew almost by instinct to get away from possible fire and to try to take cover before the Japs came.

While half crawling and staggering in a torn and bloody condition I asked some nearby Chinese farmers to lend me a hand. They apparently didn't want any part of me, for no attention was paid to my pleas as the farmers continued with their chores. I was so angry with these Chinese that I cursed them soundly with the last of my strength. Probably the reason they would not help was that the Chinese, I had heard, refrain from saving one's life because they are then obligated to care for this person financially ever afterward. These being real primitive Chinese, they no doubt went by the old traditions, for they never walked so much as a step toward me.

I was eventually picked up by one of our boys and taken to good old Dr. "Rich" Richards, an American doctor we all loved. "Doc Rich" was one of three medicos who had joined the group, and all of them were excellent medical men. Doc Rich sewed up my head and taped up my knees with yards of adhesive tape, much like casts. He had no access to an X-ray, so he wasn't able to determine whether my kneecaps were fractured.

But to hell with a little thing like my accident; the wedding went on as scheduled that night in the hostel. And I was to attend, even though painfully. My knees had become so enlarged I wasn't able to get my trousers over them, so I came in my bathrobe.

While waiting for the wedding to get under way, I was seated beside Duke Hedman (America's first ace) upon the piano bench because I wasn't able to stand for any length of time. Duke was thumping away on the piano in the hostel lobby like nobody's business, and he looked like a Gay Nineties dandy, with a cigarette dangling from his lower lip as he played on.

The ceremony finally took place, and the couple had no more than embraced when another air raid sounded. It was quite dark by then as there was no moon this night. The wedding was momentarily forgotten as everyone started to run from the well-lighted building to get into transportation of any kind to drive away from the area. Some of the people tried to lend me a hand, but I refused, for I was full of whisky for the celebration and my pain combined. Anyhow I said:

"For Christ's sake, go if you're going, but not me. The Japs can see those car headlights for miles. I'm going in back of the hostel with the Chinese cooks in a slit trench, my friends."

After this statement my would-be helpers went on their way, and I slowly hobbled out into the darkness to where I thought I had remembered seeing the cooks go during air raids. I walked with added difficulty in the dark to the place I imagined this trench was located. Then I called out. No one answered my call, but I didn't think that was so unusual for Chinese. As I sat down with painful effort, I contemplated reaching the bottom of the soundless trench with but little additional pain to my legs. But to my complete surprise, after I had slid but a short distance, I somehow had the sensation that I was in mid-air without a parachute under me. The last things I remembered were blinding lights—which in my case were stars. I had mistaken a cliff for a slit trench.

I have no idea just how long after, but two Chinese sentries helped me up the hill after the raid, then Doc Rich had his work to do all over again. And poor old Doc shook his head after he had done everything he could. Duke was standing

109

beside Doc Rich as he worked away, interrupting him by repeatedly saying: "Hurt 'm, Doc! Hurt 'm, Doc!"

Doc Rich asked: "Greg, will you do me a favor?"

"Yes, why, Doc?" I asked in return.

"I wish you would stop drinking, because if you don't, I'm afraid you'll end up dead."

"Don't worry, Doc, I promise, I've had enough."

But apparently no matter how much I planned on keeping my word, drinking was one department in which I didn't do too well, although I'm certain I had the best intentions at the time.

After a few days I was flown back to Kunming whether I wanted to go or not, and was placed in the tiny hospital beside Hostel Number One. I had very few visitors, and a hell of a lot of time to indulge in feeling real sorry for myself. And by May I could stand this hospital routine no longer, so I had my knees retaped like two casts, and went back to flying once again. My job was flying overhauled engines, putting slow-time on them, circling above the Kunming area.

While I was occupied flying slow-time, some of our fast-diving P-40s were being converted into dive bombers. A dive bomber should not pick up too much speed in a dive, therefore the engineers design dive brakes into them to slow them down while diving. But not here. They loaded the bombs on a ship that picked up speed in a dive faster than any other that existed at the time, and started dive-bombing, resulting in more pilots lost. I'd had had sufficient dive-bombing experience in the past to know that these converted bombers didn't even have to be shot down.

This was the final straw, for I'd planned on leaving prior to the July 1 induction in any event. The only reason I had hung around this long was that one of Chennault's stooges in my squadron claimed that some of our Rangoon combat reports had been lost, but they would straighten it out for pay purposes later. This was another thing, I was to find, that never did fully happen, but I told them I was going—and I went.

With my knees in adhesive casts, my body much thinner than

it had ever been, and full of yellow jaundice, I was finally on my way back to have "U.S.M.C." on my head marker. There was a terrific load off my mind, and even though I was just making another change I somehow counted on this one being the last one.

CHAPTER **12**

I WALKED INTO the China National Airways Company ticket office in Kunming with a brief case full of paper money, for the rate of exchange at that time took a few thousand Chinese national dollars to pay for a ride to Calcutta. The trip over the Hump, over part of the Himalaya mountain range, cannot be exaggerated in my opinion. The mountains, the winds, and the ice are as much a part of it as the turbulent air and lack of airways. From some of the hairy tales told to me by the CNAC pilots, added to the statistics for those who had not completed the trip, I learned of the ruggedness of the trip.

A U. S. Army quartermaster colonel was a living example that some people can survive anything. This colonel had gotten aboard a DC-3 one night, and after buckling himself in the single seat by the rear entrance he had fallen fast asleep prior to take-off. Just after take-off the DC-3 had crashed and burned just off the end of the Kunming strip, and we didn't think there was even the slightest chance of anybody surviving.

But there was a survivor. This quartermaster colonel said that the crash had awakened him and he saw the DC-3 burning to one side of where he was lying on the ground. He tried to get up and run and momentarily believed he was crippled for life because he could barely move. And it was some time before he realized that the crippled sensation came from the seat and a portion of the DC-3 that were still strapped to his body. Otherwise the only harm that came to him was a sore back, and long before he had an opportunity to get frightened the crash was past history.

The DC-3 I was on was equipped with bucket seats along each side of the fuselage, so that the passengers were seated facing one another. These passengers included three other Flying Tigers en route to the Gold Coast for new P-40s, and the rest were Chinese dignitaries of various capacities.

The four of us pilots buckled ourselves beside each other, facing some of the Chinese. There was no heat, and as the plane steadily climbed my buttocks gradually became numb from contact with the metal of the bucket seat.

Going over the high part of the Hump was the worst part of the trip. We passengers had no oxygen, and the DC-3 crew had little concern for us. In trying to climb above the rugged mountains, which occasionally loomed up from the clouds, breathing became labored at times.

Icing became a problem too, and at one time during the trip I could see very nearly a foot of ice on the spinner of the right-engine propeller outside one of the windows. In the process of the plane's going to different altitudes in the soup the ice would break loose from the spinners and large hunks would bang against the cabin. At times they sounded as if they would tear the plane apart. This was far worse than combat, as far as I was concerned, because there wasn't one damn thing I could do about anything.

The trip encountered up-and-down currents and sheer winds that caused the plane to yaw, pitch, and roll most violently, much the same as though some gigantic animal had the plane in its mouth and was shaking it to pieces. My Flying Tiger friends' faces took on a greenish color, and I knew we were going to be lucky if we held our lunch.

The Chinese dignitaries didn't seem to be as dignified as our AVG pilots. During the times when the plane rolled almost on its side, the toothy Oriental faces were hanging there above me like death masks. And at intervals they began to

113

heave. It seemed as though they always would choose the top position of the plane's roll before they let fly with the used rice. God, how I hated rice, as I continuously wiped off my face and clothes.

Believe me, there wasn't a single soul in the DC-3 who wasn't thankful when we finally got over the Hump and started the long letdown on the way to Calcutta. The climate there was the opposite to that of Kunming, for it was hot, humid, and sticky. But the two cities had a great deal in common, such as filth and even more crowded living conditions. We found a normally crowded city bursting at its seams. There were refugees from all over Asia in addition to Allied military who had arrived since the war started.

The four of us Flying Tigers had military preference, or we would not even have slept in a hotel room with eight cots in it. Here in Calcutta I was once again to run into my two old friends Jim Adam and Bill Tweedy from Rangoon.

Jim and Bill insisted upon my coming to their room for a couple of "Pegs" for old times' sake. I couldn't help feel sorry for these two sweet Scots, who, after nearly thirty years of comfortable living, were in a ten-by-twelve room with no bath.

These Scots had really touched my heartstrings by the manner in which they had taken me into their homes at Rangoon. As a matter of fact, they had been the only people who had made part of my time in the Flying Tigers enjoyable. And when I mentioned earlier, as Jim and Bill were leaving Rangoon, how relative things are, I didn't have any idea of comparing twin estates to one crummy room in Calcutta.

How can I ever forget? Jim and Bill were left sitting upon the edge of their beds clad only in shorts, balding and perspiring. They informed me that they couldn't even get any money out of England, let alone passage, for the bank accounts were frozen.

After a few days in Calcutta I was able to pick up a fare on a British overseas airline to Karachi, and I had planned upon getting a ride out of there from the Air Corps and flying back to the United States via Africa. It was an awkward feeling to be flying hundreds of miles across parched, waterless country in a seaplane. But at about the halfway point this seaplane sat down upon an inland lake and refueled, then on to Karachi.

I was not too intrigued with this desert city and its large camels, which pulled huge wagons. The camels were nasty, smelly beasts, regardless of how useful, and would just as soon bite you as look at you. And I found that my well-laid plans hit a stumbling block at Karachi. Even though plenty of United States Corps aircraft were moving, I was informed that I had to have orders from Chennault to get aboard one.

It appeared that I only *thought* I had left "Laughing Boy" behind. Anyway, I sent a wire to Chennault's headquarters for a request, for after all, I had done more than my share of fighting for the group, and in my own mind I was entitled to it. I had to check back several days for my desired answer before I was to receive an answer from Kunming, and the closest I ever came to committing out-and-out murder came through my mind as I read.

AM UNABLE TO GRANT PERMISSION FOR BOYINGTON STOP
SUGGEST YOU DRAFT BOYINGTON INTO TENTH AIR FORCE AS
SECOND LIEUTENANT STOP

This wire was signed "CHENNAULT." Who was this guy, God? Why, he had let people who had even refused to fly return by Air Corps transportation. He had given cozy jobs on his staff to others who said they couldn't take combat flying. Why should he pick on me? I had never turned down a fight in the air or, for that matter, ever turned down a fight in a barroom brawl. And I had volunteered for everything even though I knew some of these missions were plain crazy. Could Chennault be one of the old-school Army who hated Marines? If so, I shouldn't think he would even want a dead Marine's body stinking up his precious China.

But the real blow was the demotion he suggested, for all of my classmates by then were majors in the Marine Corps. This tyrant had to be taught a lesson, even if it meant my swimming back to the Corps and shooting down a thousand Japs.

After being blocked out of an airplane ride, I soon found

115

that a steamship was to leave in a couple of weeks for New York, the S.S. *Brazil*. So I simmered down, forgetting the past somewhat, and enjoyed the night life in Karachi, and then Bombay, where the S.S. *Brazil* finally departed from.

The *Brazil* was a much larger and faster ship than the *Bosch Fontein,* and it was like old home week, for I ran into most of the missionaries I had come out with, plus some entirely new ones, all of them going back to the United States. Also, there were any number of export wives returning without their husbands, as well as a few seamen who had been torpedoed and were returning for another ship.

The voyage turned out to be lengthy and crowded, but I can't say it was too unenjoyable at that. The missionaries were able to keep their morale and morals up, the same as before, but the rest appeared to have morals that suited my own. For many an orgy took place during the six weeks it was to take the S.S. *Brazil* to reach New York without an escort. And I was right in the middle of all I could handle.

In addition to the passengers mentioned there were around five hundred Chinese youths who were going over to the United States to learn to fly in the Air Corps schools, all from the better families throughout China. It seemed to me that all of them were speaking almost perfect English. During the one and only stopover where passengers were allowed to go ashore, in Capetown, South Africa, I knocked myself out trying to get these youths accommodations for the three days we stayed there. But Capetown would not have any part of them—they were Orientals, and Orientals were not allowed.

Although members of the *Brazil* explained that these Chinese were the equivalent of our own congressmen's sons in the United States, it was of no avail. I have come to believe in more recent years that the stuffy English were correct, and did know after all.

One statement aboard ship had some bearing. Even though we had knocked ourselves out to help these Chinese boys to try and get lodging in Capetown, several of them talked to me in an unfriendly manner afterwards. They informed me that we were not fooling the Chinese one bit: we weren't over to help China, we were only interested in money.

So the quarterbacks later tried to dope out who flew the Migs against us in Korea, and imagined the Russians were, although there was no evidence from crashed Migs.

At this later date I recalled picking up a Chinese cadet while at Kunming, giving him a lift into town. And we had a barrel of fun asking the cadet questions. We asked: "How do you stand in your class?"

"I am in the top five," he proudly answered.

Our next fun-poking question had been: "How long have you been taking flight training?"

After counting up on his fingers he answered in broken English: "Four years some."

At the time of the Korean conflict I pulled out of my memory facts that led me to the answer. The Mig pilots weren't Chinese, not the way they train them over in China; they were the very same Chinese we had tried to get rooms for at Capetown. These and many others following them had received the best flight training in the world, in our own U.S.A. Just another bite at the hand that tried to help—but unwisely so.

Aboard the *Brazil* I had many a spare hour to meditate while gazing out over the vastness of the ocean by day, and at the stars as I lay on deck at night. I was trying to figure out problems, most of which were of no concern to myself; not knowing time always brings the answers.

While in this deep thought I wasn't conscious of the fact that I had already established a precedence that would provide the remaining pilots amusement for years to come. I hadn't realized I was such a comical bastard when I had argued with the Asia staff like a half-assed idealist. And I didn't think everyone knew I could climb to a second-story window with a bottle of scotch under one arm to make love.

Yes, and many other things I didn't stop to think about that people have to assume as eccentric, to say the least. A number-one position on the entertainment parade was to be provided by accounts in the newspapers coupled with the imaginations of the pilots who knew me in China for many years to follow.

But it is wonderful, as I mentioned in the beginning of the book, to be able to join the few remaining pilots each year in Burbank and be able to laugh at myself and others. Bill Bartling almost goes into convulsions while telling about what was rumored around Kunming when they heard I had left Bombay by ship instead of by plane. Bill does the story like this: "You caused a lot of worry. We got the dope you left Bombay by ship with two thousand American nurses and the ship was sunk. We had visions of twenty years later, of coming upon some tropical island, where all of the people and their children would walk leaning forward at a forty-five-degree angle."

He would then add: "You know, fellows, Greg is the only son of a bitch I ever knew, who could walk leaning forward at a forty-five-degree angle and not fall down."

Time and again we have been told, or have read, how the Statue of Liberty first appears to most Americans as they sail home after having been fighting in the war zones. The old gal seems to stand there with a home-coming welcome for a job well done. But in my own case, as our transport from Asia edged her way into New York Harbor, my own thoughts were a little different from that.

As our vessel drew into the harbor, in July 1942, the Statue of Liberty appeared just as ever. But in my own heart I knew that I should not regard her welcome as a home-coming at all, but merely as a prelude to being able to go out again, and as soon as I could, and this time as a Marine.

"You have done a fairly good job," the Statue could have been saying to me. "In your year's time away you have gotten six planes, and all that. But your job isn't nearly complete. In fact, my boy, you haven't even started."

In fact, I was so anxious to get to Washington with my papers and be reinstated back in the Marine Corps that the four-hour ride by train from New York seemed far too slow. I flew instead.

The only clothes I had, of course, were my AVG clothes with their Chinese buttons and their rank epaulets. But I did not worry too much, as I felt it would not be long before these would be changed to our own Marine Corps uniforms, for I remembered only too well the top-secret papers that had been

118

signed and filed away regarding all of us of the Marine Corps who had volunteered for the AVG. We had merely been a government loan to China, so to speak, and I assumed that the reinstatement would be automatic.

So in Washington, after I put in my letter for reinstatement in the Marine Corps, I was instructed at headquarters to go to my home town on the West Coast and await my orders.

My AVG uniform, with its gaudy epaulets, seemed too conspicuous. So, when on the train for home, I removed the epaulets and put them in my hip pocket. But when in the club car, and feeling at peace with the world, I happened to notice a couple of gentlemen in civilian clothes who continued eying me. I paid no attention to their conversation, but after a while they came over and sat beside me, one on each side.

The two men started to question me, but, as I did not feel much like talking, I gave them only a few vague answers and continued looking out at the American scenery going by, for the scenery looked good after I had been away for a year.

Each time they gave me a question I absent-mindedly replied with a vague answer. Finally one of them, with a look of great satisfaction, showed me his F.B.I. card. He must have been sure that he had dug up a hot one posing in a false uniform of some sort. Nor was I the least aware that the security measures had increased so much during my absence.

But, not being aware of it, and not knowing what he meant by showing me his identification card, I merely looked at it, saw that it was okay, and then handed it back to him.

He broke out laughing then, and said: "But we're inspecting you. You're not supposed to be inspecting us."

Oh, so that was it. And it was my turn to laugh this time. And it all ended up with the three of us each buying a round of drinks. They were good people.

Yet in much this same regard I remember that, not many days later I almost had my block knocked off for not joining in the singing of "God Bless America." Why, I never even had heard the words before, or knew there was such a song. It had all been originated at home while I was out at the wars. I was at some sort of football game, with accompanying victory rally, when everybody in the stands stood up and sang this song. I stood up too, but, not knowing what they were singing, I did not sing. And this was when four or five young fellows in new uniforms, and apparently very fresh recruits, started taking some swings at me. Nor was there much I could do about it. For this time I had on no uniform, but just my flight jacket with its Flying Tiger emblem. But this meant nothing to these new boys, and we all know how a football crowd can get excited about some silly fight in the stands.

But enough of this, nor does it matter, other than that I was beginning to feel more and more lost at home, for my orders from Washington had not yet come through, and I was beginning both to worry and to wonder.

From September clear on through to November 1942 I continued both worrying and wondering, and in direct increased proportion to the days as they went by. Each day I went to the post office expecting orders to active duty, and each day seemed longer than the day before. I had to work in order to have money on which to live. But, being a reserve officer in the supposed status of awaiting orders, I could not leave the vicinity. This meant that I could not do anything, for example, like flying for airlines. There was nothing to do but to take some common labor job. I had to go to the labor union in Seattle and explain my predicament. I was informed that there were only certain positions open to me for a while.

So the following day I looked up an old friend who owned a large garage in the heart of the city. I had earned my way through the university by parking cars nights for him. When I now asked him for my old job back, the one I had had eight years previously, he said: "You don't mean it. You're kidding."

"No, I'm broke."

For two long dreary months, right in the heart of the war, I parked cars—and with only high-school boys left on the job along with me. And still no word from Washington.

A year later I was to learn the reason for this delay from Washington. It seems that, after I had filed my request for reinstatement, a renowned son of a bitch who attained his promotions by other than endangering his own life had unearthed

120

an old order, dated in 1939, that anybody who leaves the Marine Corps "in the time of national emergency" could be classified a deserter, or the words could be interpreted something like that for his needs.

However, I wasn't alone in this boat, for this same man had classified all ten of us Marines who had gone with the AVG with this antiquated order he had dug out in 1942. But the hell of it was: none of the ten was to be informed, so we could not defend our rights. This officer is well known within the Marine Corps for the sure-fire method of his own personal promotion, by cleverly but continuously knifing any officer who shows signs of some ability.

Anyway, I continued parking cars at seventy-five cents an hour, not being aware of what was going on in Washington, and ironically each noon somebody would be talking to thousands in the tremendous Victory Square adjoining the garage entrance. And ironically, too, it would be part of my job to help park the cars for military personnel who were participating in the Victory Square programs. And even though I already had seen more fighting than they had, I always was aware of the expressions on their faces: "Why aren't you in the service?"

Finally, after waiting almost three months, I could stand the strain no longer. It was a case of violating ethics, but in late November 1942 I sent a three-page night letter over the heads of everybody, and direct to the assistant secretary of the Navy. Owing to the length of this night letter, I had consumed a fifth of bourbon while I was composing the masterpiece, so by the time I had finished there was no pain in reading it off over the telephone to Western Union. I did not know the secretary personally, or anything like that, but whoever handled the night letter must have worked fast, or bawled out somebody, for within three days I had my orders for active duty, reporting to San Diego, and within no time at all I was on my way out to the Pacific again.

And ironically also, exactly three years later, the war just over, I was to stand in this same Victory Square next to this same garage, while confetti was being thrown, and there were placards: "Welcome home, Pappy."

A guy does not forget comical twists like that, of course, nor could I forget my old friend who owned the nearby garage. As soon as I could get away from the crowds in Victory Square, I walked over to my friend at his garage and said: "Have you got a job for me, Mr. Hutchinson?"

"Are you kidding?"

"Yes, right now I am. But you can never tell when I'll need one."

CHAPTER **13**

JANUARY 1943. Again I saw the shores of the United States disappearing in the distance, the last little piece of land being Point Loma at San Diego. And again it was by water, for I happened to be aboard the S.S. *Lurline,* which had been converted into a troopship for World War II.

The ship was loaded with troops who slept on bunks that were four deep all over the entire ship. I was fortunate as I shared one of the ship's cabañas, originally designed for a honeymoon couple going to Hawaii but for this trip had seven officers of field grade in their places.

The adventure and romance that were with me on the *Bosch Fontein* seemed to be lacking on this voyage. This time we had two destroyers to protect the speedy ship from possible attack by enemy submarines, so she was able to make excellent time as I recall, thirteen days to New Caledonia. Just once in the middle of the Pacific at midnight did we have a scare. It was an awesome sensation to experience the huge ship heel over on its side and complete a 360-degree turn while traveling at such a speed.

The *Lurline* remained in the harbor at Noumea, New Caledonia, only long enough to unload the troops and her small cargo, then she was off for the United States to pick up another precious load. Noumea was our first rear-area base in the South Pacific, and, as I happened to be classified as a replacement major with no command, I was free to do a bit of sight-seeing around the island. A hot and sticky feeling, a feeling that had become only too familiar, was back again. Yes, there were filth and dirty people as well, but one additional sight struck me in a repulsive sort of way.

While driving about Noumea I saw a long line of sailors and Marines, almost two blocks long, standing beside one of the buildings. Having been in the habit of waiting most of my life, or standing by, I don't know why it occurred to me to ask what this line was for.

As it was explained, there were four lone prostitutes who were taking care of this mob of men as fast as they could. Of course, they had been examined by our own medicos, and from all outward appearances these four girls were capable of doing their job fairly rapidly, at that. Pay lines, chow lines, sick-bay lines, and now a line for this beat everything I'd seen up to date.

The following day I transferred to the *General Henderson* to complete my voyage to Espiritu Santo, an island in the New Hebrides group. The *Henderson* was an Army transport that was used along with other smaller ships to make the shorter interisland jaunts. For the United States had learned out here by sad experience not to risk large ships traveling at slow speeds or in dangerous harbors. This ship was so old the termites had almost replaced the woodwork inside the metal hull, and some of its older passengers said the ship was old during World War I, when they went to France on it.

We arrived at Marine Aircraft Wing One Headquarters at a place called Tontuda, and disembarked. This area didn't look too bad even in the rain, for it always seemed to rain in the New Hebrides, which I understand have one of the highest rainfalls in the world.

But this was not my destination, and it was another splashing six-hour drive to the other side of the island to a place they called the Fighter Strip. At the time this was the first strip on the island, and the Seabees, God bless them, had constructed it out of coral with bulldozers. Many of us believed these coral white strips were the finest in the world.

This had been a French plantation at one time. Many a coconut tree had been removed in order to make way for the Fighter Strip, its taxiways, and plane revetments. The base itself, which consisted of numerous quonset huts and tents, had been set up among coconut trees about a mile off to one side on a lagoon.

The base was infested with mosquitoes and flies. I believe the Army Engineers finally rid Espiritu Santo of its mosquitoes, but what a task it was to be, because they were forced to put DDT and oil over practically the whole island. And after they were through with Espiritu, they had to do the same to the neighboring islands so the wind wouldn't blow them back or some others in. We took care of the flies by cleaning up acre after acre of rotting coconut husks, the flies' breeding place. Prior to cleaning up the coconut husks a person's body would appear coal black from only a short distance away as he was walking into a shower because of being completely covered with flies.

There were cannibals in the mountains of Espiritu Santo all the time we were there, and I rather imagine long after we left. Occasionally we would make a trip into the hills and take a look at these primitive people with bones piercing their nostrils and ear lobes. One of our trips I recall a pilot saying, "I'll bet these folks think we are crazier than hell because we don't even save heads."

These natives were typical of the others throughout the South Pacific, with great bushy mops of kinky hair, and feet that looked more like shovels than anything I am able to think of now. They had been bleaching their hair various shades of red and blond by applying lye to the hair to rid themselves of lice.

This was a rear-area base that was bothered only on occasion at night by some lone Japanese bomber. Our job was to supply the fighting squadrons at Guadalcanal with supplies, and act as a re-forming place for squadrons coming out of action or going into action.

My new job was assistant operations officer of the strip, which was about as next to nothing as I had ever hoped to be

125

in charge of in my life. I had the say of nothing. All I did was count the planes when they went out for training flights, and count them again when they returned. What a life!

The months seemed to drag on, and even though I didn't feel as if I was a part of it, the Japanese were being well taken care of. For certain, somebody had to do rear-area work, but I knew I could never be happy doing it.

Major Bob Galer, with whom I had attended the University of Washington, and flight school afterwards, had been CO of the first fighter squadron in Guadalcanal. Bob had been shot down three times but had returned through the enemy lines each time to fight again. He had been there when the Marines lived on captured Japanese food after taking the first foothold in the war, and my old friend Robert had knocked down eleven Japs when the going was the roughest.

Another friend, Joe Foss—whom I had met in Pensacola as an instructor—came in and out of Espiritu between combat tours at the Canal. Joe was truly a gaunt specimen of life while flying the Wildcats against the Japanese. Joe's final score was twenty-six before the Marines finally yanked him out of combat, full of malaria and worn down to a nub, and the first American to tie Eddie Rickenbacker's World War I record.

To me Joe has always been a great guy, even before he shot down all the planes. And I think that the people of South Dakota share my opinion, for Joe has been re-elected governor of their state. May Joe have many years to come, for there is one guy, in my opinion, who doesn't ride in the same car with politicians as I see them.

Also, there was Joe Bauer, with whom I had had the pleasure of serving in each of the only two fighter squadrons the Marines had prior to the war. And Joe Bauer, superb pilot that he was, had done a terrific job by getting twelve when the going was real rough, but was shot down at sea, never to return.

There was another old flying-school classmate who had been a corporal when I was a cadet. Ken Walsh was among the first to fly the new Corsair against the Japanese in the Southwest Pacific, and he rang up twenty Zeros before being shipped back to the States.

126

As an operation's officer the closest I got to combat was by ferrying an occasional fighter into the Canal, remaining overnight for "Washing Machine Charlie," as we called the Jap night bombers, and then being flown back to Espiritu the following morning.

Around May 1943 I finally thought my break had arrived at last, for Elmer Brackett was able to get me into his squadron as an executive officer. And we were off to the Canal. We had no more than arrived when Elmer was promoted out of the squadron, and I was assigned as commanding 222.

For four weeks—ordinarily a combat tour was six weeks—222 escorted dive bombers to various islands up the "Slot," as this chain of islands extending from Guadalcanal to Bougainville was called. Besides, 222 patrolled the Canal skies for hours each day but never saw so much as the vapor trail of a single Japanese plane.

During my stay at the Canal I spent part of my time in the famous Hotel De Gink, a real rat hole, but most of the time I lived in a tent not far from the Lunga River. The Lunga was the swift mountain stream in which so many of our valiant ground troops had drowned and shed their blood. We could see the fresh cool water from our tent area, which was concealed from the sky by tall jungle trees. Its refreshing waters were used daily to bathe and to rinse out sweaty clothes. Farther up the stream were crocodiles, and one of the sergeants I had met on the *Lurline* had been killed by one, but that didn't slow down our swimming.

This is an aviation adventure of sorts, and I am not deliberately excluding my many many ground friends. But there is one incident I chuckle about that happened in this very same jungle tent-area when the Marines had no aviation on Guadalcanal and the Japanese fleet had just finished shelling them from behind as they were in the process of getting their first foothold. Admiral Halsey had come ashore after the Jap fleet had pulled out, because he thought that he had better boost morale and visit General Vandegrift. And it was at a time when the Marines were cooking, literally, in their tin hats.

An old sergeant who had about a four-hundred-word vocabulary at the outside was helping win the war for the second time; like so many he had the right spirit but not the youth to go with it. Vandegrift had made a staff cook out of this old sergeant, who was obviously very near exhaustion. "Bull" Halsey, attired in fresh khaki, had just finished dining with the tired and soiled Vandegrift and was going into expostulations over the wonderful meal. He said:

"And that apple pie, it was out of this world."

"Admiral, if you thought it was so darn good, and want to thank somebody, why don't you thank my cook?" came back the general.

"Great idea. I'd be only too happy to."

With this statement from Halsey the general called to his cook, "Hey, Joe, come here a minute, I want you to meet somebody." And the bedraggled old sarge in a filthy T-shirt, and badly in need of a shave, came slowly over to this high-ranking pair on very sore feet. In his entire life the sarge had never been so close to so many stars as adorned the shirt collars of the pair.

"Sergeant, Admiral Halsey would like to compliment you in person on your cooking," Vandergrift said.

"Why yes, Sergeant, especially the apple pie, it was terrific," stated Halsey.

The old sergeant was embarrassed and fidgeted like a little boy, placing one sore foot behind the other while wiping a hairy forearm across his sweating and wrinkled face, and he answered:

"Oh, bullshit, Admiral. You didn't have to say that."

By now the Japs had been wiped out of the Canal, and the bulldozers had covered the last of the stinking bodies. The only Japanese thing of any use was the ice plant, which was inherited by the Marines, and they thoroughly enjoyed it. The capacity was limited, and the higher echelon had to come first, which is only natural. And there happened to be a drinking general at the time for whom we had to commence cracking ice in the middle of the afternoon. By the time it was dark and Washing Machine Charlie started to come over, our drinking general was in real good shape—he really wanted to go into action.

128

The staff would have one hell of a time with the old general as he insisted upon staggering around beneath the jungle trees shouting orders. A few planes had been lost in such a manner before the staff learned how to keep him pacified. But a great person, nevertheless, who did a great deal of good, besides having a heart that was in the proper place.

By far the greatest thrill I got from this brief and fruitless tour was Admiral Yamamoto's arrival by transport plane at Kahili, Bougainville. One night we were drinking with some Air Force pilots next door to us, and they informed us that the Allies had broken a coded message telling of the arrival of Yamamoto on the following morning.

I remember how we Marines envied these P-38 pilots, for we didn't have enough range with our Wildcats to reach Bougainville and return to Guadalcanal. We even helped the P-38 pilots plan the whole trip, and were there beside the planes to wave good-hunting as they made an early take-off, although we found out later we weren't supposed to know about this top-secret mission.

Man, oh man, what excitement in our tent area the afternoon these P-38s came back from Kahili and told us about the rendezvous with Yamamoto's transport as it was circling for a landing. They had gotten him all right. The whole world was soon to know, but we, even though we had not made the trip, were in on the very beginning. This must have been a horrible blow to Japan, not only to lose a great admiral, but also to know we could crack their code.

With this for a memento we were sent back early to Espiritu, for at this time the last of the Wildcats were being replaced by the swift Corsairs.

There had been some doubt as to whether our squadron would be sent on the usual "week's rest and recreation," as it was termed, for we had had only a very brief, no-action tour in the combat zone. However, we managed to luck out, and away we went to Sydney, Australia, many miles down under.

When the book *Snake Pit* came out, after my return from the war, I kept wondering to myself where I had heard the word before. Or in what connection. And then I remembered, and it had nothing to do with flying. It had to do with the lobby of the Hotel Australia . . . and what seems now long, long ago.

After our six-week combat tours were up, the flyers were sent back to a rear area where they were given malaria smears.

If they did not have malaria, they were permitted to go down to Sydney by transport aircraft and spend one week of what was termed on the books as rest and recreation.

I sometimes doubted that the terms were appropriate, because when the poor boys were loaded back on the planes at Sydney they had to return to the combat area to get rested up.

But just the same, on these trips down to Sydney the first thing we did (we got down there just about dawn) was to take our clothes to the cleaners and have all the mildew and tropical rain sponged out of them and have them pressed. Then we would go to breakfast and have fresh milk and eggs, something we did not have up in the islands.

Then we would get into the clean uniforms and we would go down to the lobby of the Hotel Australia, known as "The Snake Pit." Or sometimes even "The Passion Pit."

But in this lobby would always be about a hundred girls, and practically any one of them you asked would be willing to stay the whole week with you.

Some of the boys didn't stay in the hotel. Some of them preferred flats because they could raise a little more hell in the line of parties.

Also, every time we went down to Sydney, we would get an extra-large table at either one of the two night clubs in town, Prince's or Romano's. Some of the fellows couldn't make these night clubs every night, but they usually averaged about five nights out of seven in getting to those squadron parties.

It was a common saying then, even around the United States, that the Australian girls seemed to go a lot more for the American boys than for the Australians. And I think this is true, and that the reasons given for it are true; namely that American boys were more lavish with their money and we all had a good time down there. I guess the girls had a good time likewise, because they all used to write us back in the combat zone and tell us what a good time they had had, wondering when we were coming back again.

But even now, on thinking about it, I don't care to go into comparing American women with their Australian sisters. The Australian girls didn't have anything on the girls back home except that—well, except that what the Australian girls *had* they had there.

And in defense of these women I feel that it is necessary to say that most of their virile men were away fighting in Europe and elsewhere. But somehow I was happy that I didn't have to stand in line for my women or my drinks.

About the only disconcerting part of the week was that U. S. Navy Intelligence kept looking us up and asking all natures of questions. And we kept trying to avoid these officers and enjoy the fun. Their concern was to try to find out how everyone in Australia knew about Admiral Yamamoto and the code being broken. They wanted to find out who was talking about it. Everyone from Guadalcanal was suspected.

On the long trip over the ocean returning to our base weight was a very important factor, and the pilot of the DC-3 told us that we could take back with us nothing we hadn't taken down there. We had answered: "I certainly hope you are correct, my dear captain."

"No, you know what I'm referring to," he said, pointing to several cases of beer and a few bottles of whisky we had lugged out to the airport. So, to comply with our captain's wishes, we were able to get rid of our precious cargo all right by simply drinking all of it before we flew out of Sydney.

Back in Espiritu we got acquainted with our new planes. We hoped the combat tour coming up would prove more exciting than our last brief tour.

The Corsair was a sweet-flying baby if I ever flew one. No longer would we have to fight the Nips' fight, for we could make our own rules. Here was a ship that could climb with a Zero, only with a more shallow angle of climb, and one that had considerably more speed.

We flew by day if weather permitted, and the evenings were taken up by outdoor movies, as the mosquitoes were a thing

131

of the past. A public-address system would come on during intermissions at the movies, and we would hear newscasts from the rest of the world as well as home.

The actor Errol Flynn was having a lengthy session in court concerning his amours at the time with some young things aboard his yacht. And a blow-by-blow account of the trial was woven into these newscasts. I'll never forget those few hundred lonesome lads under the coconut trees at Espiritu, chanting as one, "Get that God-damn' war news off the speaker! We want to hear about Flynn."

I wonder if Flynn realized how much entertainment he was providing the troops overseas. Anyway, I give him a vote of thanks for this, and for that expression that still stands, "You are in like Flynn."

Those of us who drank, and most of us did, would spend some of these nights drinking and singing up to a point, then wrestling bouts seemed to come in fashion. This happened to be my strong point, for I dearly loved to wrestle, being a former intercollegiate wrestling champion in my day. I also loved to drink. I used to say I provided this form of entertainment, as an excuse of course, to keep the pilots from getting lonesome and thinking of their mothers.

It was just prior to 222's going back to the Canal in our new planes, and I had been one of the participants in a free-for-all when somebody tackled me from the side in the darkness with a shoestring tackle. My anklebone had snapped audibly like a twig, and the following day found me with my leg in a cast up to my knee. If fate didn't get in my way . . . then I got in hers.

The next thing I knew I was being assigned to a room aboard a hospital ship on its way to Auckland, New Zealand. I was to remain in Auckland until I was physically fit. Next to my bunk was a pilot who had lived to tell how one can spin in from one thousand feet in a Corsair and still live, but this poor pilot was in a cast clear up to his chest.

The pilot's jaws had been broken also, and his teeth were wired up solid, so he was forced to take his nourishment through a straw at mealtimes. A corpsman came into our room before the ship left and handed this fellow a pair of mechanic's pliers. As I had taken over the detail of doing the talking for the pilot, I asked: "What are these pliers for, corpsman?"

He answered: "We are shorthanded, and if the going gets rough, he is to yank his own wires out—before he strangles to death."

As the speedy light cruiser that had been converted into a hospital ship pulled out of Espiritu, I thought to myself, "Man, oh man, you have loused up the detail now!" It was beyond the realm of possibility to get into a squadron again, for, owing to my age and rank, a CO spot had been my last chance, and now that was gone, with 222 on its last combat tour without me.

CHAPTER **14**

J UNE OF 1943 found me parked safely in Mobile Six, a naval hospital at Auckland, and it was wintertime down there. This was a far cry from the excitement of Sydney; however, I was to find the New Zealanders very hospitable. Whisky was at a premium. But I had taken this into consideration when I took the precaution of having a huge cardboard box of cartons of American cigarettes shipped with me.

Of all the mediums of exchange American cigarettes, I believe, were the best. It wasn't entirely because their tobacco was rationed; they truly preferred our cigarettes to their own.

The hospital fixed my leg with a walking cast, but it wasn't too satisfactory, and I had to depend on my crutches to get anywhere in a hurry. My shoulder muscles developed rapidly. In no time at all I could walk quite a distance without tiring or getting sore arms. I used to practically run on my crutches to the Navy Club in a downtown hotel about three miles away, so I would be able to stack up drinks, which were served from five to seven each evening.

While in the hospital I received a few letters from the boys in 222, telling me how they had struck pay dirt on their last trip. The Japanese had made an all-out air effort when the Marines had gone into New Georgia. During this action the Jap

134

aircraft came so steadily 222 had been ordered to fight until out of fuel then land in the ocean. This was about the only real action 222 had, but they helped save the day by getting thirty Jap planes, which many an outfit would like to have on their record.

A few of the boys who weren't picked up by our destroyers came back later with coast watcher Kennedy's natives. Kennedy was a large, florid-faced Australian who had stayed on in the islands during the war because, for one thing, he was one of the few who could speak the native language. His native boys would paddle out in their canoes and pick up pilots after air battles before the Japs could reach the pilots in the shore boats. This coast watcher had seen to it that over a hundred of our boys had gotten home safely, so Kennedy was finally persuaded to come to Guadalcanal, where they intended to pay him homage. The purpose was to present some reward, but our headquarters got nowhere with Kennedy as he wanted nothing.

One general said: "Mr. Kennedy, we want to at least present you with a medal of some kind for your heroism."

"Thanks, no, give the medals to the chaps doing the flying."

"But there must be something you want," the general insisted.

Kennedy then laughed and said: "If you really insist upon wanting to know what I want, then I guess I'd better tell you."

"What would you like, Mr. Kennedy?"

"After thirty-six months in the bush, I would like to have thirty beautiful chorus girls arguing over my drunken carcass."

One day at the hospital I heard swearing coming from the bathroom. Upon investigating I was to find Sam Logan, a pilot from one of the last Canal engagements, and he was having somewhat of a workout in a bathtub. He had bailed out of his flaming plane, and a Zero had made repeated attacks on him as he was descending in his parachute. When the Nip had finally exhausted his ammunition, he dove his Zero into Sam, cutting his ankle so the foot had to be amputated.

"Can I help you?" I asked.

Sam answered: "No, I'm okay. It gets a little awkward hold-

135

ing this stump out while I bathe. I'm used to taking showers, you know."

I ran into Sam Logan again after the war, and he informed me that he had been the first American to obtain permission to fly with a store leg in the service.

Another young pilot, Gilbert Percy, was in bed but extremely cheerful, so I asked: "What's your trouble?"

"I got a broken pelvis."

"How did it happen?" I asked him.

"Oh, I bailed out at two thousand feet, and my chute didn't open." And I knew he wasn't kidding because I had heard about this.

"I never did get the dope on you. Just what exactly did happen to save your life?"

"My chute was trailing but it hadn't opened when I crashed into the water. I had never heard of anyone surviving, so I thought I was dead. But all of a sudden I tasted salt water, so I opened my eyes and saw a bunch of bubbles around me. I knew then I wasn't dead, so I started to swim."

This hospital seemed full of miracles. But the Navy Medical Corps captain in charge of Mobile Six was damn certain of two officers who didn't come under the miracle category.

A long-time friend of mine, a gravel-crunching colonel, was in the hospital also, and in addition to never being around for muster, like myself, the colonel insisted upon keeping his dog under his hospital bed when he was there. The dog was an odd-looking character that had been smuggled from the United States in a barracks bag, and the colonel and the dog had been together through the Canal battles. The dog had been named "Snafu" by the colonel's troops, and it stuck. The last time I saw Snafu he was dressed in a man's collar and bow tie at a dinner party at the home of this colonel in Coronado, California. The dog would hide his face with his paws or run when the colonel showed us some of his collection of firearms after dinner.

Anyhow Snafu's illegal entry in the naval hospital finally caused my friend to be placed ten days under official arrest by the captain in charge of the hospital.

I had been in a few poker games with some of the older in-
mates and was fortunate enough to win over a thousand pounds.
Because of this and other reasons the executive officer of Mobile Six had called me into his office, and said: "Boyington,
some of these fellows aren't as well off as you. They have coro-
nary conditions."

"What's all this got to do with me?"

"Some of those bets you made involved considerable sums of
money, and as a medical man I am responsible for the patients.
I have already had to treat a recurrence."

The executive officer and I talked further, then he said:
"You are not ready for duty yet, however, there is nothing more
we can do for you here. You apparently don't think much of
our treatment or you would stay around longer than just to
win a stake and shove off on shore leave:"

I wasn't able to talk the hospital out of passing me for a
flight physical before I left Auckland, but I counted on a friend
of mine back at Espiritu, to give me an okay when I got there.

Part of my time had been occupied with a divorcee in New
Zealand, a truly fine woman who mended my clothes and helped
make my stay worth while. She took in roomers to support her-
self and her young daughter. I had tried to give her money on
more than several occasions because I realized she must have
been fairly hard pressed, but she was such a proud thing and
would have no part of it.

In my efforts to find an appropriate gift for her before I left
Auckland I asked the advice of one of her friends. "What on
earth does Carrie need the most?"

And this woman friend said: "Don't say I told you, but
money."

"I have tried that," I said. Then I thought of a way to get
her to accept such a gift, one of the few things I did that seemed
to work out for the benefit of humanity, so I invited Carrie to
see me off on the plane. Before I boarded the DC-3 to Noumea,
with but one gas stop at Norfolk Island, a tiny dot on the map
on the way, Carrie said: "Please come back and see us again."

"I doubt if it will ever be possible, but here, take this," I said, and handed Carrie my roll, which contained several hundred pound notes.

"I can't accept this. You know better than that."

"I can't use this crazy money where I'm going. If you don't take it, I'm afraid I'll have to throw the worthless stuff away as I'm flying back to the islands."

The last time I saw Carrie was at the Auckland airport as I crawled on top of a number of crates in a DC-3, as there were no seats and no room to sit down anywhere. My last impression was that she was so occupied holding onto the notes with one hand and defending her clothes against the slipstream with the other that she had forgotten me forever. But she hadn't forgotten. After the war I received letters from both Carrie and from her daughter, who was grown up by then. Carrie had placed the money in postal savings and had put her daughter through school with it, and was happily remarried. The daughter wrote that she, also, had married a fine young man.

But in my true lame-brain style I had forgotten a few U.S. dollars rolled in the center of the pounds that I had every intention of keeping. My discovery of this slight error didn't occur to me until I reached Noumea, which had become real civilized. The Army mess was the only place to eat, but I didn't even have a quarter, which was the price of lunch, nor did I see anyone I knew to borrow a quarter from.

I thought I was stuck in another way in Noumea, for I found I had to pass a flight physical in order to get out of there. Beads of sweat came out of my forehead, and I was forced to bite my tongue, as part of this examination was to stand on one foot for a certain period of time with my eyes closed.

The flight surgeon had me walking back and forth while he was shaking his head, he was not satisfied with my leg. I tried to force myself to walk without a limp until I thought my leg would fold if the doctor didn't say pretty soon that I had passed. I was finally able to con the poor doc into letting me by in spite of his better judgment, and I was off to Espiritu, ferrying a Corsair as I went.

But if I thought beads of sweat had been on my face during the physical examination, these were nothing by comparison to

138

the drops that flowed when I strained and prayed for my leg not to give out on take-off, and again upon landing.

When back on the old Fighter Strip at Espiritu I was assigned to first one squadron then another, but no flying went with the work. There were about six squadrons that I went through. The pilots of each had long since been shipped back to the United States, and I was made commanding officer of each squadron briefly, so I could wrestle the paper work in order to get the ground crews and records ready to follow the pilots.

I dreaded this work because I was CO in name only, and paper wrestling bored me to distraction anyhow. Among the papers I soon discovered a lot of disciplinary action that had to be taken care of, some of it involving courts-martial. But I'll bet few Marines thanked their lucky stars a major who hated to go through channels, or didn't think they had done anything he wouldn't do himself, was the one to sort this paper out. The net result was that there were no courts-martial, and only a few who received a fatherly talking-to.

Neither criticizing nor trying to build myself up, I might have accidentally saved the Marine Corps some precious time and trouble at that, for anything I seemed to do properly was accomplished more by accident than by anything I would accept credit for as done right.

In any event this work kept me physically occupied until August 1943, but I was going mentally crazier by the day. Try as I would, I could not beg or steal my way into an active squadron or get flying of any kind. Sometimes I believed I was so hard up I would have even jumped at a chance to fly dive bombers.

The fighter squadrons up north were being used up faster than expected, and replacement squadrons that were coming in on flattops were long overdue, so this gave me a brain child. I made an after-dinner call on the group commander, who was Colonel Sanderson.

"Sandy" happened to have been an all-around great in previous years, all man, and a superb pilot. He had been called upon many a time when the services were small and they entered military pilots in the air races about the United States. I recall many a tale of his exciting past in the flying game, but two in particular.

One time while flying fighters at the Cleveland Air Races, Sandy and Oscar Brice had collided when they were doing a squirrel-cage, and both of them had to hit the silk. Oscar's chute opened and came down quite normally, but Sandy's chute had caught on the tail surfaces of his falling plane. He had thrilled the spectators, and cheated old Dame Death, by pulling himself hand over hand up the strings until he reached the tail and succeeded in jerking his chute free just in the nick of time.

Another time, during camera-gun practice above San Diego, his opposition and he came together, which resulted in Sandy being sealed in the cockpit when the upper wing was shoved back and down on top of him. But, fortunately again for Sandy, he had been able to tear off a portion of the wing and get out before his plane struck the earth.

I came up with an idea that would supply a temporary fighter squadron and fill the gap until the flattops arrived. Why Sandy didn't think I was full of hop or something I don't know, or why a person like myself had been able to talk him into this idea. But I do realize that Sandy was one of the truly great aviators in command, and no doubt he had placed himself in my position, for he knew he could have done it.

The idea was to get replacement pilots from the pilots' pool, some Corsairs used for training, and borrow a number for control purposes from some squadron not in action at the time. Lady Luck was smiling on me that night, because Sandy agreed. I hadn't approached any of the pool pilots yet, and not every pilot in the pool happened to be a fighter pilot. But I knew that most pilots wanted to be fighter pilots, if they were dumb enough.

I'll never forget two SBD pilots who wanted to go with me so badly but didn't seem to catch on very fast. About all one could say for them was that they were in the same sky with the squadron, but, regardless of that, those two were all guts.

And I'll never forget the look on Bob McClurg's face when I informed him that we had no extra time to get ready. I said as diplomatically as possible: "Bob, my boy, I'm afraid you better wait for the next trip. I am only thinking of your life, you understand?"

"You do what you have to do, Skipper. But I want you to know I'd a lot rather be dead than not go with you."

"What the hell can I do with an ape like you? Come on, Bob, you're going."

I certainly hadn't the slightest notion that this was the right thing to do, but the relief on McClurg's smiling face was worth a million dollars.

The other SBD pilot was not as fortunate with his Corsair training as McClurg, although he was trying just as hard—maybe too hard. We were always sweating Shorty out when he came around to make any landing. But on this particular landing the lad bounced and started to swerve—poured full throttle—all two thousand horses at once. The wind-up was most amazing.

It was standard procedure to inform any pilot on cockpit checkout to retard the r.p.m. setting prior to coming in for a landing. For if a burst of power became necessary to control a landing, or to make a go-around, he would be able to hold the torque produced by the extra-large, three-bladed paddle on this plane. But it was evident this boy had forgotten, or was trying too hard, for when he hit the throttle the Corsair executed a ninety-degree off the narrow runway.

The prop torque had Shorty up on one wing tip before he got off the edge of the narrow runway. The last glimpse of the plane before it disappeared from sight the propeller was doing a good job of corkscrewing the plane and Shorty in an inverted attitude through the coconut trees. We were able to raise the heavy plane up enough to free our little SBD friend from the overturned position he ended up in. Shorty was conscious, but one of Chief Sitting Bull's Indians couldn't have done a more thorough job of scalping.

I certainly had to hand it to Doc Evans, who washed the dirt and coral out of this bloody mess, afterwards talcuming the skull with sulfa powder, and doing a real neat job of hemstitching the scalp back in its proper place. Anyway, I had been re-

141

lieved of the unpleasant task of telling Shorty, the lucky fellow, that he wouldn't be going with us.

Three pilots from 222 who had gone out with me on the *Lurline* were in the pilot pool because they hadn't been able to complete the three combat tours that were mandatory. They were John Bergert, Bou Bourgoise, and Stan Bailey. The rest had never been in an active squadron, let alone seen a Japanese aircraft.

If I am giving the impression these boys couldn't fly, please forgive me, because I could see in this brief time that some were naturals. Boys like Mullin, McGee, Casey, Fisher, and Bolt, not to mention others, were born pilots in my estimation.

For three short weeks we had trained by day if the weather permitted, and talked flying combat most of the nights. I wanted all the training we could get, yet on the other hand I wanted to get going before somebody changed his mind or the relief squadrons arrived and we wouldn't get to go, period.

We had a hell of a struggle getting the bare necessities, let alone any of the regular items a squadron comes already equipped with, which all seemed as far away as luxuries at the time. I was able to see, not only feel, that some of the boys were getting dissatisfied before the three weeks were up, because I had promised many things that were slow in coming.

But we got the honey of all honeys for a flight surgeon, and Jim Ream stayed with the squadron to the bitter end. Lord only knows what we could have done without this fine Southern gentleman. Jim was young and full of enthusiasm, and fitted into our way of thinking so perfectly we were willing to stop the war on several occasions to teach the doc how to fly. We wanted him to fly combat with us.

We were also very fortunate in getting, as our intelligence officer, Frank Walton, who was a member of the police department in Los Angeles, and whom Bragdon soon nicknamed "Flat." He was a meticulous person who kept track of everything whether it was his duty or not, and thank heaven he did. The bulk of us seemed content to be scatterbrains, although actually I should speak only for myself.

In addition to Frank's obvious fine qualities was his Olympic backstroke championship in the days of Johnny Weissmuller. His name is not as well known as Johnny's, but Frank had about as many records to his credit. Frank didn't care to drink—he kept track of things for those of us who did—and, being a believer in physical fitness, he swam our asses off around the lagoon to keep us in shape, and as I couldn't take a chance on wrestling for a while it was wonderful exercise for my bum leg.

In but a short time the boys in the squadron called me "Grand-pappy," and I loved this because it came as a word of respect like the Old Man or Skipper. I was content with my nickname, for I was thirty and the rest of the pilots were from nineteen to twenty-two. Not only was there a great difference between our ages; it was considered much the same as two generations in fighter-pilot game. So Grandpappy was a natural.

I wasn't to learn until some months later the real basis for acquiring my name, which was finally shortened to just Pappy. Come to find out these boys had dragged it back from legend around flight school, long after I had sailed for China. They talked about a check pilot with a long white beard, so long that he stepped on it as he got into his cockpit to give a student a check ride in order to determine whether to continue training or send him back to college. They said they would talk prior to being checked and wish that the man with the long white beard from the North Pole could be with them, although they were not certain that he ever existed.

It made some sense when I heard this, for I never recalled giving a student a down-check, as I had found it much more satisfactory to talk him into flying an up-check.

We were loaned the number 214 from another squadron that had just completed a combat tour, but a name was needed for our squadron. The majority of names have something to do with women. But these pilots had the idea that we had been deprived of some of the things other squadrons enjoyed, so they agreed upon Boyington's Bastards and seemed pleased with the name.

I didn't bother to tell the boys that there was no need for feeling so sorry for themselves, as they had more than their share of firsts, but I certainly thought them over in my mind. They had the oldest active Marine fighter-pilot for a skipper. They had the highest rank of majors in the game, even though he had been anchor man in his class. They also had the biggest drunk in the Corps. Maybe I'd better not brag so much, and make this the biggest drunk for fighter-pilot commanders in the Corps during this period.

Our group commanders seemed to be coming and going like flies, and things finally got to the point where a fellow didn't know who was going to run the camp at Espiritu next. Colonel Sanderson had been transferred to wing headquarters, with a new colonel in his place. I had had the dubious pleasure of meeting the new colonel when I was a cadet at Pensacola, and he had given me a down-check in Squadron Three there. He had rattled me so much by screaming at me I had no idea of what he expected me to do, so I don't know how I could have flown properly.

Anyhow Colonel Lard took over, and good old Sandy was gone. As the British say, Lard was one of two bad "types" I met in the service. It's true—we also had them in the good old USMC.

This type, and one I mentioned earlier, hid under the guise of the disciplinarian: the second was the colonel who had tossed out our records in Washington, D.C., and he was the smarter individual. For he used the regulations, in addition to any other means, to scuttle people over a long period of time, slowly, with premeditation. He is very close to the top of the heap now.

The other type spends his nights pawing over the Navy Regulations and the Marine Corps Manual, trying desperately to fit the personnel under him into violations of these regulations. Then he takes disciplinary action. He is just smart enough to know that no one is perfect, and if he looks through these volumes long enough, he will find something somewhere to hang somebody with.

The colonel was fortunate in having an executive officer who played the game by his rules. His exec had had a brief opportunity at combat earlier but had found some regulation that made

144

him too valuable to endanger his life (the regulation actually applied to officers commanding ground troops), so consequently spent his only opportunity directing the action from the ground.

These buckoes were as different as night and day from Colonel Sanderson, and many others in command, for that matter. They knew how to live—I have that much to say for them. They had the most pretentious set of quarters one would ever want to see constructed on a small peninsula outside of camp—for just the two of them. Servants and the works. Nothing was too good.

Two days prior to taking my squadron up north to the combat area Lard sent for me. When I arrived at his office, I caught a fleeting glimpse of the exec going out the back door, so I didn't need my three guesses after I found why Lard sent for me. He said that someone had informed him that I was drinking quite a bit, that he hadn't been cognizant of the fact. But he was going to forward written orders to the commanding officers I would come under in combat, and if I were to take a drink for sixty days I would be subject to disciplinary action of some nature.

I shall have to admit that a number of high-ranking officers fit Colonel Lard's physical description, but there was only one Lard, and he had a very vital part in my feelings at the time. I have long since forgiven Lard, and even forgiven myself more recently.

It was indeed a relief to fly away from Espiritu and be on my way to a new strip on the Russell Islands, which are northwest of Guadalcanal. One of my pilots must have sensed my relief, for I recognized the voice, though he didn't know it, as it came over the radio: "Hey, Gramps, look out, here comes Lard!"

I answered: "Just like waking up from a nightmare, isn't it?"

CHAPTER **15**

O N THE WAY TO a new base, the Russell Islands, I was doing some tall hoping, for if this conglomeration that I called a squadron didn't see some action shortly, my combat-pilot days were over. I knew it. Age and rank were both against me now. Lady Luck just had to smile upon me, that's all.

The afternoon of our arrival in the Russell Islands I was called by Strike Command. Our first mission was scheduled for a 7:00 A.M. take-off the following morning, September 16, 1943. I had little sleep that night. For tomorrow, I imagined the ghouls would be watching and hoping to see the poor little ole squadron flub its duff.

No one, I believe, noticed how concerned I was. Probably this escaped the officers in Strike Command, because I did nothing more than smoke one cigarette after another. This was not unusual. Besides, I smelled good, because I had refused all bourbon the previous night.

Not that combat worried me, for it didn't. My great concern was that the squadron might fall flat on its face or do something ridiculous. We had had little more than three weeks together—most squadrons were trained for months in the United States before they were sent out to a combat zone—and only three of my pilots had a taste of combat previously.

It was a temporary relief to get to hell out of the briefing shack and away from the officers in Strike Command. "Moon" was waiting patiently in one of the jeeps to drive Stan, myself, and a couple of the others down to the end of the strip, where our mighty Corsairs awaited like sleek, silent steeds. Truly a picture of beauty, in my opinion, were these new ships, the Corsairs.

Twenty Corsairs—five flights of four from our squadron—and of course twenty pilots were to escort three squadrons of Dauntless dive bombers and two squadrons of Avenger torpedo planes, totaling 150 bombers in all.

The mission was to wipe out Ballale. A small island west of Bougainville, heavily fortified, and all airfield, not unlike La Guardia. The main difference was that we knew the traffic was going to be much more conjested than the New York area is today, without the aid of Air Traffic Control directing our flight patterns. Besides the lack of A.T.C., as we know and depend upon it now, our traffic would be further distorted by anti-aircraft fire, and God only knows how many Zeros.

And again, I don't believe that I gave a second thought to the fact that we had to fly six hundred miles round trip as the crows fly, up and down the old "Slot," sparsely dotted with tiny islands, most of these islands being Japanese held. The main worry was whether our seams would hold together as a squadron.

Our first problem was to get 170 aircraft off a single strip closely enough together, in time, that is, so that we would have adequate fuel to complete the trip yet leave ourselves a half hour's or more fuel for a fight at full throttle. A P & W 2000-HP engine at full throttle uses the old petrol much the same as if it were going through a floodgate.

Wandering around our aircraft, getting a nod, or seeing a wave that each one after the other was in readiness calmed me down rapidly. Soon we received the start-up-engine signal. One by one the shotgun starters audibly fired out black smoke. Each engine would go into a few convulsive coughs, afterwards smoothing out into a steady roar. Everything seemed much smoother, smooth as the perfect Venturi form of water vapor

147

formed in misty silhouette about each ship, caused by the propeller and the extremely high humidity of the island air.

Take-off time—the last Dauntless had wobbled lazily into the air, starting to turn in one gigantic join-up circle. We took off in pairs down the snowy white coral strip at about twenty-second intervals, which was a feat in itself, because none of us had more than approximately thirty hours in these powerful new speed birds.

As we climbed, in shorter radii than the bombers, we gradually came abreast of the bomber leader, pulling up above and behind him. Radio silence was in effect. We had no intention of broadcasting our departure to the Japanese. The squadron was spread out like a loose umbrella over the bombers by use of hand signals. A reminder to lean out and reduce prop r.p.m. was passed along to all hands, in order to conserve precious fuel.

We settled down to the monotony of flying herd on the bombers. Our huge paddle-blade propellers were turning so slowly it seemed as if I counted each blade as it passed by. Hour after hour, it felt. The magnetism of counting those blades was so great I was tempted on several occasions to blurt out over the radio: "Who could ever believe this damn ocean could be so damn big!"

The group commander, leading the bombers, was responsible for the navigation. I didn't have that worry. Finally the monotony was to be broken up, because we were flying above fleecy layers of stratus that demanded all my concentration to hold the shadowy forms of the bombers below in sight. Actually, the reason we had this cloud separation was that the bombers had to fly between stratus layers too. There wasn't enough space for us to fly in the visual part of the sandwich and still remain above the bombers.

Thoughts of how we might louse up the all-important rendezvous after take-off were far behind. We had made that. And the rendezvous ahead, after our mission was accomplished, certainly couldn't have bothered me. For the Brass couldn't possibly see that, only the Nips could. And I don't believe I gave too much thought to them.

A new worry took its place. The clouds being the way they were, no Nip planes could find us. No action. The high command would undoubtedly have us all back as replacement pilots, and there I'd be directing traffic once again. I thought: "Damn the luck . . . Why do I persist in planning the future when I know I can't?"

Hardly had I gotten through feeling sorry for myself when I noticed the dive bombers had all disappeared from sight.

"What in hell goes? We must be over the mission." I thought: "Jee—sus, if I lose these bombers, never showing up back at home base would be the best fate I could hope for."

I lowered the squadron through a thin layer of stratus to try to find the bomber boys. Upon breaking clear, the noise from my earphones almost broke my eardrums. One thing was for darn sure. There was no more radio silence in effect. After a few sensible words like: "Stop being nervous. Talk slower." Words came back more shrilly and faster: "Who's nervous? You son of a bitch, not me-ee." Then communications settled down to a garbled roar.

Avengers and Dauntlesses, which appeared to be streaking downward in dives at all angles, were making rack and ruin upon what, I realized suddenly, was Ballale. Some had already pulled out of their dives. Others were just in the process of pulling out. And still others were in their dives.

Huge puffs of dirt and smoke started to dot the tiny isle. A white parachute mushroomed out amid the dirty grayish puffs. Of course I realized it was at a higher altitude. Then a plane crashed. Avenger or Dauntless? How was I to know?

There were enough thick clouds over nearby Bougainville so that I did not expect any Nippon Zeros to intercept us from there. I don't know what I was thinking right at that particular moment. Or what I was supposed to be doing. Maybe, as the proverbial saying goes: "I sat there—fat, dumb, and happy." Perhaps I was watching the boys below in much the same manner as I witnessed the Cleveland Air Shows many times. Anyhow, for certain, high cover was about as close as I ever expected to get toward heaven. So we started down.

To add to my bewilderment, shortly after we cleared the last bit of fluff, I saw that we were right in the middle of about forty Jap fighters. As for us, we had twenty planes that day.

The first thing I knew, there was a Japanese fighter plane, not more than twenty-five feet off my right wing tip. Wow, the only marking I was conscious of was the "Angry Red Meat Ball" sailing alongside of me. But I guess the Nip pilot never realized what I was, because he wobbled his wings, which, in pilot language, means join up. Then he added throttle, pulling ahead of my Corsair.

Good God! It had all happened so suddenly I hadn't turned on my gun switches, electric gun sight, or, for that matter, even charged my machine guns. All of which is quite necessary if one desires to shoot someone down in the air.

It seemed like an eternity before I could get everything turned on and the guns charged. But when I did accomplish all this, I joined up on the Jap, all right. He went spiraling down in flames right off Ballale.

The bursts from my six .50-caliber machine guns, the noise and seeing tracer bullets, brought me back to this world once again. Like someone had hit me with a wet towel. Almost simultaneously I glanced back over my shoulder to see how Moe Fisher, my wingman, was making out, and because I saw tracers go sizzling past my right wing tip. Good boy, Moe—he was busy pouring an endless burst into a Nip fighter, not more than fifty yards off the end of my tail section. This Nip burst into flames as he started to roll, minus half a wing, toward the sea below.

In these few split seconds all concern, and, for that matter, all view of the dive bombers, left me again. All that stood out in my vision were burning and smoking aircraft. And all I could make out were Japanese having this trouble. Some were making out-of-control gyrations toward a watery grave.

A few pilots I had run into before, and some since, can relate every minute detail about an enemy aircraft they came in contact with. But I'll be damned if I can remember much more than round wing tips, square tips, liquid-cooled, air-cooled, and of course the horrifying Rising Sun markings.

After a few seconds of Fourth-of-July spectacle most of the Nip fighters cleared out. Then we streaked on down lower to the water, where the dive bombers were re-forming for mutual protection after their dives prior to proceeding homeward. We found a number of Nip fighters making runs on our bombers while they were busy re-forming their squadrons.

While traveling at quite an excessive rate of speed for making an approach on one of these Zeros I opened fire on his cockpit, expecting him to turn either right or left, or go up or down to evade my fire after he was struck by my burst. But this Zero didn't do any of these things. It exploded. It exploded so close, right in front of my face, that I didn't know which way to turn to miss the pieces. So I flew right through the center of the explosion, throwing up my arm in front of my face in a feeble attempt to ward off these pieces.

I didn't know what happened to my plane at the time. Evidently my craft didn't hit the Nip's engine when his plane flew apart. But I did have dents all over my engine cowling and leading edges of my wings and empennage surfaces. With this unorthodox evasive action Moe and I were finally separated, as by this time, I guessed, everyone else was. Certainly this wasn't the procedure we followed in the three-week training period.

Something else entered my mind after the initial surprise and fright were over, something I realized much more keenly than any of the pilots accompanying me on this mission. I am positive, for I had been involved in this deadly game with Mars for two long years. What I knew only too well was that the average pilot gets less than one chance in a hundred missions of being in a position to fire a killing burst. And furthermore, when this rare chance comes, the one in a hundred, nine out of ten times the pilot is outnumbered, which cuts down his chances still further. Insight into these odds came to me very vividly, for I had tried my best for over two years. Yet my score to date was six. A great number of my previous mistakes suddenly came before me. Realizing that there was meat on the table that might never be there again, as far as I personally was concerned, I was determined to make hay while the sun shined.

Long after the bombing formation had gone on toward home, I found a Zero scooting along, hugging the water, returning to his base after chasing our bombers as far as he thought wise.

BAA BAA BLACK SHEEP

This I had gotten from the past. When an aircraft is out of ammunition or low on fuel, the pilot will hug the terrain in order to present a very poor target.

I decided to make a run on this baby. He never changed his course much, but started an ever-so-gentle turn. My Corsair gradually closed the gap between us. I was thinking: "As long as he is turning, he knows he isn't safe. It looks too easy."

Then I happened to recall something I had experienced in Burma with the Flying Tigers, so I violently reversed my course. And sure enough, there was his little pal coming along behind. He was just waiting for the sucker, me, to commence my pass on his mate.

As I turned into this pal, I made a head-on run with him. Black puffs came slowly from his 20-millimeter cannons. His tracers were dropping way under my Corsair. I could see my tracers going all around this little Zero. When I got close enough to him, I could see rips in the bottom of his fuselage as I ducked underneath on my pass by. The little plane nosed down slowly, smoking, and crashed with a splash a couple seconds later, without burning or flaming.

Efforts to locate the other Zero, the intention of my initial run, proved to be futile. In turning east again, in the direction of our long-gone bombers, once more I happened on a Zero barreling homeward just off the water. This time there was no companion opponent with the plane. So I nosed over, right off the water, and made a head-on run from above on this Japanese fighter. I wondered whether the pilot didn't see me or was so low on fuel he didn't dare to change his direction from home.

A short burst of .50s, then smoke. While I was endeavoring to make a turn to give the *coup de grâce,* the plane landed in the ocean. When aircraft hit the water going at any speed like that, they don't remain on the surface. They hit like a rock and sink out of sight immediately. For the first time I became conscious that I would never have enough fuel to get back to home base in the Russell Islands, but I could make it to Munda, New Georgia. Ammunition—well, I figured that must be gone. Lord knows, the trigger had been held down long enough. Anyhow, there would be no need for more ammo.

But the day still wasn't ended, even though this recital of the

152

first day's events may start seeming a little repetitious by now. And God knows I was certainly through for the day, in more ways than one. Yet when practically back to our closest allied territory, which was then Munda, I saw one of our Corsairs proceeding for home along the water. I tried to join up with him.

And just then, as if from nowhere, I saw that two Nip fighters were making runs on this Corsair at their leisure. The poor Corsair was so low it couldn't dive or make a turn in either direction if he wanted to, with two on his tail. There was oil all over the plexiglass canopy and sides of the fuselage. Undoubtedly his speed had to be reduced in order to nurse the injured engine as far as possible.

In any event, if help didn't arrive quickly, the pilot, whoever he was, would be a goner soon. I made a run from behind on the Zero closer to the Corsair. This Zero pulled straight up —for they can really maneuver—almost straight up in the air. I was hauling back on my stick so hard that my plane lost speed and began to fall into a spin. And as I started to spin, I saw the Zero break into flames. A spin at that low altitude is a pretty hairy thing in itself, and I no doubt would have been more concerned if so many other things weren't happening at the same time.

It was impossible for me to see this flamer crash. By this time, I was too occupied getting my plane out of the spin before I hit the water too. I did, however, shoot a sizable burst into the second Zero a few seconds later. This Zero turned northward for Choiseul, a nearby enemy-held island, but without an airstrip. The only thing I could figure was that his craft was acting up and he planned upon ditching as close to Choiseul as he could. Anyhow I didn't have sufficient gas to verify my suspicions.

Also, I was unable to locate the oil-smeared Corsair again. Not that it would have helped any, or there was anything else one could do, but I believe Bob Ewing must have been in that Corsair. For Bob never showed up after the mission. And one thing for certain, that slowed-down, oil-smeared, and shell-riddled Corsair couldn't have gone much farther.

This first day of the new squadron had been a busy one, all right. It had been so busy I suddenly realized that my gas gauge was bouncing on empty. And I wanted so badly to stretch that gas registering zero to somewhere close to Munda I could taste it.

I leaned out fuel consumption as far as was possible, and the finish was one of those photo ones. I did reach the field at Munda, or rather one end of it, and was just starting to taxi down the field when my engine cut out. I was completely out of gas.

The armorers came out to rearm my plane and informed me that I had only thirty rounds of .50-caliber left, so I guess I did come back at the right time.

But I was to learn something else, too, in case I started to think that all my days were to be like this one, the first one. For this first day—when I got five planes to my credit—happened to be the best day I ever had in combat. However, this concerned us nought, for one would have thought we won the war then and there.

Opportunity knocks seldom. But one thing for certain, peo-ple can sense these opportunities if they are halfway capable of logical thinking, and, of course, are willing to take the conse-quences if things go dead wrong.

Lengthy delay in arrival of relief squadrons from the States plus my ability to con Colonel Sanderson into making a squad-ron out of thin air were the necessary ingredients—and bluff. This was the shady parentage of my new squadron. Born on speculation. An operation strictly on credit had been approved: Airplanes, pilots, and even our squadron number, 214, were borrowed.

That night, I recall vaguely, the quartet of Moe Fisher, Moon Mullin, George Ashmun, and Bruce Matheson harmoniz-ing on the cot next to mine. Tomorrow, the future, meant little to me then. Not even the possibility of a hairy hangover both-ered me the slightest. So I took aboard a load of issue brandy, which our flight surgeon, Jim Ream, had been so kind to sup-ply. I took this load of brandy, along with yours truly, to another world.

Sandy couldn't possibly have known that our first mission would work out this way—or could he?

CHAPTER 16

DAYLIGHT WAS STREAMING through the Dallas-hut windows, and I could sleep in for a while, and I wanted to fall back to sleep, shutting out the world a little longer—but I couldn't. There were many problems on my mind. But first I had to gather my boys together and wise them up to a few things that hadn't been carried out to my satisfaction.

While I was pulling on my fatigue clothes, a two-piece jacket and trousers, I was thinking of things I would have to explain to the pilots. These fatigues were green cotton affairs I believed were the most comfortable clothing a fellow could wear after they had been laundered a few times, and very easy to shed if one were to have a forced landing in the water, which happened to be about the only place we could expect to have one.

The first man I saw this morning—or noticed, I should have said—was Major Stanley Bailey, my executive officer. Stan had been recently promoted to major, and what a proud one he was; I was positive he polished his gold leaves daily. There Stan was in fresh starched khaki with rank insignia on his collar and on his hat, which few of us ever bothered to wear. When I observed that he was also carrying a small swagger stick I thought I was seeing things, but no, I was not. He gave the impression he had just been waiting for the day he made major and would be entitled to pack this "riding crop" from there on in.

Stan was a swell person as well as a good pilot—naïve, yes, and a sincere-type lad with whom we could have a great deal of fun. The other pilots in the squadron remembered him from Pensacola, where he had taught instrument flying, as he had been stationed there after graduating from flight school. When my exec would get wound up a bit, the boys in the squadron would say:

"Now settle down, Major. All you have to remember is—needle—ball—air speed."

Moon Mullin, who was our flight officer, called the boys at 9:00 A.M. for our little get-together. The faces that surrounded me in the ready shack were of happy, joking boys, not the serious do-or-die-type lads we are accustomed to watching in the motion pictures of war. I started: "Before any compliments or corrective criticisms, there is something else I believe should be decided upon immediately. We are going to have to choose a squadron name that is fit to print, my friends."

"Just what do you mean, Gramps?"

"I mean Boyington's Bastards. In the first place, I don't think a squadron should be named after a person. And in the second place, a correspondent said last night, they would balk at printing it back home."

There was a great hassle following this, and some of the many suggestions followed:

"Outcasts?"

"Forgotten Freddies?"

"Bold Bums?"

"To hell with 'em, we'll do such a job they'll have to print it and like it." So it appeared we were right back where we had started.

"No, Gramps. We have thought it over, suggested names, but we like the one we already have. Besides, we have been treated like bastards, and our name rhymes."

I had an answer, but I didn't tell the boys where it came from, for fear they would laugh me out of the ready shack.

Since my childhood the noises made by trains and motors of various types had played a little jingle with my thinking upon many an occasion. My recollection of these occasions when I had

156

been pleasantly occupied with daydreams was most enjoyable. My childhood jingle was, "Baa Baa, Blacksheep, have you any wool, yes sir, yes sir, three bags full."

So I said: "Say, fellows, I got an idea! Something we could use in polite society. Something society already accepts."

"Okay, spill it, Gramps."

"Try this for size. Black Sheep. Everybody knows that it stands for the same thing. And yet no personality is involved, and they can print Black Sheep."

"By golly, we like that, Gramps. We can make up a bastard coat of arms like they used to do in England. And we can put it on a shield and use it as our insigna."

Several days passed before the boys obtained all the authentic dope they needed for drawing up the shield, or insigna. Someone explained that the bar on a bastard shield ran diagonally in the opposite direction from the legitimate. So we made ours this way. They also decided a black sheep was to be on the shield, but, search as we might, we could not locate a drawing to copy one from. Finally we came across an artist of sorts, and the sergeant promised to draw our sheep for the squadron.

I'll never forget their delight when the boys saw the drawing the sergeant came up with, it was ideal, the most woebegone-looking black sheep anybody ever saw. It had taken him such a long time to bring our black sheep that my curiosity had been aroused, so I asked: "Where in hell did you get the idea to draw this from, Sarge?"

"I searched high and low, and was about ready to give up, when I happened to run across a cartoon in a magazine."

The sergeant then handed me a worn sheet from the magazine he spoke about, and I immediately broke into laughter. The cartoon was two G.I.s on their hands and knees camouflaging themselves in sheepskins, and one G.I., in a black skin, was watching a ram approach the flock where the two were hiding, and the face looking out from under the head was saying: "Look, Joe, I'm not so sure I wanna go through with this or not."

Anyway, this sad-looking sheep the sarge had drawn, with

the position it was in, and the name Black Sheep were to stick. And we were free to go on with the business at hand.

My talk concerning the mission to Ballale, our baptism in combat as a squadron, was given to protect our lives and yet shoot down more enemy aircraft at the same time. There had been far too many probables. I realized, though, that the unexpected manner in which we had gone into action was the excuse for not following up. I also realized how bad I'd been in my first fight.

I informed the squadron of my own efforts in the past, all the hours I had flown searching and trying my best, that this was the first time in nearly two years I had been given an opportunity, that one has to plan, before the time arrives, just exactly what one is going to insist that his plane do when the infrequent opportunity presents itself.

And when one gets some of these few chances, he has to know ahead of time how he is going to get into position. When in position, which is the furthest thing in the world from being permanent, he doesn't have seconds. There is just a split second where everything is right, for the target is going to remain anything but stationary. During this split second the range has to be just right, the deflection has to be accurate, and the first squeeze of the trigger has to be as smooth and perfect as humanly possible.

In other words months of preparation, one of those few opportunities, and the judgment of a split second are what makes some pilot an ace, while others think back on what they could have done. Some of the boys took this message to heart, while others did not—or could not. I will never know. Or does it really matter?

Bob Ewing hadn't shown up. We knew Bob was down. But whether he had made some island, of which there were few, and most of them Japanese-occupied, or, more than likely the wide, wide Pacific Ocean, we did not know. I couldn't help thinking that he was in the beaten-up plane I had tried to help. Patrols of fighters were sent for several days until, at last, one of our pilots brought back a report. He had sighted a one-man raft, the type carried by fighters, and there had been a motionless body aboard. The pilot had flown within a few feet above the raft but had gotten no response, saying that the body appeared black and lifeless. We relayed this information to "Dumbo," a PBY rescue amphibian that went out and circled the raft for twenty minutes at a speed much slower than the fighter's.

Dumbo had wisely decided not to risk four lives landing in high waves so close in enemy waters, just to pick up a dead companion. Anyhow, whether this was Bob we never knew, and Bob Ewing had to be declared missing in action, like the majority of people who chose to fight in the air.

It has been said: "Who knows the man you are sitting next to."

Bob McClurg, who was doing his best when he stayed in the same sky with his squadron, had blasted two Nips from this very same sky. His section leader had had to return to base with engine trouble prior to the fight, but Bob stayed with the formation as best he could, and he said afterwards that every time he joined up with a plane he discovered it was covered with angry red meatballs. The character. How in hell did he ever get home? There has to be a Supreme Power; that's all there is to it!

Bob Alexander, who was from Davenport, Iowa, a fellow with perfect white teeth that matched his clean-cut, youthful appearance, seemed definitely out of character as he gave his version of the encounter. He related: "I sent three bursts into this Zero, but it didn't want to go down, so I flew alongside to see what was holding him up. It was really something. I could see the Jap's face. His hands were flailing like windmills, batting at the flames in the cockpit. I was only a few feet away, staring right at him, as he burned to a crisp."

McGee was standing there as he was always dressed, except, possibly, when we were on shore leave at Sydney. "Maggie" had swarthy features and always wore a bandana around his neck, and, except for the lack of golden earrings, I'd have sworn the gent under the mop of curly hair was a gypsy. And he had also drawn blood the first fight but was not the demonstrative type by any stretch of the imagination.

159

It was almost securing time that afternoon, when a jeep drove up to the ready shack with the colonel in charge of the strip and his driver. Stan and I were off to one side of the shack talking, the occupants of the jeep had asked some questions, and some of the boys were pointing in our direction. The colonel walked over to where we were standing and started talking to my exec, leaving me completely out of the conversation. The pair conversed for quite some time, while I stood listening and chewing on a piece of straw. Finally Stan blushed so red it shined in the polished insignia on his collar, and he said:

"Colonel, you must think I'm the commanding officer."

"Why, yes, aren't you?"

"No, that's Boyington, in the fatigue clothes."

"Well, both of you are invited up to my quarters for dinner this evening," the colonel skillfully replied, and then he shoved off.

Before the two of us drove up the hill to dinner, I wished that I had not been recognized at all, so that I could enjoy the evening with my boys, and some of Doc Ream's brandy. But I got dressed in khaki and up the hilltop we went to accept the hospitality of the colonel in charge.

This colonel was one of the sweetest guys I've ever met, and he was full of enthusiasm, as much so as any of the small fry in the squadron. He was all wrapped up with our tales of the action the day before in the skies under his command. Here was a fellow I believed when he stated: "I wish I could be demoted a couple of ranks so I could have gone with you."

As soon as I entered the colonel's quarters, I spotted several bottles of Old Taylor sitting beside some glasses and ice cubes on a drink service, and immediately my mouth began to water. My brain was going a mile a minute. I was thinking of the brandy I had enjoyed after the mission last night, and wondering if he could possibly know anything about this. And I wondered if Colonel Lard could have been so mean as to have forwarded those orders he had told me of.

While all this was going over in my mind, I heard my host say: "Water, soda, or straight, like the men you have proved yourselves to be?"

"Water for me, please, Colonel?" I vaguely remember hearing Stan's voice. Although I was thinking a great deal, words didn't seem to want to come out of my mouth.

"I know how you like yours, Boyington—the same as I do." And the old boy poured two water glasses over half full after handing Stan his mixed drink. There before my eyes was this straight bourbon staring me in the face, waiting for me to accept it from my host's hand.

"Well, come on, take it, drink hearty."

"Thanks," I mumbled, and reached out, taking the offered glass from his hand. I thought: "What in hell is this, a trap of some kind?"

I sat there, not paying much attention to the conversation, just toying with the glass, when the colonel finally brought me back to this world.

"Come on, drink up. Don't worry, there is lots more where this comes from." He winked at me and pointed to a wooden case in the corner of the room.

I thought: "To hell with Lard. He will never be around where there are any bullets. So why should I let him worry me now?"

After the first large swallow had gone down my neck, the others took care of themselves; not the slightest worry concerned me. But as we three were leaving to go to dinner, the colonel informed Stan that we would be with him in a minute, as we had something to talk over privately. I found that Lard had sent those orders after all.

I thought: "What a hell of a world this is, a nice fellow like this trapping me," and I believe the greater part of the delightful glow left.

The colonel said: "Have no fear, Boyington. I'll show you what I think of Lard and his orders, 'to be forwarded.'" With this statement he tore the orders to bits, extending a hand in warm friendship.

I had broken faith with Lard, but I was more determined than a little bit not to let an understanding gent like this down, and many others like him. Come to think about it, I didn't

161

have to worry, because a man like Lard had already lost his faith in everybody, himself included.

But it would seem that these white coral strips on the Russells were, like so many more, constructed only to be completed too late to be of much use. The Japanese were not sending their aircraft down this far any longer. For the equipment we were using it was an ungodly long way from here to where the Nips were operating out of Bougainville. So we had to be content with escorting TBFs up the Slot afternoons until darkness set in, then we would fly to base, leaving them to go the rest of the way in the dark to bomb shipping and anything else on the schedule.

One of these TBF outfits we used to escort was commanded by Major Dooley, who was a cadet when I instructed at Pensacola. This young man had been badly burned as he bailed out of a flaming trainer with his instructor, and it had been doubtful that the Navy would permit him to continue training. I remembered that he had wanted his wings above anything else. And it was evident that he had stuck to it, for here he was, a major leading a squadron.

About a half hour before sunset Dooley would motion for me to fly alongside, so the two of us could use sign language and not have to open up on the radio. The gutty character would then pat the top of his head for taking over command, give me a cat-eatin' grin, and blow me a kiss good-by with a gesture from one of his crippled hands. Then, as our fighters executed a 180° for the Russells, I would be thinking: "God, what a man!"

At Munda the obliterated Japanese landing strip was being reconstructed as soon as the Japs had been pushed off the field. When I thought of the thousands of tons of bombs dropped on this gutted place, I wondered how anything could have survived. But human life is very difficult to knock out, even though the terrain is pounded to a pulp. The cost in lives had been dear for the combined Army and Marine forces that went in by sea to take care of the final arrangements, as always. All airpower had accomplished was the removal of enemy aircraft, and our flyers had done a good job of clearing the air.

162

The Munda strip was being enlarged and lengthened while the fighting spread to the jungles of New Georgia—a repetition of Guadalcanal. Many of the Japanese ground forces had been able to get away to some of the islands near New Georgia and dig in, intending to make it costly to the Allies if they intended to take the islands. By this time the Allies had no intention of doing anything but silencing enemy airdromes and taking only steppingstones wherever they felt necessary.

We patrolled and went along with the dive bombers to strafe gun positions on the islands surrounding the Munda area. The enemy was sending almost daily raids from Bougainville, but we never seemed to be around the area at the right time to tangle with these Jap air raids. But in a manner of no time at all, it seemed, the Seabees had made it possible for Navy Hellcats and Marine Corsairs to operate from the old Jap strip at Munda. These fighters that first operated out of Munda were having all the luck—damn the lucky devils. We continued escorting. This escorting can be paralleled to the lineman's duty on the football field—a lot of work and the backs make all the touchdowns.

With this escort work the Black Sheep had not bagged a single enemy plane since the first mission, and I was becoming desperate. I wasn't the least bit content with patrolling our area under the supposition that we were keeping it free of enemy planes. Or even the slightest bit thankful that the Munda fighters were not permitting the Nips to come down as far as we were. This was bothering me so much I had to do something to change the pattern. I knew only too well that our squadron might be disbanded after the tour, and the number 214 returned to its rightful owners.

Then one day we escorted TBFs to Kahili, with weather none too favorable for bombing. Our bombers had to release the bombs through a small hole in the clouds over the target, afterwards turning back for home like a bunch of contented cows, as no Nips came up to heckle them. It was our duty to protect the bombers, but there was nothing in the rules saying that we had to land with them. When the TBFs had gone as far as I felt was a safe distance, I took the boys in 214 back to

Kahili by themselves. We were able to play a game of hide-and-seek around the clouds, as the fighters were no longer encumbered by bombers.

The enemy ground-control radio had our frequency and decided to join the little game. They were pretending to be American pilots on a mission in our locality. But we were willing to gamble on just who was going to fox whom.

"Major Boyington, what is your position?" came in as clear as a bell without the slightest trace of an accent. I doubt that I would have recognized some of those American-sounding voices on the radio if they hadn't used such perfect English, or if I hadn't known in this particular case that we were out of range of our own aircraft.

Our pilots used a variety of slang expressions that would be extremely difficult to imitate. For an example: "Hey, sheriff, give a gander at the lower forty," and similar expressions were all the code we needed—and they certainly came natural enough.

I played along with the ground radio and the Japanese who were speaking to me in English. Help from some cloud formations at several different levels made the game of hide-and-seek even more interesting. I was aware that their fighters were in the air and trying to locate bombers.

"Major Boyington, what is your position?"

"Over Treasury Island," I came back with, which was a short distance southeast of Bougainville, and then told him exactly where we were above the clouds.

"What are your angels, Major Boyington?"

"Twenty angels, repeating, twenty angels."

"I receive you five by five," which means loud and clear, and then they ceased transmitting. I had lied about my altitude angels, for we were at twenty-five thousand, and were putting an extra grand on for luck while I was talking.

The next thing I saw, about the most beautiful sight a fighter pilot can dream of, climbing in an easterly direction coming from beneath a white cloud, was a formation of thirty Nippon Zeros. We were fortunate in having the midday sun coming over our shoulders, pointing down in front of us upon the backs of our climbing enemy, which is another thing a fighter pilot desires if possible.

I recall placing my finger to my lips to caution silence, while throttling back to lose altitude as I tried to keep in line with the rays of the sun. Whether my signal was passed on visually made no difference, for my boys remained as silent as the little lambs they were. As we eased down, getting closer and closer, a thought that maybe I was hoggish and our prey might get wise ran through my mind. But no. Almost everybody in the squadron got a shot on our first pass.

It felt as though I had the Nip leader in my sights for at least an hour. When I reached the point where I could wait no longer I let go with the six .50-caliber machine guns, and their leader practically disintegrated in front of my eyes. I didn't dare to turn right away because I could see the tracers from my mates sailing past both of my wing tips, and I would run into some of the spare rounds by turning in either direction. So I continued straight ahead completely across the top of the Jap formation.

Flames and debris from several of their planes were visible as they started into a steep left spiral, which reminded me of watching the soapy water whirl out of a bathtub in Sydney. Water rotates counterclockwise down under and clockwise in the Northern Hemisphere, but aircraft have been in the habit of turning left in either hemisphere ever since their invention.

When it was clear to join the mad whirlpool, I too joined the left spiral. The Jap bailed out of the second Zero I fired upon, not more than a second after my burst hit his plane, and I could see a dark-colored chute stream by in a blur. For some reason the blurred form on the end of the trailing chute didn't appear human at this particular instant. By continuing with the spiral until I had completed nearly 360° I was able to get a third Zero to flame. All through this complete circle there were tracers on all sides of me, and I knew they came from my own Black Sheep's guns. But, as plentiful as the tracers were, I was too occupied at the time to worry.

Our Nippon friends disappeared into the clouds as if they had been erased from a blackboard, after what I felt had been

165

a lengthy action. But after our return to base I discovered that one of the boys had timed the action with a stop watch, for there was always some guy who had to do the unusual. The entire action, from beginning to end, had taken just thirty seconds.

A hell of a lot of thoughts can pass through one's mind, not to mention how much air action can take place, in thirty seconds.

CHAPTER **17**

THE BLACK SHEEP were in high spirits after getting twelve more planes to their credit. I realized that taking this most recent opportunity into my own hands could have resulted in the reverse effect just as well as not, but no one argues about protocol when the enemy loses planes and you do not. This was especially true because the bombers had gotten an additional break by being able to bomb through the clouds.

The Munda airstrips were ready to accommodate more aircraft by October, and we were extremely happy to go, because we would have an opportunity for more action. This was anything but a paradise as far as living conditions were concerned, but a hell of a lot better than it had been a month earlier. In the month of October we were to be flown to a frazzle. There was no such thing as rest, or a day off, a situation I had never experienced before.

The invasion of Bougainville was planned for the first of November. This suited me to a tee. Their objective was to wipe out Japanese aviation on Bougainville during the current month, not exactly a small chunk to bite off.

The time the Black Sheep were to fly as a complete unit had passed by the boards, for Strike Command would ask how many flights of four each squadron had available each night, then

167

assign these flights in the command. There would be so many flights for patrol, for escort, or for fighter sweep; and besides pilots would be assigned to stand by for scramble alert. We were flying throughout each and every day, as there were plenty of aircraft available and sufficient ground crew to take care of the planes.

The Navy had F6F fighters, TBFs, and SBDs in addition to the Marine aircraft. The Navy ground crews worked side by side with the Marine ground crews; some of the Casu crews worked upon Marine aircraft, and vice versa.

These turned out to be hectic days for all concerned. One morning as I was walking by a line of planes I saw a Corsair catch fire, and a young sailor was standing beside it just watching. Believing the youth was merely frozen to the ground he stood on, I tried to jar some action into him and said: "Get the lead out, sailor. Grab a fire extinguisher and turn to."

He answered: "I'm not responsible for Gyreen planes."

On the spur of the moment I picked up a heavy extinguisher and heaved it at the pimply-faced youth as I screamed: "Turn to, you stupid son of a bitch, or I'll swab the fire out with you."

This situation was corrected in a hurry as soon as I was able to get hold of the commander in charge of the Casu outfit and inform him of what had taken place. I said: "For Christ's sake, Commander, will you please tell your men to wait until the f——king war is won before they resume fighting with the Marines?"

Haphazard maintenance at Munda nearly cost my life on two occasions, but this wasn't what caused me to fret like I did. The thing that really got my goat was that these two incidents came at times when it should have been a comparative cinch to shoot down some bombers. As it turned out, I never once got a chance with a Japanese bomber; the only planes I tangled with were fighters.

On one of these alerts I scrambled west of New Georgia when we got the word that Jap bombers and fighters were on their way. Instructions to get our altitude close to the field was given to allow less chance of their sneaking by somehow and getting a crack at Munda. The events following my take-off could have well been my most frightful flight if it hadn't been overshadowed by surprise and anger.

The Japs arrived much sooner than expected, for they had come in low over the water until they were fairly close to us, so the mountains would blank out our radar warning or make it inaccurate. However, contact was made in ample time to turn them away from anything of importance in the vicinity of Munda. I was all set up in the middle of a juicy dogfight when my engine sputtered and cut out cold, leaving me no alternative but to dive. As I dove away, I had plenty of company, which I can't say I appreciated the slightest. For it's not the easiest thing in the world to dive away from any plane with a powerless engine. I no doubt wouldn't have gotten away if there had not been help from some Navy F6Fs.

To make a long story short, I was completely out of the running as the fight progressed in the direction of Bougainville. The reason for my predicament was obvious, as I discovered shortly after diving clear that my plane had not been refueled after its previous flight. With nothing but the few gallons remaining in the reserve supply there was nothing to do but to give up the chase and return to base.

There was just one more daytime attack, and although checking the gas gauges in my alert plane had become an obsession, it so happened that it didn't change things a damn particle. When the alert sounded and announced bombers and fighters again, I felt my opportunity had arrived as we were making our mad dash for the planes. But how far from true this was.

As I was one of the first to climb out of the field, everything seemed to point in my favor, and I guess part of it was in spite of all that went wrong. Somewhere in the neighborhood of ten thousand feet the engine cowling tore loose, and then hunks of the exhaust stacks started flying out from beneath the torn cowling. This time I wasn't even in sight of the enemy as I throttled back and proceeded to turn to our field in utter disgust.

Upon taxiing up to the flight line a ray of hope lighted my spirits, for there was a plane in commission with no one to fly it. What a break, I was thinking as I again tore down the runway with Moe Fisher and his plane kicking up coral dust next to mine.

The radio was jabbering as always when contact with the enemy had been made, pilots trying to get through to locate where the fight was taking place. The location was between Kolombangara and Vella Lavella over the water. The Japanese had dive-bombed a new strip that was being constructed by the Seabees out of the side of a mountain at Vella. A ground radio operating on the Vella strip had been giving a blow-by-blow account while Jap torpedo planes were dropping bombs on the new strip and a few ships loaded with supplies.

A shore radio was directing a PT boat out to pick up a Corsair pilot who had been shot down by Zeros. When Moe and I flew over the place where the action had just taken place, we found only a half-dozen or so oil slicks left on the water, one much larger than the others. There wasn't a single survivor near any oil slick, but I knew that the large one was where the Corsair had plowed into the sea, taking its pilot to the bottom, as had the Zeros where I saw the smaller slicks.

Moe and I knew that the Japs had completed any bombing they had in mind, so we headed straight for Bougainville even though we weren't able to spot a Jap plane. Our throttles were floor-boarded for over half an hour as the two of us sped for Bougainville. But we missed the Nips, or maybe they had too great a start on us, for we saw nothing but a few Navy and Marine fighters returning to Munda.

In addition to the heavy flying schedule we were becoming more exhausted every day from being kept awake half the night by Washing Machine Charlie. Charlie was more than just bothersome, because he had damaged a number of aircraft and killed several of our ground crew who had been camped near the field. Night bombers raised hell with us.

Our Corsairs flew patrols commencing with take-offs early in the morning before sunrise, and ending the day with what we called "Moonbeam Patrol," landing after sunset. Our pilots slept in tents up on a hill in back of the field, open tents with wooden flooring to keep our feet out of the dirt. The tent in which six of us were quartered had a box for a table in the

170

center of the floor covering a foxhole underneath. None of us had had time to explore around much, let alone give the foxhole much thought. We had taken for granted that the hole would be waiting in case it was needed some night when the bombs were too close, as we were able to judge by the whistle whether it was time to take cover. Otherwise we paid very little attention to the bombs.

The first occasion we had to put our foxhole to use was a couple of days after our arrival. We were half awakened by the sound of anti-aircraft guns. Then we were still further awakened by the drone of a Jap bomber and the whistle of a string of bombs coming too near for comfort.

All six made a wild leap from under the mosquito nets covering the bunks. The first man out had kicked the box table to one side and jumped in the hole. I was the last to drop into the foxhole; because of my bum leg I wasn't able to move as fast as the others.

The boys preceding me had already experienced what I was about to, but they didn't have time to warn anyone even if they had thought of it. We wound up in roughly two feet of muddy ooze and stagnant water in the bottom of the pit. How fortunate I was I had entered the hole in the decking feet first, for some of the others had not!

The bomb string spaced itself across the tent area, but in the stinking ooze there were six naked bodies that were more irate concerning their present unpleasantness than they were about the bombs. I swore that I was going to teach the Nips a lesson by flying all night the following night.

There didn't seem to be any difficulty in obtaining the permission to fly this night, which was to have a quarter moon. With no radar equipment in the planes and a moon of no value to me I would have to count upon the ground radar for everything. The ground station was to direct me by magnetic vectors in which the night bomber would be approaching Munda, for there were no city lights like back home to direct one by locality. I was fully aware while planning the flight that I stood little chance without moonlight; a night shoot-down in the dark without radar had been a rare thing.

171

Our anti-aircraft batteries were informed that a plane was to be up and had orders not to fire when their searchlights picked it up because it might be a Corsair. I said: "I certainly hope you inform all of the anti-aircraft in the outlying areas, too."

With the arrangements complete as far as we were able to think of I welcomed operations giving me the rest of the day off so I could get some sleep before my flight. I went to my tent and shed my fatigues and tried to catch a few winks on my cot. But I found that I could not fall asleep even though dead tired; maybe the mosquito net stopped any breeze from touching my body. There were no mosquitoes during the day, but the flies were impossible, so if I wanted any rest I had to stay under the netting.

A stiff drink would have helped me to relax, but I didn't dare to take a drink because I knew only too well that my eyesight had to be at its sharpest that night. I wandered about some of the other tents, not looking for anything in particular, as I recall, merely to pass the time, or perhaps to see how the rest of the boys were living it up.

It wasn't difficult to figure out who lived where, for there were photographs of nice-looking girls in the tents with "all my love" or something written to so-and-so on each picture. There were the usual souvenirs about, like Jap automatics, swords, Nippon flags, and ammunition of various calibers with Japanese writing on the brass.

One tent I entered, with my mind miles away from Munda, caused me to take a walk into the jungle and get away from camp. Here beside a bunk, placed on top of a small wooden box, was a sightless, grinning skull staring from underneath one of Junior Heier's baseball caps. I asked Junior later: "How can you stand that thing around you? Where did you get it?"

Junior had grinned and said: "Just outside of camp. And don't think I didn't have a time finding one without any extra holes in it."

As I walked away from camp, I was reminded of walking along one of the cattle trails in Idaho as a boy, when I walked with my head down for fear I would miss any Indian arrow-heads or pretty rocks. My thoughts were evidently back in the peaceful valleys of Idaho, recalling how I used to imagine the battles of the American Indians of yesteryear, for I had traveled miles back into the New Georgian jungle without realizing how far from camp I had wandered.

All of a sudden I came across the body of a Japanese soldier lying on the trail. No danger of the Japs being about, for this man had been dead for some time, and the maggots were busy taking care of him. Some person, or persons, had smashed his helmet and crushed in the entire face in a little added flurry of hate. Also, the soldier's rifle lay in broken pieces beside the body.

I continued along the trail without being able to define any of my thoughts one way or another. Soon I came across two more dead Japs who had been mowed down by a cross-fire action as they were defending a lookout post of some nature, judging by what evidence remained. These too had been clubbed after being shot. Little wonder Junior had such a diffi-cult time acquiring a perfect skull to make a hatrack for his bedside.

Farther on down the trail I was to learn what the outpost was protecting, for here I came upon a vacated camp in a silent little valley in the jungle. By browsing around I found how the enemy lived in the jungle, and how they slept. There were no dead here, so the outpost had served its purpose, when the camp heard the firing, and was able to move on to a safer place. It was a good thing the Japs had decided to move in a hurry, or for that matter maybe I was walking among booby traps and didn't know it.

The thought came to me that this was one hell of a place for a pilot to be, and that I'd better return to the flying field where I belonged, as the sun was better than halfway down to the horizon. There were a number of stray Japs roaming about during the mopping up of New Georgia, so I was doing any-thing but being sensible. I dog-trotted back to get prepared for my night skirmish with Washing Machine Charlie that evening.

The engine was purring like a kitten as I rolled faster and

faster down the Munda strip, and continued to purr as I climbed in the darkness above the field. Every plane light was turned off, inside and outside, not only to enable better visibility but to minimize Charlie's chances of spotting the plane. Nothing could be done with the exhaust, but anyone would have to be on top of a Corsair before the glow could be seen.

Control had agreed not to communicate until a positive image appeared upon the screen, and then I was to remain silent so the enemy wouldn't get wise. Leaned out to my finest to lengthen the stay aloft to the utmost, I must have been up over an hour before I heard Control directing anti-aircraft and searchlight batteries on a bogey miles out on a certain vector. In easing around without getting any of the quarter moon behind my plane and the reported position, I focused my eyes so as to avoid missing Charlie. The fact that the searchlights were instructed not to light until he was close enough to track was probably reason for him to suspect something unusual. Charlie chose to be cagey, in any event.

For six hours I was vectored to the fringes of our radar screen, and only twice was I able to catch a glimpse of some object at an altitude different from mine. By the time I changed altitude and tried to close, there was nothing but darkness to be found. Not knowing about flying saucers when I was doing this, I mentioned that it was like chasing ghost riders in the sky.

Finally I was ordered to land, and even though I had a dejected feeling, there were a number of people who had a good night's sleep for a change. I had taxied up to the flight line and was enjoying a very welcome cup of coffee and a cigarette just as Washing Machine Charlie returned. Whether it was the same bomber or not doesn't matter, but for some reason he was no longer suspicious. A string of eggs came whistling down on the field as the Jap decided to let all go at one time and head for home at dawn. My coffee and cigarette sailed into the darkness as I dove into a slit trench with the others and listened to the string of bombs galumph along the strip.

I was standing in front of the ready shack one morning when I noticed a familiar face from the past. The two stars on each

174

side of his shirt collar were about the only change, and he was the general in command of Munda. A striking man with wild eyes that looked through one from beneath thick, bushy brows, and he had been nicknamed "Nuts" by his buddies many years before. Of course I didn't take the liberty of addressing him as "Nuts," though the older officers of his rank did, and I knew that the general was no more nutty than a fox.

The general was a character, however, who was always seen carrying a cane—for good luck. He had never let the cane out of his sight since the Shanghai Marine days when he had been stationed in China. Once he had been stunting a plane during an air show put on for the benefit of the Shanghai public, and the wings came off his biplane fighter. The openmouthed spectators had watched him as he descended over the stands, pulling a bit of air from the side of his chute to avoid landing on top of them. Just before he sat down in front of the grandstand, he shouted: "Yip Ho-ee," and the thrilled spectators saw that he was twirling a cane in one hand.

Nuts was so genuine, in my estimation, that I simply adored the man, and he had always impressed me as a father rather than a superior officer. I recalled years before when I had been standing an officer-of-the-day watch one Sunday at North Island, San Diego, when a colonel had just flown in and I had gone out on the field to greet him. He had just completed a cross-country from Washington, D.C., and I might add that the colonel happened to be the highest rank in Marine Corps aviation.

I had saluted and started all the fawl-de-rawl procedure I was supposed to do, but Colonel Moore had stuck out his hand, and said: "Hello, son, gosh it's good to see you!" For he was the kind of a person who could make one feel wanted when I'm certain he barely recognized him.

Anyhow we renewed our friendship, and the general wanted to know if I would strafe the Kahili airfield the following morning because the bombs didn't appear to be destroying the enemy aircraft; furthermore he had a deadline to meet. I said: "General, you don't have to ask for anything; you just name it."

"I know it, son, but you are busy now. How about having dinner with me tonight after you secure—about six, let's say?"

"Invitation accepted, General, thank you." As we were not getting enough to eat at this particular stage, I figured I could use a good meal even though I didn't know how well he was eating.

My boys gathered around me and wanted to know what this was all about after the general and his cane drove away. About all I was able to say was that I had been invited to dinner at his quarters that night. Their faces looked like little children's as they said: "Gee, Gramps, that's great! Will you see if you can bring us back anything?"

Although I had not the faintest idea of what it could be, I promised just the same. The general had a meal that tasted all right by comparison, but I enjoyed the drinks before and after dinner more while he was talking over the intended mission the following morning. What I appreciated so much was that Nuts Moore told you the problem and then would sit back and listen while you told him how to go about getting it done.

As he was in the process of wishing us luck, and I was about to return to my brood empty-handed, the general asked: "By the way, how are you lads fixed for whisky?"

"The whisky situation is rough," I lied, thinking that maybe I would not have to return empty-handed after all. "We have been completely out of it for some time."

I could see the funny look that came into his eyes as he pointed with his cane to a wooden box underneath a bunk. He said: "This must be a coincidence. Here's a case with no name on it. I don't know who it belongs to, but take it with you."

Not wanting to take a chance on this being an oversight, I thanked the general profusely while in the process of backing out into the darkness outside his quarters with the wooden case clutched in my arms. I didn't figure that Nuts Moore's eyesight wasn't what it had been, for I could plainly see that this case was addressed to another major general whose judgment in fine whisky had been respected for a good number of years. My conscience was clear as I walked back to camp with the heavy box across my shoulder, for the general had given this to me; I had not stolen it. Not until after the war was over did I mention the addressee, then Nuts got that funny little look again and said: "Yes, I was aware of it, but I thought my buddie had been drinking too much."

When the boys ran out to greet me upon my return from dinner, I felt that this was the closest I had ever come to playing Santa Claus. They had faith in me, and it showed in their expressions. They must have known far better than I did that I wouldn't return without bringing them some goodies. We were laughing and joking as we planned the dangerous mission for the following morning.

Twelve of 214 took off the next morning as planned, and flew low over the water along the north coast of Choiseul. This was according to plan. We didn't want the Kahili Nips on Bougainville to pick us up on radar, and knew that the long east-west range of mountains on Choiseul would act as a shield. There were Japanese troops on Choiseul, but they would believe that we were on a reconnaissance mission by our flying so low along their coast line—we hoped.

When past the westernmost tip of Choiseul we were but a short distance over water north from the strong Kahili airstrip, a matter of a very few minutes. At this point eight of the pilots who were to be top cover climbed gradually above the four of us who would strafe. The Kahili strip ran east-west, one end of it being almost on the eastern shore line of Bougainville. Not choosing to attack the field from the seaside where the Japs would be expecting an attack, we continued on west for a short distance before circling around behind their field, hugging the jungle as we went. Once over land, we added full throttle to pick up all the speed possible before making the low strafing run, as the Nip ground troops would be firing rifles and machine guns.

When I figured I was close to the west end of the Kahili clearing, I pulled our flight of four abreast up ever so slightly, so I could sneak a last-second check that would enable a perfect line-up with the runways. This gave the maximum amount of target over the full length of the field as we strafed eastward with guns and throttles wide open.

For my money's worth things could not have worked any more successfully than they did. The Japs had no fighters in the air, and it was apparent that they hadn't even heard our Corsairs until they came whistling over the treetops on the edge of the clearing. We had taken Kahili by complete surprise in broad daylight and clear visibility. Our incendiaries and armor-piercing were a special load for this work, and they worked to perfection. But I had to thank the Nips for having the majority of their parked planes lined up for us, as it is almost impossible to change your sights when traveling at any speed over the ground.

It wasn't in the original plan, but when Moon, who had charge of the top cover, saw that there were no Nips upstairs, he quickly decided to join the strafing with the rest of the boys. I believe that every piece of equipment on the field got sprayed, at least, and flames were coming out of some twenty aircraft as we sped across the field for Munda. It was a great feeling to be able to report this successful action to General Moore.

At first I thought we had accomplished all this without anyone getting hurt, but shortly after landing I realized that one of the twelve was missing. Junior Heier was not with us, and no one had seen him crash. We didn't have a chance to send a search or even worry very long, for news of Junior came in from the new strip being constructed at Vella Lavella. The boy had landed at Vella among the bulldozers, roughly but safely.

Later I saw why the lad had been delayed, and it was a miracle that the plane ever flew, with thirty-six inches off one wing tip and forty inches off the other. Junior had been so intent on strafing Jap planes that when he finally decided to pull up it was too late, and he was forced to fly between two coconut trees at the end of the Kahili strip. These trees, combined with the plane's momentum, had done a far better job than Junior could have with a pair of scissors and a model plane. Even though he had continued at full throttle, there was no keeping up and he lagged behind, and finally became so short on fuel he tangled with the bulldozers.

CHAPTER **18**

AS FAR AS I WAS CONCERNED the Black Sheep were able to write their own ticket through the medium of General Moore after we pulled such a successful job on the strafing mission. However, I certainly hoped Moore would not get a notion that the war could be won in this manner, for Lord knows I should have learned a lesson in China that this is far from true. So I quickly followed up with some ideas of my own, which I was certain would be satisfactory yet not foolhardy, or as dangerous.

As a matter of fact I was able to talk Strike Command into permitting their bombers to sit out of a few missions so we could go on fighter sweeps and not be tied down with bombers. To my way of reasoning, based upon what I had seen and read, the procedure used by both the enemy and ourselves should have been reversed many times.

Not only did I present statistics, but in a small way my Black Sheep had provided Strike Command with a couple of concrete examples as well. In the earlier stages of the war the bombers had been sent over heavily defended areas without fighter escort by both sides when they needed escorts in the worst way. The extreme range in many cases made escort prohibitive. But by the time new strips were acquired closer to the targets, the need for fighters had lessened considerably, or in some cases became almost unnecessary.

If it were possible to send some fighters over a target prior to the bombers arriving there, the enemy would dissipate some of their interceptor aircraft. The outcome would be that the enemy fighters would be short on fuel about the time our bombers arrived, and be forced to land without making contact, thereby adding the chance of our blowing up a few more on the deck. A few results and one swell general, and, I may add, a deadline, all put together enabled the hired men with the clear blue eyes and rippling muscles to have a say in affairs for a change.

We were on one of these fighter sweeps, and entertaining the idea, more or less, that it might be possible to hold another conversation and a repeat of the time before with the Japs. It was by no means the same. The Japs were talking and asking our position, but our circling around waiting for an interception proved futile, and finally I knew that gasoline had to be the deciding element in any longer wait.

"Major Boyington, what is your position?" came in again.

I tried to taunt them off the ground as I knew that soon a fight would be impossible with our gas supply. I said: "Right over your airport; why don't you yellow bastards come up and fight?"

It became apparent the Japs were not falling for any more of this, and answered: "Major Boyington, why don't you come down if you are so brave?"

As we circled above the strip at twenty thousand feet, the Japs tried their best to knock us down with anti-aircraft guns. The black bursts would start in a little behind and a thousand feet above or below our formation, and after correcting the range and deflection they would start laying the bursts closer to us. Our planes would then reverse course and change altitude quickly, and immediately, the Jap gunners would be presented with an entirely new tracking and range problem.

When it became evident that words or insults were not going to make them take off, Casey and I dove down and strafed two of the gun positions, leaving the rest of the fighters upstairs.

180

We didn't get too low on this insult strafing because we knew the Japs machine guns were extremely accurate at short range. We were content with just spraying the parked aircraft, knowing that if there were any damage it would be more luck than anything else.

"All right, you devils, I was down," I challenged. "Now, how about you coming up?" But no Zeros took off this day to accept our invitation. This was a hell of a note, a fellow having to change his tactics daily in order to get a nibble. I should have been thankful the enemy was not in a complete rut, and killing me with monotony.

This day ended like so many other days, with me scratching my head and racking my brain for the answer: what to do next time. I had lost Casey for a brief spell during our strafe on Kahili, but he finally caught up and was flying on my wing. I imagined Casey had broken his seat, as he was sitting so low down in the cockpit I was barely able to see his eyes over the edge. The reason I had noticed this in the first place was that normally he would have the seat jacked all the way to the top position for better visibility. Casey didn't happen to be the tallest guy in the world, and I hoped he would be able to land safely, as the Corsair, with its long nose, was as blind as a bat on landings.

He had made the landing without mishap, and was walking over to the ready shack, helmet and goggles in hand, when I decided to throw a gibe. I said: "Say, Casey, I thought for a few minutes I had lost you."

"You damn nearly did, Gramps." And he wasn't smiling.

"When you finally did join up, you were out of sight, I had to fly above you to see if there was anyone in the cockpit."

He said: "Take a look for yourself," offering the removed helmet while he rubbed a knot on the top of his crew cut.

Upon inspecting the helmet it was apparent that a 7.7 slug had cut a slit completely through the fabric approximately four inches in length. But outside of a small welt and a wee bit of skin missing from the center of his crew cut, he looked as good as ever to me. I can't say I blamed the lad for never flying again

181

with his seat any higher than just enough to look through the electric gun sights.

One night the Japanese decided to evacuate Kolombangara by small boats. They had counted upon darkness and early morning fog to conceal the movement, and fortunately it did for the majority of the boats. Some of 214 with parts of other squadrons caught the last of the Nip boats on the early morning patrol, and strafed the poor devils at sea. I was just as happy that I had been fortunate enough to miss this action.

The evacuation of Kolombangara was assumed to be complete by the Allies and they had no intention of sending any patrols ashore, which happened to so many of the unimportant islands of the Pacific. The Japanese had spread themselves thin by trying to protect all the islands, so when the Allies came to control the sea and air, the troops on these islands were of no value to the enemy; they were stranded. They remained there until the end of the war, to exist as best they could off the land itself. I am certain that this was no picnic on any of the islands I saw.

The day of this evacuation of Kolombangara was a sad one for the Black Sheep. Not that it was any great military action, but the loss of one Sheep, no matter what the cause, was of great concern to us—and to his loved ones back home. A mistake happened this day, as did many others during this long war, but actually no one can be blamed—or should be blamed.

One of our patrols of four spotted a boat from altitude near the north shores of Kolombangara, and the flight was signaled to dive down. The leader had recognized that this was not a Nip boat, but one of our own PT boats patrolling the island a lot closer than it was supposed to be. The leader had pulled up, and expected his three wing men to do likewise, but they did not.

Bob Alexander was in this flight, and apparently couldn't hear his section leader, firing a burst at the PT boat. One of the pilots on this flight said he saw one of the U.S. sailors trying frantically to wave the Corsair away, and as he was watching the sailor wave from the bow, the Corsair fired his .50-calibers, cutting the sailor in half as he was waving.

Another sailor handling the twin .50s from the stern of the PT boat fired back as Bob continued to fire. It was automatic reflex, more or less defense action. Bob Alexander's Corsair didn't pull out, but crashed in smoke and flames a few yards back of the beach in the jungle.

One thing I have noticed about letters, especially letters exchanged with parents whose sons were lost with us or missing, is that the parents do not want the answers to contain gush or platitudes. In other words the parents, and quite rightly, do not have to be sold on the worthiness of their own boys. What the parents or relatives do want is the minutest details of the boy's last fight, or how he came to be knocked down, or what he was doing when last seen. And this information, to obtain or to know or to give, is the hardest of all. I tried, but only in a few cases in regard to lost flyers did I know, or does anyone know.

We would take off on a mission, we would cover lots of miles over ocean or jungle, and we would be shot at, we would have our own individual fights maybe, we would go through clouds. And those of us who did not come back just simply did not come back. And the ocean tells no secrets. This roughly was how it was when we lost people, or, as a more personal example, when I myself was lost later.

Or as in the case of Bob Alexander, another example, but one where we did have a clue: we saw him go down. We saw his plane burst into smoke and flame, and we saw him crash. But he crashed on an enemy-held island. So the remainder would have been a secret.

I wrote his folks, of course, and told them exactly what had happened, and that the island was held by the enemy. And this is all that I could do at the time, or anybody could do. Yet it so happened that the case of Bob Alexander is the one and only, while I was squadron leader, in which we were able to recover a body later—and could complete the tragic letter to the folks. For in December, some two months later, after Bob had gone down on the island, our troops had forced the last of the Japanese to evacuate, and we were transferred to the nearby Vella

183

strip. Immediately I formed a small party among us, and we got a PT boat's crew to take us over to this island.

We maneuvered around the north end of Kolombangara where we had seen the plane go down, and finally saw traces where the terrain had been torn up. We swam ashore with machetes and shovels, and finally located the spot where the plane had crashed.

The place was a jungle, but we searched through it, climbing through the brush and the vines, and finally found Bob's body. What was left of Bob's mortal remains had been slammed into a tree trunk there in the jungle.

The day was so hot with that sticky tropical heat that all of us were soaked with sweat by this time, and we finally managed to edge out a grave. We placed Bob's body within the grave and, remembering what a fighter he had always been, we decided to place his body so that he faced Tokyo. He had wanted so much to get there. Then, after covering the grave with jungle earth, we took one of his bent propeller blades, painted his name on it, and placed it at his head.

Bob Alexander's funeral services were brief. Three New Zealand boys who had accompanied us on this mission stood on one side of his grave, and I placed three of Bob's comrades on the other. I had all intentions of giving a befitting prayer. But as I started out, in my memory I saw Bob standing before me. He was such a well-built boy. I could see his perfect teeth and his hair, which was more golden than red, and I could see in my memory his everlasting smile also. So, as I started to give the prayer, words would not come. The best I could do was give a right-hand salute. We all saluted, and then I mumbled: "So long, Bob." And that, for some reason, was all I could say.

Yet, for once, and only once, we had found one of our lost Black Sheep. We had found Bob, and could write his folks so.

After we swam back and had gotten aboard the PT boat, heading back for Vella, I was mentally chastising myself for the lack of delivery in the prayer department. In my lifetime it was nothing unusual for me to try to rebuild the past, forgetting the present. I turned to Moon Mullin, the handsome

184

lug, because he seemed to possess such great faith, and started to talk.

"If only I could have gotten a prayer out."

Moon must have been reading my thoughts, for he placed his arm around my shoulders, smiled kindly, and said: "Don't worry, Gramps. We all understand. We feel the same way."

The command at Guadalcanal had been recently turned over to the Air Corps, and we had many an occasion to escort B-24s and B-25s. It was on one of these Air Corps B-24 missions that I came very close to being decorated with my first medal. As it happened, I wasn't, and, having left China in a huff, I had collected no medals from there, either. I didn't know that I was eventually going to be given up for dead before I was to receive what I termed "booby prizes."

The Black Sheep squadron was one of three designated to escort B-24s from Guadalcanal on a strike to Bougainville. Air Force P-38s were to be top cover, Bell Aircobras were to be low cover, and 214 was to be medium cover for the 24s. 214 rendezvoused with the 24s and their other pursuit over Munda, then proceeded on the mission.

A storm front was beginning to make it appear unlikely that the bombers would even find their target, let alone bomb it, so, one by one, the two Air Corps pursuit squadrons peeled off, returning to their respective bases. But not the Black Sheep, good old USMC stuck right with these Air Corps bombers, and it was a good thing we did, for the Nips were able to get up plenty of Zeros in the clear weather on the other side of the storm front.

None of our planes was shot down, bombers or fighters, although several of them were struck by 20-millimeter cannon fired from the defending Zeros. My Corsair came back with all its ammo intact because I was never presented with a decent shot, but 214 was not goose-egged, as Casey, Moon, and Bolt scored. The Nips gave our fighters but few opportunities; they could see that we were intent upon escorting properly and wouldn't break off and chase them.

Quite some commotion was created in Air Corps Headquarters at the Canal by our sticking with the 24s when their own pursuit had left them. I've long forgotten the name of their CO. It was something like General Hill, but I am not certain. And it really doesn't make much difference now. Anyhow, the general was all set to come over to Munda and pin a Silver Star on me. He had even gone so far as having the papers written up for the decoration. But in trying to be ethical the general had informed Navy Headquarters of his intention, and somebody there squelched the dear general, informing him that the Navy was capable of decorating its own Marines. This was the closest I ever came to being considered for so much as a Purple Heart until it was believed that I had been killed, although I had no way of knowing this at the time.

I thought: "To hell with medals," as I sincerely believed there were other things a person can give that are far more important. Memory is the only means of getting these things out and enjoying them over again.

Words or gestures of encouragement come in strange ways. In the same sense that we often may be unaware of giving them to others, so, too, others may be equally unaware of giving them to us. This goes not only for the war. It goes for today as well. And I am especially thinking of a man who, possibly without realizing it himself, has bucked me up at both times.

The second time was after World War II when I, after being returned to the United States, was trying to get my personal things squared away after my long absence as a captive, and during a specific period when nothing seemed to be going right for me at all. But the first time this same man encouraged me was long ago when the going was truly rugged in Munda.

With all the flying and little sleep at night we had to take a little shut-eye during those moments when we could grab it. Next to drinking I liked to sleep as much as anything else in the world. I always have been that way about sleep since I was a kid. My mother thought I was going to come down with sleeping sickness before I was graduated from college.

At this particular time I had no idea that later I would be a so-called hero. And the next month, just depending on the morning's paper, one might be something else for a while, yet at heart all along he is still the same person. Then it is natural for some people, even military higher-ups, to be on the safe side and watch one carefully from the sidelines, or avoid him altogether like a leper, until the publicity (or whatever it is) blows favorably in his direction again.

It was another hot sticky morning on Munda, and I was stretched out on a cot in one of the tents beside the white coral strip. One of my boys came in and nudged me and said: "Hey, Gramps, somebody outside to see you."

Being tired and a little crabby, I answered: "My God, what in hell does someone want to see me for now?"

Trying to push the sleep out of my brain, I walked out of the tent blinking under the glare of that white coral strip, just like looking at an everlasting field of white snow. The light was blinding.

I finished rubbing my eyes and got them focused, and saw an array of stars on collars. Two admirals were standing before me, and two Marine Corps major generals. Without a cap I could not salute, but I nodded and said: "How do you do." And one of the admirals stepped up in front of me.

I was a little nervous at first, but was soon put at ease. This grizzled-looking admiral who had stepped forward was Admiral Halsey. He stuck out his hand and said: "Nice work, boy."

After that I felt just as much at ease as though I was talking to my own father.

At the time water was scarce around Munda. In fact, we had hardly enough to drink, let alone to shave with, and the weather was so hard on our faces in that hot climate and the slip-streams and everything from flying that I did not like to shave more than about once a week anyhow. But I was put right at ease with this too: I noticed that Admiral Halsey had not shaved for at least a couple of days.

Another gentleman I talked to in this group of visitors ashore was Harold Stassen, at the time a commander in the Navy. I had only about a five-minute chat with him there on the field at Munda.

All of us cannot return to States-side life knowing all the answers as readily as if we had lived there all the time. For even some of those who have lived here all the time do not know all the answers either. This is the way with everybody, of course. We may not change, but the publicity momentarily may change, and that is all. But we are helpless against it for the brief while it lasts. And one evening I could not help thinking of all this a little, and perhaps contemplating it a little too, as one does —and just then the phone rang in my home.

The call was an oral message relayed from Halsey that, when he reached the coast the next day on his way to Mexico, he wanted most of all to have my wife and me attend a small dinner with him.

He had not, then, forgotten the unshaven guy on Munda when the going had been rough. And he had not forgotten him later, for I was still the same guy, though older, of course, and more dilapidated, but nevertheless the same guy to whom Halsey that morning had said: "Nice work, boy."

So, at least, I got a turn later to think of a man like that with the words: "Nice work, Halsey."

Maybe this can make you understand, as I did, that tokens of true friendship that words are inadequate to describe mean so much more than all the hundreds of thousands of tiny chunks of metal they could possibly design. Men like Halsey, Moore, and my own Black Sheep spurred me on, although I had not the slightest notion of where I was going to end up, or even where I was going.

Living had become more normal around old Munda. Even the nights were at last free from Washing Machine Charlie, because an old Navy friend, Commander Gus Woodhelm, had a squadron of night fighters based at Munda. These night fighters were Corsairs with a large, bulblike fixture on the wing, a radar, and these planes proved to be very effective too.

Gus and his boys patrolled by night and slept by day. Most of the Nip bombers were being knocked down long before ever getting close enough for us to hear the guns or see the tracers. I found that Gus and I had different problems on our hands, for he chased a dot around on a radar screen within his cockpit, never looking past the instruments, not until the dot that represented a bomber got very close to the center of the screen.

He said that they were in no hurry, as we were; they tracked

188

a bomber, checking its speed, enabling a nice slow closing rate where either a miss or a chance of ramming a bomber was highly improbable. With these night fighters, which involved more thinking than action, the nights were cleared, so I had more time to rest, and think too.

I often wish today that in some of these big fights where we had twenty or thirty Corsairs and Hellcats, and about forty or fifty Zeros, that I could have had a moving-picture setup that would have taken in the whole affair. The little cameras connected up with one's guns took only the actual firing at a plane. The film never showed a plane go all the way down to the sea. But if I had had a camera that could have taken the whole thing, it would have been a sight to behold for today's public records.

In these bigger battles you could see planes going around in circles, half circles; you could see Zeros, Corsairs, Zeros, all firing at each other; you could see the red balls from the tracers, just like Roman candles going every which way in the sky. The battles would cover an area from about three thousand feet above the water to about twenty thousand, and equally as wide. Every time somebody pulled any g-load in turning or pulling out, it would form a vapor streak that would get larger and larger.

When one is off away to one side, these vapor streaks resemble a bunch of hoops placed in the sky, and, as I have said before, sometimes when one is directly below, they resemble chicken tracks that have been made in wet mud and allowed to dry.

After a while our prey got a little rougher to get, because the Japs wouldn't take to the air when we had the advantage. Instead, they dispersed their aircraft on the ground, so it would have been foolhardy to try to strafe them.

Strafing in the middle of the day is truly a rough proposition at best because every ground gun in the place, including rifles, can be trained upon one when he comes down to strafe. So, we had to devise different methods for getting them up in the air. Any semblance to the laws protecting ducks is purely coincidental, my friends.

One highly successful caper was pulled in October as twenty-

189

four of us flew to Bougainville in "V" formation at high altitude so the Nips would think we were unescorted dive bombers and might possibly take off. We were talking back and forth to one another about where we intended to bomb as we approached Kahili. And best of all of the ruse—the Nips fell for it.

The trouble with anything good was that it usually worked only once, never more than two times at the outside. This was one of those firsts—and what a first.

We waited until about half of the Nips had climbed out of Kahili, and the rest were in the process of taking off or taxiing up to the end of the strip. I don't believe that any of the first Nips off ever got much higher than five thousand feet. But they had committed themselves, and that was all we wanted them to do. We quickly changed the formation from bomber Vs of three into fighter pairs, then we streaked down upon our unsuspecting foe.

We started nailing the first Nips at about five thousand, as they were climbing up at a considerable disadvantage. Even the Nips on the ground were practically helpless because they could not fire for fear of hitting their own aircraft. By following the dust streaks down the field we were able to see others taking off. Some of these Zeros were knocked down before they even had a chance to take up their landing gear after take-off.

Off the end of the Kahili strip, which stopped right on the edge of the ocean, I saw eight splashes, with oil gradually spreading in larger circular patterns on top of the water. This must have been a demoralizing sight for the ground Nips, watching their gallant air force take off up the field and before completing a half-circle ending up in the drink, right in front of their noses.

But it is at times like these when people get overanxious, or maybe careless, and I include myself as one of the greatest violators. I heard several calls coming through the multi-jabbering over the radio. One was for help. It came from Moffett, who was from another Marine squadron.

"How about giving me a hand?" he said. "I'm having engine trouble. Two Zeros on my tail. Hurry."

BAA BAA BLACK SHEEP

Someone said: "Hold on a minute, I'll be with you."

Moffett came back: "Oh, skip it, I'm going in." Then silence. When the cards were all face up, some of these last words became classics.

There was really only one other Corsair I could positively identify in the wild flurry on more than one occasion, and this was Bandana Maggie. McGee didn't seem to be wasting much extra lead this day, as I saw him flame three on first bursts.

This happened to be a good day for me, as I too was able to flame one at five thousand feet, and another just below while he was busy making his turn off the end of the strip, climbing out. A third Zero nosed down to pick up some speed and tried to outrun me by flying straight ahead after he had taken off the strip. He didn't make it, for I shot him down, but he did get me into some serious trouble.

We could fly to Bougainville at any altitude we chose. The main thing to remember was always to be on top of the enemy before starting to work on him, and never stay on the bottom of one of these heaps any longer than absolutely necessary.

In regard to breaking this latter axiom, I certainly broke it in shooting down the third Zero, for I chased him all the way down to the water and was just starting to climb sharply, looking for more targets, when five Zeros jumped me.

Thank God, there was a small cloud nearby, and about all I could do was to keep going in and out of it. Every time I came out, two or three of the Nips nailed me with lead. Then I would have to execute a flipper turn and duck momentarily back into my cloud again. This routine seemed to go on until my whole body seemed to become dry. The dryness, starting in my mouth, gradually worked down my throat, then down to my stomach. Finally, despite all the gymnastics I was doing in that cockpit, I got so dry I had to fumble down to my web belt, get my canteen off, and take a drink of water.

In the midst of all this some clown up in the sky hollered out over the radio: "Where's the fight? I want to get into the fight."

This is when I made that answer to him that the pilots repeated to me later, after we were down on the ground. It seems that during my thirst and my trouble, I had yelled back over the radio: "Jesus Christ, you silly son of a bitch, if you want to shoot Zeros so damn much, come down over the Farro Islands at three thousand feet. I've got five of 'em cornered here."

But I still wish that today we, or somebody, could have made full-sized motion pictures of some of these bigger fights. It would have been good to know whether my Black Sheep, among others, had really been so photogenic, after all.

CHAPTER **19**

I N THE LATTER PART of October the Allies had counted
upon seeing the last of Japanese air resistance on Bougainville,
but instead we were to receive word through our intelligence
that one hundred replacement fighters from the Rabaul area
had been flown in recently. This seemed to verify the Chinese
saying "One cannot kill a dragon by chopping pieces off its
tail." This was like my own life: When I counted upon something being completed, so that I would be able to loaf, new
problems always came up.

One of these B-24 escorts, a total flop as far as a mission
went, turned out to be one of the most thrilling as far as 214
was concerned. The bombers had taken us somewhere in the
neighborhood of Bougainville in some bad weather; they had
tried to get above it and could not; they tried to get below it
and could not. The lot of us were completely surrounded by
clouds, and this was all there was to it.

I had kept a dead-reckoning track as best I could, but with
the task of following someone else in this weather I knew it was
far from accurate. The bomber leader would not answer when
I called: "Bomber One from Fighter One—take the fighters
back to base."

Two thoughts were bothering me: one, the bombers would

mill around long enough to lose us over that vast ocean, and the other, the fighters stood a good chance of running low on fuel. Time after time I tried to make contact with the bomber leader, who was supposed to be navigating and was in charge of the whole formation. His radio was working, for I could hear his communications with the other bombers, and these were loud and clear. Again I called: "Bomber One, please take the fighters home."

No direct answer was to come, but there was an answer, so to speak, because the next transmission I heard left no doubt as to what was going on.

"Break formation. Every man for himself."

I could see the bombers breaking formation. This was it. Then I called the fighters, ordering them to close up on my plane immediately, for I knew the bombers were lost, and that none of my pilots even had a prayer of plotting a track while escorting a formation.

This was a stunt most of them did when they had the feeling of really being lost. Everybody would break up and each one would try to find his own way home, which a lot of times ends up pretty sadly for someone, usually the fighters. In such a case the fighters have little or no idea as to where they are, added to their lack of navigational equipment.

Below was solid overcast. There was solid overcast in all directions. I very calmly gathered my boys together, because there was a chance of exciting a few. From my plot of the track-out it became obvious that we were going to have to navigate like a crow, or our gas supply would never take any of us to our home base.

Still not wanting to make anybody nervous, I gradually lowered the outfit down through the clouds, down more than twenty thousand feet, until I came to the water. You could see from about fifty feet above the water. I watched the whitecaps through my rain-swept windshield.

I knew from my dead reckoning that we would have to fly north in order to hit any islands. I flew due north and ran into a spot on the south shores of Bougainville. Bougainville, I knew, had some mighty high terrain. I followed the white coral beach around until I flew directly over the heavily fortified airstrip of Kahili, in order to get an accurate fix. I was paying no attention to any ground action in a mess like this, for I had a difficult enough time recognizing the airstrip from fifty feet up.

Nobody fired at us because no one on the ground could see through this fog either. But at that point I turned due east and flew over another familiar airstrip, the Japanese-held island of Ballale. Everyone was familiar with the course home from these targets, I knew, so in going across this water between these two enemy airstrips I was proving that I knew where I was just to keep confidence in my squadron.

Though I often referred to these boys as "my clowns," it was with the same sort of affection that they referred to me, I presume, as Gramps. But because of my age and longer experience I was able to save them from a lot of silly mistakes that young pilots make and thereby lose their lives.

The majority of pilots in the war were not shot down by the enemy; they were killed in operational accidents in taking off from the fields, in getting lost in the fog, and so forth, not by enemy fire.

Between the two airstrips we saw five fairly large Jap AKs. It was a temptation to stop and shoot at them, but I knew that if I ever took a shot at these I would have my clowns all spread out, and then they would never get back home.

So I forwent the pleasure of shooting at these Jap ships, although a couple were within forty feet of us. We didn't fire at them, but from then on flew practically two hundred miles in solid overcast. Once in a while we could see whitecaps, just fifty feet below us, and this was about all we could see. But my boys remained all bunched in, not more than twenty feet apart, and that was the only way we kept together in that weather.

Finally I got them all home except Emrick, and he made a water landing right off Vella airstrip. He was picked up by a PT boat and saved.

This feeling, this trust they showed, that I could take them home through the fog was one of the greatest I ever had in my life. Or perhaps anybody could have. I wish I could experience it again—now—in some of their present anxieties.

195

BAA BAA BLACK SHEEP

One of the chaps in this flight was a fairly savvy boy, and without any orders from me or from operations, the high command, he got his plane regassed and took off. Of course nobody knew what he was doing, but he flew back through those two hundred miles of fog and found those Japanese AKs and strafed them until he was out of ammunition. I rather imagine that he killed practically everyone aboard all five.

When Jack Bolt finally returned to our field and made his report, it was up to me to bawl him out. I called Jack into my tent, my office, and told him that what he had done was strictly against my orders, and that it was up to me to chew him out.

"I'm not going to bother chewing you out, Jack," I told him. "You know yourself that you disobeyed orders. But I'm going to write you up for a Navy Cross."

This boy was awarded the Navy Cross.

Or, as I was told by "Chesty" Puller years ago, there is only a hairline's difference between a Navy Cross and a general court-martial. As far as I was concerned, Louis Puller had the habit of always hitting the nail on its head, and is the greatest Marine I know of.

It is not my intention to take credit for being a great navigator, because I was far from it. My only idea was to instill confidence and lessen panic. Furthermore, I was always breaking established rules the same as they were, and we would all have to look out for each other, for the good of ourselves and the good of the war.

For instance, I mentioned once before how I liked to sleep, how during these long days in the hot tropics I never seemed to get enough sleep, especially when going on these long tiresome missions up into enemy territory, mile after mile over South Pacific waters. It was a tiresome ride. The only comparison I can make is to someone's being strapped up in a chair in the living room and told not to move for five hours. This might give some idea of what it was like to go on one of these missions.

During these missions into enemy territory I used to envy the bomber pilots, who had automatic pilots in their planes. So, for lack of an automatic, I would take along rubber bands and pieces of string, and I would rig these up on the instrument panel and on the brackets on the side of the cockpit, and I would have them all fixed up so that I could sleep most of the way going up to enemy territory. I would loosen my safety belt and half crawl out of my parachute straps, and then I would doze off.

Rarely would I have to glance at the altimeter, for I was able to tell by the sound of my engine whether I was going up- or downhill. So, without opening my eyes, I would just reach out and tap the rear string, and everything would sound right and I could doze off again.

If one wing dropped, I would lurch over to that side, gently tap the rubber band, and when the adjustment was made and I was sitting on an even keel, I would doze off once more.

It may seem funny that someone would go to sleep on the way to enemy territory where there were enemy planes, but I knew that I had many young eyes in the squadron that could see farther than I could. There was one young chap named Bourgoise, who could spot enemy planes forty miles away. I never could see them until I got within about twenty miles of them. So I had no fear of ever being jumped by planes as long as I had all these young eyes with me.

Another thing, we were not supposed to smoke in planes because of the fire hazard. But I am an incessant smoker and I liked to smoke at any time I was in the plane, except when I was in actual combat. So I would wait until the Japs got in the right position. During this time, though, I would be smoking. But just before we started to go down on these planes, I would crack my hood open on my plane and toss out my cigarette butt.

But back in the rendezvous of our tent McClurg, who had been flying on my wing for a while, told me one night: "I always know when we're going into combat. I always know because you always flop back your hood and flip out your cigarette, and something is going to start in the next few minutes."

So accustomed do we become to our habits that I would have been unaware of this cigarette gesture being a signal if Bob McClurg had not told me during one of these gab-fests.

197

In a previous chapter I mentioned how equally unaware people can be of giving encouragement. An accidental word, or a thoughtful gesture, may mean everything to somebody at some time—perhaps months later.

I have been on the receiving end of such words. But just to demonstrate how, during these gab-fests, we also may give them without fully realizing what significance they may have for others at some future pinch, I will tell about "Murderous Manny" Segal, now a well-known Marine Corps ace.

He was not with my squadron, but with one of those whose members used to drop into our tent to talk things over, how to solve mutual problems, and how to get away from various types of planes.

Years later, and after I was released from prison, I happened to see Segal again. And his words were:

"I always wanted you to come back," he said. "I wanted to thank you. On that mission you were shot down on I came back with over four hundred holes in my plane. A Jap got on my tail, and I remembered one thing you said one night in the tent on how to get away from a Toni. I did what you told me and finally shook him. If I hadn't remembered, I would still be out there."

Naturally I had forgotten all about having told him. Nor can I clearly recall the incident of the telling. But it goes to show how help can be distributed around, and without being formal about it, without going to classes or lectures. We just talk informally, now the same as then, and from these talks—well, who knows?

One of the other things for which I am most grateful to my Black Sheep is something else they taught me. They taught me that—and it may sound stereotyped, but it isn't—they taught me that you can get along fine with the American boy if you show him and lead him and do not try to order him or drive him.

Never send somebody out on a mission that you, as squadron commander, would not go on yourself, and always take the first of what promises to be ugly or bad missions. Strafing missions are missions that pilots always dread. Whenever you had one of these, if you took the first strafing mission, you would find that eventually, instead of trying to ditch these missions, all of the pilots practically would be begging to go on them.

Instead of talking about you had you not gone on them, all the pilots might be talking about you because you had not let *all* of *them* go.

Just a case of reverse English that further helps to explain the American boy.

Those hundred fighters that were sent into Bougainville prior to the November 1 invasion had to be liquidated. After we got our beach-head and could build a Marsten-matting strip on the beach, the situation wouldn't be too bad, but something had to be done about these planes in the meanwhile.

Strike Command planned a little deal in late October that worked out to perfection. Three groups of fighters would take off for Bougainville one hour apart. The idea was to run these Nips short on gas with the first group then, at least, the second and third groups would have these planes at a sizable disadvantage when they arrived.

Lady Luck made the Black Sheep part of the third group over the target. Believe me, this was pure luck, as I didn't pull any strings. For by this time, as one might well imagine, I was beginning to be suspected of having a hand in sorting out the best missions as they came along.

I was able to hear the jabber that accompanied the fight long before I ever reached Bougainville on this mission. And from bits of conversation the fight had to be between Kara and Kahili airdromes, which were but a short distance apart. It was also more than likely close to the ground, because as a dogfight progresses it usually gets closer to the ground. Many pilots missed these fights while they were trying to find them by the noise, by going over at such an altitude they couldn't spot the fight below them.

The first thing I saw, and was too late to be of any help, was a Corsair proceeding at rather slow speed in more of a glide than anything else. And right on his tail was a Zero firing his 20-millimeter cannon, which fired at a much slower rate than our .50s. Before I was able to get even close to the Zero, this

199

Corsair plowed into water, making a huge splash near the Short-land Islands. The Marine never got out.

Revenge is truly a hollow quantity, I thought as I sent the Zero into the drink beside him.

Immediately I trained my sights on another Nip who was scooting for Kara over the water, and I fired a short burst. I couldn't be sure I ever hit the plane because it rolled over as if to reverse direction, but obviously didn't have sufficient altitude to clear the water, for it crashed and sank out of sight in the mirrorlike reflection of the still water. Calm, bright waters have always been treacherous to maneuver about, whether in combat or not.

Having already learned my lesson, in addition to watching this Corsair prove it again, that it was unhealthy to scout for enemy planes too low off the water, I climbed to some altitude. While I was looking about for a target, occasionally covering up the sun with my little finger to make certain no Jap had me bore-sighted, the fight had apparently spread over quite an area, which was not unusual.

A feeling was going through my mind in this perfectly clear weather, almost like the lull before a storm. Actually, I couldn't spot any Nips for some time, but I knew that I would shortly as there were dust streaks moving about down on Kara, and I knew that some more Nips were taking off. I anticipated the time, altitude, and a conventional left-hand climbing turn, and sure enough, when I lowered down to three thousand feet, there was my Zero.

Taking advantage of the sun's rays was so automatic, as I coasted down, that I almost forget to mention it. It was about as simple as making a landing, as I came down and sent a burst into the climbing Nip, setting the plane ablaze.

Shortly after this I spotted a Corsair and motioned for it to join up, for our fuel was getting down a way on the gauge. Bruce Matheson smiled when he knew I was close enough to recognize him through the plexiglass hoods, and the two of us started for home over the water.

On our way we spotted a dark-colored Zero, circling low over something in the water. I decided to blast this plane out of the sky, so I pointed at it and then looked at Bruce, who nodded "Let's go." At close range we saw that this plane was circling somebody in a Mae West jacket, floating in the water. Both of us opened up on the circling Jap plane, which ducked down as low as it could and scooted for Kahili. We didn't think it was wise to give chase, and therefore we have no idea whether he made it or not.

Actually there was a second reason for not following this Nip, a selfish reason, because 214 was to be relieved the day following, and we weren't taking any more chances on losing our trip to Sydney for rest and recreation.

As Bruce and I flew back to Munda, we heard a familiar voice, "Where is everybody?"

I knew that this was Harper and tried to give my position as best I could, so he might be able to join us. But we didn't see him until after everybody had landed. Poor "Harpo" had gotten a slug in his buttocks near the spine, which very nearly ended his career. I understand it was years before he fully recovered.

And talking about getting slugs in the butt, the Black Sheep seemed to have a corner on the market. It didn't happen on this mission, but a few weeks earlier, Rinabarger had come in to Munda with a slug that had traveled just under the skin from one hip across to the other, and poor "Rinny" didn't have too much butt to spare, either. When I was there trying to console him while Doc Ream was probing for the bullet, Rinny said: "You bastards, please get out. You're just giving me another pain in the ass, besides the one I already got."

But, this being supposedly our last mission of the busy and tiresome tour, we were more than ready to turn in our chutes that very same afternoon. So we did turn them in, and our bedding as well.

None of us wanted to take the slightest chance on missing the DC-3 out of Munda the following day by attending to any last-minute duties, so we didn't give a hoot if we had to sleep on a bare cot for one night.

Before the afternoon was over, we talked Jim Ream into parting with all that remained of the issue brandy and medical alcohol. We decided to drink it all up that night, because we were going back where there was more. And besides, we would have an entirely new supply if we came up on another combat tour. The Black Sheep had one hell of a good time talking over the hairy times behind them, and they sat around drinking and singing our own adaptation of the Yale Whiffenpoof song, which we had adopted as our own.

Late in the evening, when 214 had been sound asleep for a few hours, sleeping upon bare cots because the bedding had been turned in already, I was awakened by the telephone in my tent. I had to shake my head. This must be a joke. But no, General Moore orders: "We have to have a flight to strafe Kahili and Kara in the dark."

I said: "Don't you know 214 has been relieved? Why don't you ask the squadron that replaced us to go?"

"They have never been to Bougainville in daylight, let alone at night, and there is a little weather, besides. They would be lucky if they didn't get lost. It's a cinch they couldn't find either airport."

"Okay, okay," I agreed without thinking—for I knew that I couldn't let Nuts down under any circumstances—even before I could clear up my befogged mind enough to realize what was going on.

I walked up and down between the cots for some time, trying to think this out, occasionally looking at some of the nude bodies that were completely crapped out underneath the mosquito netting. These perspiring and motionless forms were dreaming of anything but a night strafing mission, I was positive. I didn't have the heart to order a flight, or to even ask the members who were assigned to my own flight, to go with me.

As I was thinking, I heard my own voice, not too loudly, and it said: "Are there any three clowns dumb enough to want to strafe Kahili and Kara with me tonight?"

It seemed almost as if a prayer was being answered as I stood there and watched three of these motionless forms come to life and crawl through the mosquito netting without a stitch on their bodies. There was no doubt about this being real when

202

Ashmun, McGee, and McClurg walked up to me, and one after the other said:

"I'll go with you, Gramps."

Thank God there was a moon, but there was also a little rain to go with it. I was walking about in the mud with nothing but a pair of rubbers on my feet. The four of us pulled on our fatigue clothes and started down the hill in a jeep in the rain. Jim Ream appeared worried about me, as if I might catch a cold or something, and asked: "Aren't you going to wear shoes?"

I looked down at the muddy rubbers I was wearing and said: "Doc, if this mission is a success, I won't be needing any shoes until tomorrow."

The weather seemed to grow better rapidly as we approached Bougainville. The moon began to stay out nice and bright. Maybe the fact that the brandy was wearing off was making things look brighter, I don't know, but I do know that I was happy for this change.

I called McGee on the radio, for the Japs couldn't possibly think anyone could be crazy enough to attempt what we were about to do, and I gave some brief instructions: "Maggie, you and McClurg take Kara. George and I will take Kahili."

We were flying without running lights, so one airport would have been a bit overcrowded with four of us in one landing pattern. I had to assume that McGee and McClurg had left me; for that matter, I wasn't able to see my wing man, either. I was able to make out the Kahili strip all right, although at altitude I couldn't see any aircraft. I could not seem to forget Junior Heier's clipped wings as I was going down to the field.

As I approached the field I was able to observe parked aircraft with such remarkable clarity it surprised me. It wasn't possible to line them up as we had done the other day, but I had little trouble in making my pass down the strip, controlling my aim with just tracers, much the same as one might play the water from a hose. In fact it worked so well I reversed my direction and sprayed tracers back across the field in the opposite direction. I could see George's tracers, and a couple of planes on

203

fire. How the two of us had missed one another on our turn-arounds is too late to worry about.

During the few seconds George and I were working over Kahili I could see tracers and ground fires over at nearby Kara, and I knew McGee and McClurg had been able to locate their target okay also. I couldn't see any tracers coming up from the field, but my imagination, or my better judgment, compelled me to say, "Let's get to hell out of here."

In the process of turning east for Munda I saw that there was a Jap destroyer anchored in the Kahili harbor. This was no doubt one of the last that ever came to Bougainville. I found out later that the only means the Japs had for getting anything into most of this islands was by huge cargo submarines.

I wasn't worried about the terrific fire power a destroyer is capable of turning on a plane, feeling that the night had me well protected, and decided the "can" could not see me coming until I opened up on her with my .50-calibers. I put an ungodly long burst into the can on my way out of Kahili, which resulted in an explosion and fire. But whether it sank was of little concern to me then; I was intent only upon arriving home in one piece.

I was ready, willing, and able to celebrate in those wee small hours in the morning because all of us had gotten back safely, but no one wanted to celebrate with me and I could find no brandy around camp, or I'd have done it by myself.

CHAPTER **20**

THE MOST TIRED and rundown herd of Black Sheep anybody ever wanted to see landed in the DC-3 on the fighter strip
back at Espiritu Santo just before sunset. It was dark before we
were given a lift by truck to the group mess, which had been
open for this late arrival of ours. Many of the pilots were too
pooped to enjoy good food now that they had it, and plenty of
it for a change.

The lot of us were either too tired or sleepy—just plain lazy
in my case—to bother to make up our bunks, piling into them
as best we could. One thing was for certain: we weren't going
to be bothered with routing out a quartermaster sergeant at
that time of night to get bedding and mosquito nets. Besides,
after the outstanding work by the Army Engineers, mosquitos
had become a thing of the past in Espiritu long before November. So most of us fell fast asleep in our skivvies as soon as
we peeled off our clothing.

It must have been close to midnight when I was awakened
by a very bright light, shining squarely into my face, blinding
my eyes so much I couldn't see anything. I tried to turn my
head to get away from the glare, but the light seemed to follow
me whichever way I turned, so I could not see who was holding it.

A gruff voice came from behind the light, one that was only too familiar to me—and not pleasantly familiar, either. The farthest thing from my sweet dreams was there breaking up my sleep, none other than Lard himself.

At first I naturally assumed he was sore about my disregard for the orders concerning drinking, like they were so much confetti—because I'd witnessed these orders being torn up by another colonel up the line. But during the ranting about I soon discovered what this was all about as he kept mumbling: "Netting," among other things, to be written down by the capable executive who was always standing one pace behind Lard.

"Don't you know, Boyington, that there is an order against anyone sleeping without a mosquito net?"

"Yes, sir," I answered, but I thought: "This fat son of a bitch really had to dig deep in the old records to come up with this one on nets." There were no mosquitoes then, and besides, we had taken atabrine while in the combat zone until we were almost the same color as the Japs, just so we wouldn't miss a trip to Sydney. I don't believe this joker ever destroyed an out-of-date order for fear he might have some use for it some time.

As he and his stooge with the pad and pencil moved away in the darkness with the flashlight, Lard was also mumbling something about restricting the lot of us from making the trip we had so dearly earned.

However, we did get our trip to Sydney, for there was no way he could logically prevent us without going through wing HQ. He was also aware of the fact that we had to have a negative smear for malaria before being allowed to go to Australia. Perhaps he was counting on some of us not taking our atabrine—if so, we would have been dead ducks for sure.

And I do not wish to bore you with more sex, as this trip was almost a repetition of the last trip, only different women in most cases. But women were a vital part of a combat pilot's life, if only in his songs and thoughts, so I shall let it remain that way.

One thing was different from other trips for me because, although I had a date somewhere around the Romano night club, I shared the entire evening with General Nuts Moore. Everyone else but the general and myself who had been seated at the table had shoved off by either direct or indirect invitation, leaving the two of us alone to entertain ourselves after a fashion.

Moore informed me that the Bougainville invasion had been a success, although costly as usual, and that just enough of the island was taken to construct three airstrips. What remained of the island the Japanese were welcome to, for we didn't want it at any price.

The reason that the other guests were forced to leave the table, one by one, was that the general and I were using the entire tablecloth for a war map, leaving only enough space for the two of us long before the club closed. We really had everything all doped out, but things didn't quite work out in the exact manner we had planned. But come to think of it, the majority of these things did come awfully close. If only MacArthur and Halsey had been present, there would have been no need of further alterations, and then we could have rolled up the tablecloth and taken it along with us.

I was the most dumfounded person in the Corps when, because of my seeing eye to eye with the general, or vice versa, I was called into Lard's office upon our return to Espiritu. This was three days prior to the date set for my squadron to go back into combat.

I must say, too—and almost every military person will appreciate what I mean—that there are times when we have to fight to be able to fight the enemy. This has occurred to many of us all along the line, and perhaps from time immemorial. We break all kinds of rules, local or standardized, in order to be able to do what we think we can do best. We certainly are not encouraged to go over people's heads, even if the purpose is simply to get into combat during time of war. But as an early example of this, if I had not gone over people's heads I still might be parking cars near Victory Square in Seattle.

Or another is that the Black Sheep Squadron would not have come into being. It was a case of doing what one thought was right, or what one thought just had to be done, and to take a chance on being reprimanded by some paper-wrestler who was a stickler on regulations.

There is a heel or two in every outfit, regardless of what it is. So in this connection I will again remember some good advice from Chesty Puller. He gave it back in basic school to us second lieutenants:

"A word of advice to you men. Many times in your Marine Corps career you are going to feel like resigning. But don't forget: one son of a bitch or four or five cannot ruin the Corps."

Through the years I always remembered those golden words whenever confronted by somebody who seemed deliberately to go out of his way to show his authority by keeping things stymied. Then fortunately his superiors would not be that way at all, and the higher they were, the more understanding they were, and also the more capable. And, in order to help get a war won, it frequently was up to the lot of us to take the chance and say something—as delicately as we could, of course —but where it would count.

All of these things were rolling over in my mind on the way to Lard's headquarters.

After I arrived at group headquarters, I was permitted to cool my heels for the prescribed amount of time outside the door of Lard's sanctum.

Finally somebody said: "You may go in now, Major Boyington. The colonel is free."

I entered and said: "Good morning, Colonel. You sent for me?"

"Yes, I did, because I'm going to have to jerk you out of 214, as I have a new job assigned for you."

"But—but—I thought it was all settled when I talked to General Moore."

"I'll have you know I'm running this group, and I'll be giving the orders around here, understand? We have to place senior majors into staff jobs as they come up, and that's what I have to do in your case."

"But, Colonel, who is going to command 214? They have to go back to combat in a couple of days."

"Don't you worry about that. Anybody can do it."

"What is my new job, then?"

208

"Oh, it's—er—ah—I'm not at liberty to say just now. This will be all for the present. I'll get in touch with you later."

I left Lard because I was at a loss for words, and besides I realized there was little use in talking any longer to anybody so stupid. My 214 had already destroyed over a hundred enemy aircraft, not to mention a bit of shipping, and had done loads of escorts and patrols. He had not explained his reasons, because he had none. Nor did he have any new job in mind, or he would have said what it was. He didn't even have a squadron commander in mind to send in my place.

The pilots in the squadron were about as stunned and disgusted with the odd turn of events as I was. I had destroyed somewhere in the neighborhood of twenty planes personally, and I was anxious to keep on knocking down some more, for, after all, that was the reason I was out there.

I could not quietly sit by and watch my Black Sheep leave old Espiritu and flight out for a combat tour again without me, nor could anyone else have, under the circumstances. What causes some people to change orders like that, without a reason or even an explanation, is something I cannot understand. It may have been jealousy over my record, or it may have been something else. But I did not know. I went to see General Moore, who happened to be on the other side of the island at wing headquarters.

I did not go to his office directly, for I had to be more subtle than that. I sort of timed myself to cross his trail while he was walking to his office. He was a great general, that man was, and after we greeted each other he wished me the best of luck on the next combat tour, coming up in three days.

"But I'm not going, General," I said.

Moore looked puzzled; he invited me into the office and asked me why. He probably thought it was something personal.

I explained calmly that I did not know why but that my orders had just been changed today. In no time at all Moore reached for his telephone, called a certain office, asked for a certain group commander, and I sat there—still with a poker face—waiting for an explosion, I guess. But there was no explosion. Moore very quietly told this person he didn't want any changes, adding that he might drop over to see him before he went north again.

But I was so happy about my reinstatement with my Black Sheep, and it occurred immediately, that the moment I left the general, I could keep my poker face no longer. Three of my pilots had accompanied me on this little mission of sorts across the island and had been waiting patiently for the outcome, one way or another. There was only one thing to do, and that was to celebrate another Black Sheep victory with this official good news. So we celebrated. And we celebrated too long. For when we finally broke up at the wing club, the time was midnight, the rain was a deluge, and we had to cross the island in a jeep to our quarters on the fighter strip.

I was driving in the downpour when a sentry stopped me. He was as wet as I was, and in the darkness we could not see each other very well. But he said:

"Major Boyington, you're wanted at Colonel Lard's quarters immediately, regardless of how late you get here."

In the hard rain I could barely make out the poor guy's features, even when he was standing in the glare of the headlights. He was more than ankle deep in muddy water, and probably chilled to the bone. Knowing this was no ordinary challenge, I asked:

"What's up, sentry? And how come you were able to know me so well?"

"Oh, that's easy. It's none of my business, but as long as you asked, I guess I can tell you."

"Certainly, you don't have to worry about me, spill it."

"Well, the colonel called first on the phone, but because I couldn't understand him over the wet line, he drove out here in a jeep. He was so damn mad I thought he had gone completely crazy. He was swearing and waved his arms around so hard he slipped and fell flat on his ass in the mud."

"Yes, yes, but what did he say?"

"I didn't know what he was yelling about, but he said he would handle it, and I was to have you report IMMEDIATELY. He also said I could smell when you were coming because you would be like a bourbon factory. He said you were

210

a bull-necked, flat-nosed son of a bitch who would have no cap or raincoat because you didn't have brains enough to wear them."

So I reported, and learned I was to consider myself under technical arrest for having violated some local code such-and-such for having seen the general without having gone through certain channels, and having done it for the "betterment of my own command," or similar wording. I forget just what now.

Anyhow Lard's executive officer typed another set of orders for me to take along up north with me for the coming combat tour. Words to the effect that I was to be permitted to lead my squadron but was not to be allowed such privileges as going to the movies or any officers' club, as if we had any where we were going. This was to be effective for a certain period of time. I forget now but took a copy of the set of orders along to remind myself.

The following morning, while I was still in my tent, Bragdon and some other pilot entered my quarters all excited after an early breakfast. Bragdon said: "Hey, Gramps, we had a visitor real early this morning."

"What do you mean by visitor?" I asked.

"The gent with the cane intercepted Lard as he was coming down the trail from his penthouse to breakfast. I saw him standing beside the trail and wondered what he was doing over here so early."

"What happened?" I asked, getting excited along with the pilots.

"Believe us, it was a one-sided conversation, with the general on top."

"Well?"

"It went something like this, and we pretended not to be eavesdropping.

" 'Good morning, General——'

" 'Say, Stud, I thought I'd better drop over and pay you a little visit; I've been neglecting you. I understand from more than several sources you like to keep the combat pilots in close touch. Well, I fixed it up so you can go up to the new strip and be with them as an operations officer!' "

211

These pilots said Lard's mouth kept opening and closing without making a sound until the general was through, like a big fish out of water.

I asked: "What did Lard say when the general was through with him?"

"Nothing but 'Aye-aye, sir,' because Nuts wheeled around and left him when he was through talking."

This was great as far as I was concerned, for Lard would be where he couldn't do any good for himself or be of any harm for us. His feathers had surely been plucked. I wondered how he was going to get along without the palatial estate on the peninsula, or without a staff to help dig up dirt on anyone.

Here was December, two years after Pearl Harbor, before the Allies were on the roll in the opposite direction for a change. We were thinking about the long way to Tokyo as we were flying in the DC-3 back to combat. We were to have a new home there this time, for the Vella Lavella strip had been completed.

One of these big deals General Moore and I had worked out on our tablecloth down in Sydney was put into action. This was quite an operation and, because it involved passing a certain longitude, Halsey had had to obtain permission from MacArthur prior to our going on the mission, which involved all the Allies in the Pacific. Anyhow, with all the lengthy screwing around, I'm convinced the Japanese were let in on it too, for they were certainly waiting for us like they never had before.

The long-planned operation, containing over a hundred Allied fighters, struck the Rabaul area in a fighter sweep. We had topped off our fuel on the new strip at Bougainville, and had started taking off on December 17 at the crack of dawn. This mass fighter sweep was led by Wing Commander Freeman of New Zealand in the P-40s, and included Aircobras, P-38s, Hellcats, and Corsairs.

Whether the Nips had gotten previous word makes no difference now, but the strike was balled up from the very beginning. The Allied fighters were of so many different types, we might just as well have been escorting bombers. Because the five large airfields on New Britain and New Ireland were spread over a large area, the mission at least should have been restricted to fighters with the same flying characteristics.

Commander Freeman and his P-40s were first off, and hit the Rabaul area without waiting for their high cover to get into position. They probably figured they had to chance it because they had been first off and knew their gas wouldn't last for much more than the round trip. The individual take-offs from the new strip had been awfully slow to begin with, and we were too late to prevent Freeman himself and many other P-40s from being knocked down that morning.

With all our fighters not more than a half-dozen Nips had been accounted for, at best, while the Allies lost close to thirty planes that day. Only one member of 214 had any luck, and he got two Nips. I came to the conclusion that these long-drawn-out affairs may have their place, but definitely not in aviation.

This mass boober was just another thing in my life I couldn't be proud of, for, even though I had not led the attack, my brain was to blame for thinking up this Frankenstein monster. But there was no way I could get back to that tablecloth at Romano's and have the chance to start all over again.

I was to brood over this more than I should have and was itching for an opportunity to square accounts somehow. I got it, and on Christmas, on the peace-on-earth-good-will-to-all-men day, I went around the skies slaughtering people. Don't ask me why it had to be on a Christmas Day, for he who can answer such a question can also answer why there have to be wars, and who starts them, and why men in machines kill other men in machines. I had not started this war, and if it were possible to write a different sort of Christmas story I would prefer to record it, or at least to have had it occur on a different day.

Come to think of it, there was undoubtedly some basis for my feelings this day, for as far back as I could remember Christmas Day was repulsive to me. Ever since my childhood, it had always been the same. Relatives were forever coming to our house and kissing my brother and me with those real wet kisses children dread so much, and making a number of well-wishing compliments that none of them ever seemed to believe.

And then it started after everybody had a snout full of fire-water, fighting and speaking their true thoughts. All Christmases were alike, my brother Bill and I ending up by going to a movie. And even after I was old enough to protect myself, I did the same damn thing, leaving the house and celebrating the occasion with people I didn't know, in some bar.

I was leading a fighter patrol that was intended to intercept any enemy fighters that followed our bombers, which had preceded us to Rabaul. We saw them returning from their strike at a distance, and saw that Major Marion Carl's squadron was very capably warding off some Zeros, and before we got within range I witnessed three go up in flames from the .50-calibers triggered by Carl's pilots.

We caught a dozen or so of these fighters that had been heckling our bombers, B-24s. The Nips dove away and ran for home, Rabaul, for they must have been short of gasoline. They had been fighting some distance from their base, with no extra fuel because they wore no belly tanks. They had not expected us to follow, but we were not escort planes and didn't have to stay with our bombers.

Nosing over after one of these homebound Nips, I closed the distance between us gradually, keeping directly behind his tail, first a thousand yards, then five hundred, finally closing in directly behind to fifty feet. Knowing the little rascal couldn't have any idea he was being followed, I was going to make certain this one didn't get away. Never before had I been so deliberate and cold about what I was doing. He was on his way home, but already I knew he would not get there.

Nonchalantly I trimmed my rudder and stabilizer tabs. Nonchalantly I checked my gun chargers. As long as he could not see me, as long as he didn't even know I was following him, I was going to take my time. I knew that my shot would be no-deflection and slowly wavered my gun sight until it rested directly upon the cross formed by his vertical tail and horizontal wings. The little Nip was a doomed man even before I fired. I knew it and could feel it, and it was I who condemned him from ever reaching home—and it was Christmas.

One short burst was all that was needed. With this short burst

214

flames flew from the cockpit, a yellow chute opened, and down the pilot glided into the Pacific. I saw the splash.

Using my diving speed with additional power, I climbed, and as I climbed I could see off to my right two more enemy planes heading for Rabaul. One was throwing smoke. I closed in on the wounded plane, and it dove. His mate pulled off to one side to maneuver against me, but I let the smoker have it—one burst that set the plane on fire—and again the pilot bailed out.

His mate then dove in from above and to the side upon my own tail to get me, but it was simple to nose down and dive away temporarily from him. From a new position I watched the pilot from the burning plane drift slowly down to the water, the same as the other had done. This time his flying mate slowly circled him as he descended, possibly as a needless protection.

I remember the whole picture with a harsh distinction—and on Christmas—one Japanese pilot descending while his pal kept circling him. And then, after the pilot landed in the water, I went after the circling pal. I closed in on him from the sun side and nailed him about a hundred feet over the water. His Zero made a half roll and plunked out of sight into the sea. No doubt his swimming comrade saw me coming but could only watch.

This low altitude certainly was no place for me to be in enemy territory, so I climbed, but after searching for a half-hour I saw no more of the little fellows in this vicinity.

I next decided, since I was so close, to circle the harbor of Rabaul so that I could make a report on our recent bombings there. Smoke was coming from two ships. Another had only the bow protruding from the water, and there were numerous circles all around that had been created by exploding bombs.

While I was looking at all this, and preparing mental notes, I happened to see far below a nine-plane Nip patrol coming up in sections of threes. Maneuvering my plane so that I would be flying at them from the sun side again, I eased toward the rear and fired at the tail-end-Charlie in the third "V." The fire chopped him to bits, and apparently the surprise was so great in the rest of the patrol that the eight planes appeared to jump all over the sky. They happened to be Tony's, the only Nip planes that could outdive us. One of them started after my tail and began closing in on it slowly, but he gave up the chase after a few minutes. The others had gotten reorganized, and it was time for me to be getting home.

On the way back I saw something on the surface of the water that made me curious. At first I thought it was one boat towing another but it wasn't. It was a Japanese submarine surfacing. Nosing my Corsair over a little steeper, I made a run at the submarine, and sent a long burst into her conning tower. Almost immediately it disappeared, but I saw no oil streaks or anything else that is supposed to happen when one is destroyed, so I knew that I had not sunk her.

My only thought at this time was what a hell of a thing for one guy to do to another guy on Christmas.

CHAPTER **21**

VELLA LAVELLA is a beautiful tropical island, though I wasn't capable of appreciating it at that time, owing to the business at hand. But I enjoyed roaming the wooded hills near the camp occasionally, with what little time I had. It was during the walks that I seemed to be able to think more clearly than at other times.

Vella had an abundance of fresh limes. I believe these were wild, although I am not positive. They certainly made a wonderful punch when mixed with crushed ice, medical alcohol, and issue brandy. There was only one drawback as I saw it: the island had far more of these tasty limes than Doc Ream had alcohol or brandy. My afternoons and evenings were free for these walks and drinking, while my mornings were occupied with flying.

Daily routine from Christmas until January 3, 1944, was a predawn take-off, flying to the airstrip on Bougainville, refueling, then flying on over to the Rabaul area. It seemed monotonous.

The day after Christmas I was awakened in the dark with some of the other pilots at three in the morning, and I had one hell of a tussle pulling myself out of the old rack. Too much celebration, no doubt. I was staggering about the tent, searching

217

for my fatigues without much success. Knowing this would never do, I wobbled out of the tent to a rain barrel that was kept constantly full by the waters shedded by the tent top, and there I submerged my head and shoulders into the cool water.

I repeated the dunking several times, blowing bubbles from my mouth and nose until I was able to steady myself down a bit. This little aid had become standard procedure with me by then, for the pressure was really on me, I felt.

Some phenomenon of nature would cause some of these islands to have a very heavy rainfall, while others, for no apparent reason, seemed to be lucky if they received a little. In many cases these islands were only a hop, skip, and jump apart. These conditions I took for granted while I dunked my head. I had no idea that I would soon be on an island, not too remote from Vella, praying for water to drink.

I was feeling really rough as I drove in silence down the hill to our ready shack by the strip with a load of duty pilots. They were trying their best to cheer me out of my silent mood, but because I was anything but happy I just couldn't laugh. After our arrival beside the ready shack Moe Fisher finally succeeded, by putting on a funny act while standing beside the bulletin board. It was his duty to keep it up to date and he was tearing some typewritten papers down, trying to keep a straight face. He said: "Gramps, I don't believe we have any more use for these."

Glancing at the orders he was referring to made me break out laughing, for these happened to be the orders Lard had composed for my benefit and had sent up the line with us. Moe had thumbtacked these for a joke along with the so-called important material for the day. He pretended to be making a decision of great importance and said:

"I believe these have been complied with because you haven't attended a movie, and there is no officers' club. It doesn't say you weren't supposed to shoot down four Japs while being under arrest. Anyhow, the time's up, Gramps."

On one of these daily fighter-sweep jaunts over the Rabaul area we seemed to be parked at about twenty-four thousand feet, playing the usual hopscotch with the anti-aircraft gunners. I was

218

busy scanning the sky looking for Nip aircraft, occasionally moving the squadron to get away from bursts as soon as they seemed to have our address. Far below were two Jap seaplanes, so I imagined they were looking for submarines near the mouth of the harbor. I guess the Nips had every intention of keeping Rabaul, because there was one place that put up bursts almost thick enough for us to walk on.

As I watched the two seaplanes, too far down even to recognize the make or insignia, I saw a landplane approaching one of them. There was nothing out of the ordinary about this until the landplane opened fire and the other burst into flame and crashed in the water a few seconds later. At first I thought, "Can't those dumb jerks recognize their own planes?" And before I knew it the landplane had disappeared from my vision. I then took a visual roll call up in the sky and found that I had one plane missing. While I was busy scratching my head and trying to remember everyone who was supposed to be along that day, I noticed a Corsair climbing up underneath the squadron. All of a sudden everything became perfectly clear to me when I looked through the canopy of this climbing plane. There was McClurg, with a cat-eatin' grin that spread from ear to ear.

This was the only plane shot down that day, and I thought that, for a clown who had so much trouble checking out in a Corsair, he had turned out to be quite a boy. I shook my fist at him, because I knew he had been lucky to get away with this stunt. There was no use arguing with him later when he said: "I didn't think the Japs would bother with one lone plane if they knew the Black Sheep were circling up above them."

While gassing up at Bougainville for the return trip to Vella I had a little talk with the three members of my flight, especially McClurg.

"I have some dope, fellows, about a few seaplanes operating out of the Shortland Islands. They're probably anchored, as they've been reported only at night and in bad weather. I'd like to go over low and take a look-see, provided you clowns would like a chance to get some seaplanes."

As one they said: "What are we waiting for, Gramps? Let's

219

get going." All three pilots had a light in their eyes, much the same as if I'd promised them a million bucks, especially Mac.

The four of us were skimming the jungle at full throttle, and were closing in on the harbor where the seaplanes had been reported. Like the Kahili escapade, we pulled up just before leaving the jungle trees to get last-second bearings. We found no seaplanes anchored. The Japanese must have had them well concealed from view, if there were any about the harbor to begin with. But we were not to be goose-egged, for there was an interisland steamer, approximately two hundred feet long, proceeding into the harbor at low speed.

With four abreast we poured our .50-calibers into the boat as long as we dared, because we were gradually converging as we approached the same target. A screenlike curtain shot up, probably steam from a boiler. I saw a few people leap over the side as we passed over. Then we opened up on the village beyond, strafing anything we thought might be of importance. As we left the area we hugged the water in order to present as poor a target as possible, heading for home.

Shortly after leaving the target, I saw a fairly large projectile sailing past my left wing tip, and it was traveling end over end, like a tomato can. It must have been a faulty round of some kind, because I couldn't fathom any gun bore being that smooth.

McClurg had spotted a gun emplacement and its crew, and claimed that his tracers caught one of the crew's pants on fire, because he saw him slapping at the flames. I had to believe this because he also stated: "Just after I passed over the gun crew, I felt something burning my foot. It got so damn hot I had to take off my shoe."

The boy had a slug the size of one of our .50-calibers, which he showed about the camp with a great deal of pride. After inspecting Mac's plane we discovered how this had happened without injury to him. The round had entered the forward part of the plane and had torn through several pieces of aluminum, then bounced off the seat, and finally dropped down beside a skinny ankle inside of a loose-fitting shoe top.

During one of these daily hops over Rabaul I had reached

a definite climax in my flying career without too much effort. I shot down my twenty-fifth plane on December 27. And if I thought that I ever had any troubles previously, they were a drop in the bucket to what followed.

There was nothing at all spectacular in this single victory, but it so happened that this left me just one short of the record jointly held by Eddie Rickenbacker of World War I and Joe Foss of World War II. Then everybody, it seemed to me, clamored for me to break the two-way tie. The reason for all the anxiety was caused by my having only ten more days to accomplish it; 214 was very near completion of its third tour, and everyone knew I would never have another chance. My combat-pilot days would close in ten days, win, lose, or draw.

Everyone was lending a hand, it seemed, but I sort of figured there was too much help. Anyway, I showed my appreciation by putting everything I had left into my final efforts. I started flying afternoons as well as mornings, and in bad weather in addition to good weather.

One predawn take-off was in absolute zero-zero conditions, and all we had for references were two large searchlights on the end of the Vella strip, one aimed vertically and the other horizontally. I wasn't questioned by the tower whether I had an instrument ticket, like I am today. My last words to my pilots before I started my take-off through the fog were: "Please listen to me, fellows, and have complete faith in your instruments. If you dare to take one look out of the cockpit after you pass the searchlights, you're dead."

As I had always been unaccustomed to help or encouragement in the past, all the extra help did nothing more than upset me. But I couldn't have slowed down or stopped if I had wanted to, simply because nobody would let me.

One fight made me desperate when I could not see to shoot with accuracy, because I wasn't able to see well enough through the oil-smeared windshield. After several fruitless attempts I pulled off to one side of the fight and tried to do something to correct it. I unbuckled my safety belt and climbed from my parachute harness, then opened the hood and stood up against the slip-stream, trying my darnedest to wipe off the oil with my

221

handkerchief. It was no use; the oil leak made it impossible for me to aim with any better accuracy than someone who had left his glasses at home.

Soon I began to believe that I was jinxed. Twice I returned with bullet holes in my plane as my only reward. Twice I ran into a souped-up version of the Zero known as the Tojo. Though not quite as maneuverable as the original, it was considerably faster and had a greater rate of climb. Still no shootdowns, and I was lucky the Nips didn't get me instead.

Doc Ream was really concerned over the way I was affected by the pressure, suggesting we call a halt to the whole affair. He said that there were plenty of medical reasons for calling all bets off. But I knew I couldn't stop. Whether I died in the attempt made no difference. Anyway, my last combat tour would be up in a few days, and I would be shipped back to the United States. I said: "Thanks for the out, Doc, but I guess I better go for broke, as the Hawaiians say."

I knew that I was tired, and covered with what we called the tropical crud for lack of a medical word. Running sores were in my armpits, on my chest, and in my crotch so badly I wasn't able to sleep much when I had the time. My ears would be sealed tight with caked pus by morning, and Doc would have to break this away and blow sulfa drugs into them with a straw. He hated to do this painful operation daily, but if he hadn't I wouldn't have been able to hear a word over the radio.

In direct proportion to all the shoving from my own side the Japanese were making my way equally difficult from their side. During one of these fights I felt positive that the Jap pilots were getting better, or that I had lost my touch. It turned out to be no imagination on my part, for far below, bobbing like corks upon the swells, I could see two Nip aircraft carriers that looked about the size of postage stamps from altitude.

I had been told that Jap navy pilots were far superior to those based on land. And I thought what a time it was for me to prove this. But because I was worn out I wanted to have the tough ones first. Maybe it was just as well, for if pilots this good had caught me in my first fights, I no doubt wouldn't have been around to do much worrying.

I couldn't turn back, I kept telling myself, even though I honestly didn't give one hoot in hell about breaking any record by then. But I was helpless. And even during this strain I came to realize that a record meant absolutely nothing; it would be broken again and again in spite of anything I did. I was worried only about what others might think of me.

This worry about what others think has only caused me to get into one predicament after another, all my life. I have driven myself half nuts, trying to imagine how far I could have gone if I had taken my time and not let others bother me. But now I am content with not worrying over the past, of which I have no control, and not worrying about the future, either. I am content by handling the one thing I have control over, one day at a time, the present, and I find I derive a considerable amount of happiness from this way of life.

But what odd things most of us do when under stress. We do things or say things for which we later feel ashamed or at least embarrassed.

I, for instance, once caused a plate of salad to leave my table and fly over into the lap of a correspondent. I had not intended to do this, and I know that the correspondent also knew. But just the same it happened. Frequently during the days after the war, while answering my mail, I felt tempted to write a letter to him apologizing. For then maybe both of us could have a laugh and forget about it.

It had all started one October day in 1943 while I was working out of Munda. I had at that time twenty planes to my credit, and was called into a tent for an interview with this war correspondent, an able one from Chicago who had been a Pulitzer Prize winner.

After talking to me for a while, wanting to know how I had gotten these planes, and going through all the description and whatnot, he inquired into my personal life.

I was hesitant to tell him about it, as I didn't see why these particular questions had anything to do with the war.

He answered: "Oh, that is what the great American public wants."

But when I informed him of my age, and told him I had

been divorced and had three children, and that at that time there was no lady in my life, he ended up his interview with me by saying:

"Well, I can frankly state, brother, that you just aren't news!"

I said: "Yes, I realize that. And it's all right with me. I am some thirty years old, and without some so-called lovely young sweetheart. But I didn't come out here to make news. I came out here to fight a war."

He abruptly ended the conversation and stalked off. I don't blame him.

But in late December, when I got to the place where I was only one plane less than a record, my score being twenty-five, I miraculously seemed to become what is called "news" anyhow, even though I was divorced and had three children and was some thirty years of age. During this era correspondents approached me every place I went, out in the field, up in my tent, anyplace, wanting to know: "When are you going to break that record?"

I tried to explain that it wasn't like going out and grabbing a couple off the line and bringing them in, like they were a pair of socks. My duties were to run a squadron and run it properly, and that was what I was doing. So I had to say to them once again: "Just leave me alone. When I beat the record, I'll tell you all about it." Yet even this didn't seem to be enough explanation. Everywhere I turned there was a correspondent waiting for me and asking the same old question, and it began to get on my nerves something terrific. The best description I can give for this situation is that of having the reporters in the dugout with the players while the World Series is being played. One day I came right out and said to a group of them: "God damn it, you don't give a damn whether I beat that record or not. It will make just as good a story if I get killed in the attempt to beat it or if I tie it." The way it turned out, I was right on one of those counts.

When I got back home out of prison, I had no idea of all the publicity I had gotten, the stories had been written just that way, just as I had told some of them, that they didn't care whether I beat it or tied it.

BOYINGTON DIED IN TYING RICKENBACKER'S RECORD.

Oddly, though, it so happened that I not only had tied the record but had beaten it, but this was not to be known officially until later, when all the circumstances of my last fights were reported and tabulated. After beating the record I didn't return to Vella.

But I am way ahead of my story about the correspondent, Fred Hampson. When I had twenty-five planes to my credit, Frank Walton, the intelligence officer, took me over one evening to give him the dope he wanted, and this is when I was sorry later for talking to him the way I did. Anyhow, he was supposed to leave me alone until the record was broken, and there wasn't anything more to be said.

After spending some time talking with him in his tent, I went up to the mess hall, and, lo and behold, there, to the vacant seat right across from me came Hampson, the correspondent.

Immediately he wanted to know once again when I was going to break the record, and I said: "God damn it, pal, I thought I told you that when I did I would let you know and you weren't supposed to bother me in the meantime."

Saying this, I slammed the table for emphasis but by accident hit the edge of my plate. The plate ricocheted in the air, crossed the table, and the entire contents dropped squarely into his lap.

Frank Walton said to him: "Damn it, I told you to leave him alone or he would flip his lid. You can't blame anyone but yourself."

Hampson, however, was such a worthy reporter he realized at last that he had been crowding me too much. I saw the story he had written on me after I had broken the record and was "killed." I saw the story, of course, not until two years or so later, but it was a "savvy" story.

Even today it is hard for many people to believe that we, or anyone else, were not out there fighting a war for medals or publicity. Almost all the boys were fighting the war because it had to be fought and had to be won. They didn't give a damn whether their names ever hit the print or whether they ever received a medal.

Many men who never received mention gave everything they had—they're still out there.

CHAPTER **22**

NEVER HAD I FELT as tired and dejected as I did when
I flew into Vella one afternoon in late December. Another
futile attempt was behind me. The bullet holes in my plane
were a far cry from the record I was striving to bring back. I
was dead tired, I had counted upon the day ending, but a pilot
had crawled up on my wing after I had cut my engine, and he
had something important to say.

Marion Carl was scheduled to take several flights that afternoon to Bougainville, where they were to remain overnight,
taking off on the following morning for a sweep. He said:
"Greg, I want to give you a chance to break the record. You
take my flight because you're so close I think you are entitled
to it. I've got seventeen, but I still have loads of time left, and
you haven't."

Carl had been out previously in the Guadalcanal days as a
captain, piling up a number of planes to his credit, and was
then back for the second time, as a squadron commander. He
had just been promoted to major, and it was true that many
chances were coming up for him. Great person that Marion
Carl is, he was trying to give a tired old pilot a last crack at the
title, even though it was at his own expense.

I can never forget George Ashmun's thin, pale face when I

mentioned where I was going, and he insisted that he go along as my wingman. Maybe George knew that I was going to have to take little particles of tobacco from a cigarette, placing them into the corners of my eyes to make them smart so that I'd stay awake.

Those close to me were conscious of what kind of shape I was in, and they were honestly concerned. But I was also happy to find others I hadn't thought of at the time who were concerned for my welfare as well, though in most cases I didn't discover this until after the war. And that was by mail.

Some of the letters were clever, but I especially remember one from a chap who I imagine must have been about eighteen. He wrote me that, after I was missing in action, his partner, "Grease Neck," who worked on a plane with him, had said that I was gone for good, and the first chap said: "I bet you he isn't." The outcome of the discussion was that each bet a hundred and fifty dollars, one that I would, the other that I would not, be back home six months after the war was over. The six-months business referred to the fact that if you are missing six months after the war is over you are officially declared dead. And at one time I had said, just as a morale builder to the other pilots so that they would not worry about me: "Don't worry if I'm ever missing, because I'll see you in Dago and we'll throw a party six months after the war is over."

I had said it by coincidence just before taking off on what turned out to be my last fight, but the words apparently had stuck in their minds.

But to get back to this letter from the young chap, he told me how thrilled he was about my being home, and he told me about this bet he had made with "Grease Neck," and how he had just collected that hundred and fifty, and that he was going to spend the entire amount on highballs in my honor in San Diego.

It was a great feeling to get those letters and know that the boys really wanted to see you home—bets or no bets. I also hope, because I never heard any more from this young fellow, that he didn't end up in the local bastille while celebrating in my honor.

My thoughts then are much the same now in many respects. Championships in anything must be a weird institution. So often there is but a hairline difference between the champion and the runner-up. This must go for boxing and tennis, football and baseball. In my case it was something else, the record for the number of planes shot down by a United States flyer, and I was still having quite a time trying to break it.

After getting twenty-five planes, most of them on missions two hundred miles or better into enemy air, I had gone out day after day, had had many a nice opportunity, but always fate seemed to step in and cheat me: the times there was oil on the windshield and I couldn't see any of the planes I fired into go down or flame; the times my plane was shot up. Nothing seemed to work for me. Then everybody, including the pressmen, kept crowding me and asking: "Go ahead; when are you going to beat the record?" I was practically nuts.

Then came the day when the record finally was broken, but, as so often happens with one in life, it was broken without much of a gallery. And in this case without even a return.

It was before dawn on January 3, 1944, on Bougainville. I was having baked beans for breakfast at the edge of the airstrip the Seabees had built, after the Marines had taken a small chunk of land on the beach. As I ate the beans, I glanced over at row after row of white crosses, too far away and too dark to read the names. But I didn't have to. I knew that each cross marked the final resting place of some Marine who had gone as far as he was able in this mortal world of ours.

Before taking off everything seemed to be wrong that morning. My plane wasn't ready and I had to switch to another. At the last minute the ground crew got my original plane in order and I scampered back into that. I was to lead a fighter sweep over Rabaul, meaning two hundred miles over enemy waters and territory again.

We coasted over at about twenty thousand feet to Rabaul. A few hazy clouds and cloud banks were hanging around—not much different from a lot of other days.

The fellow flying my wing was Captain George Ashmun, New York City. He had told me before the mission: "You go

229

ahead and shoot all you want, Gramps. All I'll do is keep them
off your tail."

This boy was another who wanted me to beat that record,
and was offering to stick his neck way out in the bargain.

I spotted a few planes coming up through the loosely scattered clouds and signaled to the pilots in back of me: "Go
down and get to work."

George and I dove first. I poured a long burst into the first
enemy plane that approached, and a fraction of a second later
saw the Nip pilot catapult out and the plane itself break out
into fire.

George screamed over the radio: "Gramps, you got a flamer!"

Then he and I went down lower into the fight after the rest
of the enemy planes. We figured that the whole pack of our
planes was going to follow us down, but the clouds must have
obscured us from their view. Anyway, George and I were not
paying too much attention, just figuring that the rest of the
boys would be with us in a few seconds, as usually was the case.

Finding approximately ten enemy planes, George and I commenced firing. What we saw coming from above we thought
were our own planes—but they were not. We were being
jumped by about twenty planes.

George and I scissored in the conventional thatch-weave way,
protecting each other's blank spots, the rear ends of our fighters.
In doing this I saw George shoot a burst into a plane and it
turned away from us, plunging downward, all on fire. A second
later I did the same to another plane. But it was then that I
saw George's plane start to throw smoke, and down he went
in a half glide. I sensed something was horribly wrong with
him. I screamed at him: "For God's sake, George, dive!"

Our planes could dive away from practically anything the
Nips had out there at the time, except perhaps a Tony. But
apparently George never heard me or could do nothing about
it if he had. He just kept going down in a half glide.

Time and time again I screamed at him: "For God's sake,
George, dive straight down!" But he didn't even flutter an
aileron in answer to me.

I climbed in behind the Nip planes that were plugging at

230

him on the way down to the water. There were so many of them I wasn't even bothering to use my electric gun sight consciously, but continued to seesaw back and forth on my rudder pedals, trying to spray them all in general, trying to get them off George to give him a chance to bail out or dive—or do something at least.

But the same thing that was happening to him was now happening to me. I could feel the impact of the enemy fire against my armor plate, behind my back, like hail on a tin roof. I could see enemy shots progressing along my wing tips, making patterns.

George's plane burst into flames and a moment later crashed into the water. At that point there was nothing left for me to do. I had done everything I could. I decided to get the hell away from the Nips. I threw everything in the cockpit all the way forward—this means full speed ahead—and nosed my plane over to pick up extra speed until I was forced by the water to level off. I had gone practically a half mile at a speed of about four hundred knots, when all of a sudden my main gas tank went up in flames in front of my very eyes. The sensation was much the same as opening the door of a furnace and sticking one's head into the thing.

Though I was about a hundred feet off the water, I didn't have a chance of trying to gain altitude. I was fully aware that if I tried to gain altitude for a bail-out I would be fried in a few more seconds.

At first, being kind of stunned, I thought: "Well, you finally got it, didn't you, wise guy?" and then I thought: "Oh, no you didn't!" There was only one thing left to do. I reached for the rip cord with my right hand and released the safety belt with my left, putting both feet on the stick and kicking it all the way forward with all my strength. My body was given centrifugal force when I kicked the stick in this manner. My body for an instant weighed well over a ton, I imagine. If I had had a third hand I could have opened the canopy. But all I could do was to give myself this propulsion. It either jettisoned me right up through the canopy or tore the canopy off. I don't know which.

There was a jerk that snapped my head and I knew my chute

231

had caught—what a relief. Then I felt an awful slam on my side —no time to pendulum—just boom-boom and I was in the water.

The cool water around my face sort of took the stunned sensation away from my head. Looking up, I could see a flight of four Japanese Zeros. They had started a game of tag with me in the water. And by playing tag, I mean they began taking turns strafing me.

I started diving, making soundings in the old St. George Channel. At first I could dive about six feet, but this lessened to four, and gradually I lost so much of my strength that, when the Zeros made their strafing runs at me, I could just barely duck my head under the water. I think they ran out of ammunition, for after a while they left me. Or my efforts in the water became so feeble that maybe they figured they had killed me.

The best thing to do, I thought, was to tread water until nightfall. I had a little package with a rubber raft in it. But I didn't want to take a chance on opening it for fear they might go back to Rabaul, rearm, and return to strafe the raft. Then I would have been a goner for certain.

I was having such a difficult time treading water, getting weaker and weaker, that I realized something else would have to be done real quickly. My "Mae West" wouldn't work at all, so I shed all my clothes while I was treading away; shoes, fatigues, and everything else. But after two hours of this I knew that I couldn't keep it up any longer. It would have to be the life raft or nothing. And if the life raft didn't work—if it too should prove all shot full of holes—then I decided: "It's au revoir. That's all there is to it."

I pulled the cord on the raft, the cord that released the bottle of compressed air, and the little raft popped right up and filled. I was able to climb aboard, and after getting aboard I started looking around, sort of taking inventory.

I looked at my Mae West. If the Nips came back and strafed me again, I wanted to be darned sure that it would be in working order. If I had that, I could dive around under the water while they were strafing me, and would not need the raft. I had noticed some tears in the jacket, which I fully intended to get busy and patch up, but the patching equipment that came with the raft contained patches for about twenty-five holes.

"It would be better first, though," I decided, "to count the holes in this darned jacket." I counted, and there were more than two hundred.

"I'm going to save these patches for something better than this." With that I tossed the jacket overboard to the fish. It was of no use to me.

Then for the first time—and this may seem strange—I noticed that I was wounded, not just a little bit, but a whole lot. I hadn't noticed it while in the water, but here in the raft I certainly noticed it now. Pieces of my scalp, with hair on the pieces, were hanging down in front of my face.

My left ear was almost torn off. My arms and shoulders contained holes and shrapnel. I looked at my legs. My left ankle was shattered from a twenty-millimeter-cannon shot. The calf of my left leg had, I surmised, a 7.7 bullet through it. In my groin I had been shot completely through the leg by twenty-millimeter shrapnel. Inside of my leg was a gash bigger than my fist.

"I'll get out my first-aid equipment from my jungle pack. I'd better start patching this stuff up."

I kept talking to myself like that. I had lots of time. The Pacific would wait.

Even to my watch, which was smashed, I talked also. The impact had crushed it at a quarter to eight on the early morning raid. But I said to it: "I'll have a nice long day to fix you up."

I didn't, though. Instead, I spent about two hours trying to bandage myself. It was difficult getting out these bandages, for the waves that day in the old South Pacific were about seven feet or so long. They are hard enough to ride on a comparatively calm day, and the day wasn't calm.

After I had bandaged myself as well as I could, I started looking around to see if I could tell where I was or where I was drifting. I found that my raft contained only one paddle instead of the customary two. So this one little paddle, which fitted over the hand much like an odd sort of glove, was not of much use to me.

Talking to myself, I said: "This is like being up shit creek without a paddle."

Far off to the south, as I drifted, I could see the distant shore of New Britain. Far to the north were the shores of New Ireland. Maybe in time I could have made one or the other of these islands. I don't know. But there is something odd about drifting that I may as well record. All of us have read, or have been told, the thoughts that have gone through other men under similar circumstances. But in my case it was a little tune that Moon Mullin had originated. And now it kept going through my mind, bothering me, and I couldn't forget it. It was always there, running on and on:

"On a rowboat at Rabaul,
On a rowboat at Rabaul . . ."

The waves continued singing it to me as they slapped my rubber boat. It could have been much the same, perhaps, as when riding on a train, and the rails and the wheels clicking away, pounding out some tune, over and over, and never stopping.

The waves against this little rubber boat, against the bottom of it, against the sides of it, continued pounding out:

". . . On a rowboat at Rabaul,
You're not behind a plow . . ."

And I thought: "Oh, Moon Mullin, if only I had you here, I'd wring your doggone neck for ever composing that damn song."

About six months after World War II was over, and before I had a chance to answer a letter I received from Moon, who was then stationed in Japan, I read of his death in the newspaper. I still felt that it was my duty to write his parents, so I wrote a kind of letter different from my others, as I was as much in the dark as they were concerning Moon's last flight.

CHAPTER **23**

T HE PAST APPEARS TO BE the present sometimes, as I may have mentioned before. And the present sometimes appears to be the past. And there is the future in mind, also, for all of us, but I personally find myself much better off not worrying about either the past or the future. Merely taking care of the present is all I can handle.

But perhaps this tiny medallion I always wear from my neck on a slim gold chain is a sort of connection with all three. Or even, perhaps this is what all religions, the same as all talismans, are expected to be—a connection.

Unlike so many flyers I know, even those in my own outfit, I have not always worn a good-luck charm. Today, as we know, a good many such so-called charms are on the bottom of the ocean. So I do not consider this medallion one as such. At least not in the ordinary sense, for it represents to me something even bigger than that, and I never will part with it.

Nor did I have it even at the time I was knocked down. It was given to me afterward, long afterward, and after a series of circumstances that, if described the easiest way, would have to be described as "peculiar."

In regard to the word so loosely described as "religion," I used to go to the Protestant services sometimes with some of the

Protestant pilots in the squadron, and at other times I'd go to Mass with the Catholic pilots. Indeed, I once heard a padre in Guadalcanal give one of the meatiest Easter sermons I ever heard. Instead of going on at great length on something that didn't interest the boys, he spent about an hour telling the boys why they should write home more often to their folks.

"Explain to your folks," he said, "that Guadalcanal is not a hellhole any more," which it wasn't at that time. "Your people back home think that you're living an awful life out here. Let them know that you're getting along fine, that you have plenty of food and are not *always* being bothered by Japanese bombers. It isn't fair to let your people think that you're suffering when you're not."

It was about one of the most sensible Easter talks one could expect to hear. And even now, today, so many of us who were out there are expected to answer such questions as which made the best chaplains, the Catholics or the Protestants. My answer would be that it depended on the circumstances as well as the man.

Because on my records I was listed as a Protestant, and still am, it was up to a Protestant chaplain to preach my funeral services after I had been "killed." Nor was it until years later, after I was released from the Japanese prison camp, that I had the opportunity to thank him for the nice things he had said about me. He was quite a boy. At our airstrip, while we were flying, he had lived in a tent with the Catholic padre and a rabbi, and I had asked him, "Gee whiz, how do you three get along?"

He had just laughed and said: "Well, I'll tell you. We've gotten along wonderfully here for months. I get along fine with them as long as they don't try to convert me!" I liked him for that.

The Japanese military have a little prayer of their own, too, which I was to learn later. Any chaplain, whether Protestant, Catholic, or Jewish, would have to agree that even this Japanese prayer had something in it too; I say this even after I had listened to it in Japanese for some eighteen months. It would be given each morning and afternoon while all of us were in formation.

236

At first I could not figure out the prayer, so I asked someone what it meant. He told me that it meant that they would be kind to those less fortunate than they were, and guide the weak, and so forth. The way he described it to me it meant just anything that would be similar to one we would give in any of our own religions. So any one of them who would live up to that prayer, the same as any of us who could live up to the Lord's Prayer, could not be too far off his base.

Mentioning our own assortment of padres, I cannot help think that the Catholic chaplains had a knack usually of stealing the show. They seemed extraordinarily congenial in their special efforts to get along with the boys. They seemed to try hard to talk the boys' language and to try to understand them. In fact, some of their language couldn't be used after the boys got home here.

There was one Catholic chaplain, in Espiritu Santo, whom I used to like to go over and talk with on rainy nights, and we never talked about religion. From him I learned something about their organization and how they had helped the Allies in the Pacific. He told me that the Church had known all about this Pacific war long before it ever started, and that the Church knew what islands were going to be taken, and how the Church quietly had removed all the German priests from these islands ahead of time, even from the islands we were on then, and had replaced them with American and French priests. The reason the Church had been able to do this, the padre explained, without any of the German priests being suspicious, was that instead of transferring them they gave them all promotions and moved them back to the Vatican. This was to prevent their helping the Japanese, of course, and yet they had no idea at the time of what was going on. Whether they would have or not, the Church removed all temptation very cleverly.

On one of the down-pouring nights, as I was trudging along through the coconut trees near the fighter strip, I was very nearly drowned in my attempt to get to my cribbage-playing pal's tent. In order to get the proper coral for constructing a runway or taxi way the bulldozers had taken the coral from the ground, leaving behind long pits. Some of them were ten or

237

twelve feet deep, and they were left open. The pits had been completely filled with rain water, and in the darkness they resembled many of the roadways, which were also covered with water. By accident I happened to walk into a water-filled pit on my way to the padre's, wearing hip boots and a heavy raincoat. The suddenness, combined with the extra weight, made it almost impossible for me to crawl up the vertical sides submerged in the water. I must have struggled nearly twenty minutes before I got out. While I sat beside the ditch, waiting to catch my breath, I realized that I had had a near miss.

It was pleasant while talking or playing cribbage with my friend. We occupied ourselves until the wee hours of the morning by smoking long black cigars and quietly sipping brandy. I never seemed to get drunk when I was with this man, though. Apparently I must have been seeking something, although I wasn't quite certain what it might be. This man seemed to possess what I needed.

Even at that time, I am positive, I realized that fame or fortune could not be the answer. I was seeking happiness and peace of mind, but the way to get these eluded me. Fortunately, for me, I know now that spiritual things are the only answer.

Yet out of it all, and in regard to this tiny medallion of mine, I hardly know just how to classify my attachment to it, whether faith, or trust, or part of something I believe I am just beginning to understand.

When, after being shot down, I finally got aboard my little raft, and no clothes on, I found that I had something clutched in my hand. It was a small card that had been sent to me by a Catholic nun from Jersey City. The card was soaked with sea water then, of course, as I held it and looked at it and wondered why I had it. And it was then I remembered how, when a couple of years previously, when passing through Jersey City, I had given a talk to a Catholic orphanage, and a couple of little girl orphans took a fancy to me. So, when I was out in the South Pacific long afterward I had sent this nun some money to buy dresses for these two little orphans, and the nun had mailed it to me.

Please don't get the idea that I had turned noble, because I

238

hadn't, not in the least. I had won a considerable sum of money playing poker with some starry-eyed second lieutenants who had more money than they knew what to do with. But it bothered me, and I would have gladly given the money back if I'd thought they would accept it. Nor was I the type of person who gambled with his own squadron mates, for I didn't like the idea of people firing guns behind me when they owed me money. I gambled with people I didn't have to fly with.

So that is how I happened to think of the nun. But I didn't think of her and the orphans until I had spent all I could on whisky while in Sydney.

I had paid little or no attention to the card when I received it, but absently had stuck it in my jacket pocket, the pocket that happens to be above the heart. But why now on the raft I had it in my hand, water-soaked though it was, I never will know. Yet, for some peculiar reason, I now looked at it more closely than I had before. It was a picture of a lady with a baby in her arms, and there was a boat on a stormy sea. On the back of it I could make out the blurred lettering of a lengthy prayer. I read it over time after time, while drifting there. I probably read it over forty or fifty times, and it seemed to give me a great deal of company, and I was sickly unhappy when later the Japanese, after taking me, also took the card away from me.

While floating about the Pacific I had time to meditate. I wondered how it was possible for me to be saved from death so many times when people I considered so much better than myself had to die. I hated myself, but it was for the first time that I realized a Higher Power than myself does with one as it wishes. I truthfully wondered why a Higher Power might be saving a bum like me.

I look back now and realize that this was the first time I had ever prayed without asking for something, the first time I had ever prayed honestly, or properly, in my entire lifetime. I wasn't asking for a deal, although I wasn't conscious that it is impossible to make a so-called deal with one's Higher Power.

I prayed: "I don't know why I was saved, and I don't really care, but you have my permission to do anything with me you want. You take over. You've got the controls!" And, oddly enough, this seemed to help me through the next two hectic months.

After being released from the prison camp, at the end of the war, and returning to the United States, I sent a letter to the nun and told her about the card and that it had come to be in my hand at such a time, when there seemed no chance at all of getting out. I wrote all this to her as best I could, and when I was in New York City sometime later the little nun presented me with my medallion to replace the card. And this is why I always will wear this medallion. It is about the size of a dime, or even smaller. On one side is the Virgin Mary, and the edge is bordered with stars.

CHAPTER **24**

HOW MUCH SIMPLER LIFE would be for all of us if we could turn our lives over to some comic-strip cartoonist and say: "Here you are, mister. You take on from here." He would leave us in all kinds of tough situations, of course, but it also would be up to him to get us out of them. He could not very well let us, his main characters, be drowned or killed, for he himself would then be out of a job. His strip would have reached an end.

I was not thinking of this while floating around on that raft. But I am thinking of it now, and the whole string of incidents does seem to parallel some of those strips we have seen. The cartoons are not always funny, and neither was my own case, but always the last panel of each strip leaves me suspended again with a sort of "to be continued" motif.

Strip sequence: Have pilot finally break American record but be last seen going down in flames.

Next strip sequence: Have pilot in last moment save himself by parachute but be last seen swimming in water and being strafed by enemy.

Next strip sequence: Have badly wounded pilot save himself by finally getting rubber boat inflated but be last seen floating around a long distance from nowhere.

241

And so on, and it would now be up to the cartoonist to get me out of this fix but immediately into something else equally suspenseful. It would be his worry, not mine. But on looking back I must admit he did a rather pat job of it and should be congratulated.

After I had been floating around on the raft for something like eight hours, I happened to see something come to the surface nearby. I looked at it and realized that it was a submarine —a large submarine.

Only a cartoonist could have thought of that, and also of the idea that it should not be an American submarine but one belonging to the enemy, which it turned out to be. But I didn't know this until the sub came alongside. I figured that in those waters it could very well be one of ours and started to take hope. But then, as it drew alongside, I could see a tarpaulin stretched by four lines to the conning tower, and right in the center was that angry red meat ball.

"Oh God, Boyington," I said, and heaved anything I thought might be of military value over the side of the raft. The only things I didn't heave over the side were my jungle pack, which I knew would float and they would pick up anyhow, and my medicine kit, which I thought might be of use later on.

As the sub pulled closer, out of the conning tower came a lot of funny-looking little men. They had on all the same kind of hat. I later saw that these hats were all one size and had a kind of shoestring affair in the back to adjust them so they would fit anything from a fathead down to a pinhead.

After the sub came alongside, a line was tossed to me, and when I grabbed hold of it they pulled in the little raft. The men helped me aboard, took my rubber raft and jungle pack aboard, then sat me down on the deck. One of them, in English, asked my name.

I was going to give him a phony name and a phony rank because I didn't have on any clothes. A thought ran through my mind that it wouldn't be too conducive to longevity to tell my real identity. Just as I was about ready to give this phony information, I happened to glance at my jungle pack, lying there on the deck, and on the back was stenciled: "Major G. Boyington,

USMC." So I decided to give them my correct name instead. I didn't think they would know me in their navy.

The one person who spoke English was a pharmacist's mate, and he said to me: "You don't have to worry about anything as long as you are on this boat." That made me feel about as comfortable as the old turkey does before Thanksgiving. It left me to wonder what the hell was going to happen when they took me ashore.

Strangely, I was given the best treatment I ever had while I was a captive. The sub stayed surfaced all the way into Rabaul Harbor, more than a two-hour trip, and anchored just after darkness. But meanwhile they offered me sweet tea and cookies, and gave me cigarettes, which didn't taste good at the time, and matches.

Later I found out that the cigarettes they gave me were their better brands; Sakara and Cherry were the words in their language. This was the only time the Nips didn't stand around and gawk at me. The majority of them proceeded about their business and paid no attention to me.

When we anchored in Rabaul Harbor, a small boat similar to one of our navy Higgins boats came alongside and was secured to the sub. This time they blindfolded me, tied my hands, and marched me over the gangway into this small boat. I didn't know it then, but I learned later that, when the Nips so much as took a prisoner across the street, they always blindfolded him first.

Before being blindfolded I had noticed that about twelve Nippon sailor boys with rifles were in this small boat, and now, as I sat there on the deck blindfolded, they kept clicking the bolts in those rifles. It seemed to me, by this sound, that they deliberately were trying to tell me they comprised a firing squad for after we got ashore.

When we landed, they led me up the coral streets of Rabaul. I couldn't see a thing and I was limping along on a shattered ankle. To help me along, they would boot me in the hind end with rifle butts. Finally they stopped me in front of what must have been some kind of building. My bare feet had been cut something terrific, because coral is just like walking on broken glass to feet that are not used to it. In front of wherever it was that we stopped an Americanized voice addressed me: "How would you like to be with your friends?"

"Jesus," I thought, "maybe he means these fighter pilots we've been knocking off all the time. That wouldn't be too good." And then I thought: "Well, maybe he's referring to where I'm going, either up or down, after they're through with me." Finally I answered: "I don't believe I know what you mean."

He said: "Oh, you'll find out soon enough."

In the house or building, or whatever it was, I could hear a lot of tinkling of glasses, a piano thumping, and women's hilarious voices in a language I didn't understand. I wondered if they were going to take me in there and put me on display without any clothes on. It was horrible enough, but the blindfold made it seem so much worse by turning one's imagination loose upon himself. I gave a sort of prayer while I was forced to stand there: "I hope to God they give me a couple of drinks for the road from one of their sake bottles before they do away with me."

Finally they threw me in a truck and drove me on up some street. I was then taken out and put in a small wooden building, and the blindfold was taken off at last, and then a feeling of complete relief came over me for a moment. This, I was to find, was their third-degree room. Off on my left about two feet stood a goon I imagined must have been the world's champion judo boy, because he possessed a pair of tremendous cauliflower ears and had a pair of hands that, when he pounded on you, felt like a pair of boards.

The Americanized voice I had heard before was there in front of me again, and I later found out he was a boy who had gone as far as high school in Honolulu before his parents had sent him on to Japan for further education. The first question they asked me through the boy was my name. I already had given that, so I told them. Then they asked me my rank, and I told them. Then they asked me my serial number. Now this, by international law, is all they are allowed to ask you. But I was probably the only one in the Marine Corps who didn't have a serial number because I had not received one after I had been

244

reinstated. When I maintained after an hour that I didn't have a serial number, they finally believed me and stopped slugging me and twisting the ropes like tourniquets, the ropes that were holding my hands together. They had another quaint trick in the third-degree room, that of putting out cigarette butts on your neck and shoulders.

They brought in first one area commander and then another in the course of that evening, and they asked me this question and that question. Of course, as I was a fighter pilot, there was not a darned thing I knew that could help them, and I began to realize the fact. I didn't have any idea that the Marshall and Gilbert campaigns were coming off soon; they had to tell me all about that. Then there was one snaky-eyed individual with about ten pages of radio calls. Of course, we used to change these calls from time to time, but just the same he read off each one and then looked at me and his eyes twitched behind his glasses as he said: "You know, don't you?"

Finally I just threw up my hands in disgust and said: "Honest to God, I don't. How the hell could I?"

Some of these officers were able to speak a fair brand of English, although I was certain they had never been in the United States, but they didn't seem to be capable of understanding my brand of English. They had to rely, partially at least, on their interpreter's version. Between officers there was usually a short break, and I welcomed the chances to talk to Suyako, which I came to find out means interpreter.

I came to like Suyako in a very short time, and finally appreciated that he was in much the same boat as I found myself. He gave me as much of a tip as he dared real early in the game, by saying during one of the periods when the two of us were alone:

"Why don't you make it easy on yourself? I keep telling 'these Japs' what you fellows know and what you don't know. But they think they are so damn smart, they insist you do."

"What do you mean, make it easy on myself?" I inquired.

" 'These Japs' are going to question you, and question you again. So whatever you tell them, always stick to the same story.

As long as you more or less pass the time of day with them, you will get along okay and lose nothing."

"Thanks for the tip, Mac," I said.

"Don't call me Mac, call me Suyako," he said, rather sternly, to impress me.

"Okay, okay," I said, trying to simmer him down a bit.

By now, I was fully aware that I was no comic-strip hero, and I understood that I knew absolutely nothing of any military value that they probably didn't know more about than I did. So I decided to stop playing Dick Tracy. I decided to be truthful in matters I wanted to tell them, so I could remember what I had said in the next question period.

Real late in the night a very elderly gentleman came in. I later found out that he was the commanding general of the entire Rabaul area, which at one time included all the Solomon Islands, Bougainville, New Ireland, New Britain, and what the Japanese held of New Guinea, so he was quite an important person. When he came in I noticed that the interpreter bowed about twelve times.

I was sitting on the chair with my injured leg crossed over my good one, holding onto it with both hands. After the interpreter was through with his bowing spree, he turned around and slapped my injured leg off the other one. Scolding me, he said: "Don't you know it is impolite to cross your legs in front of the commanding general?"

But I was in pain and kind of punchy, and I said: "God damn it, tell him my leg hurts like hell!"

So the interpreter turned around and went chop-chop-chop to this big boy, and the answer came back to the interpreter, who turned around to me and said: "The commanding general says if your leg hurts you can cross it."

I answered: "Thank you," nodded to the elderly gent, and crossed my leg and held onto it with both hands.

Now this old boy didn't ask me questions like the underlings had done. He wanted to know who started the war. My answer was: "Why, you people, of course."

He wanted to know where.

"Why, Pearl Harbor."

Then he wanted to know what I thought of the Japanese people. Well, I was diplomatic enough to say that I personally didn't have much against them, but then I went on at great length saying what I thought of their militaristic government, and what I thought of the atrocities I knew were committed in the Philippine Islands and in China.

The interpreter told me that the commanding general was about ready to leave but would like to tell me a fable and would I mind.

I answered: "Why, no, certainly not."

So the commanding general told this fable, and as nearly as I can recall—for I was shot in the head and everything else, and was punchy, shot, and exhausted—the fable went like this:

"Once upon a time there was a little old lady and she traded with five merchants. She always paid her bills and got along fine. Finally the five merchants got together and they jacked up their prices so high the little old lady couldn't afford to live any longer. That's the end of the story."

So, after having said this, the general bowed to me and went out of the room. I couldn't help ponder that there just had to be two sides to everything, and I just couldn't help admiring this distinguished old gent a little bit.

To show how one's mind can become set on some idea, one of the first things I wanted to learn after being taken captive was the whereabouts or possible fate of Lieutenant Colonel "Indian Joe" Bauer.

Joe was a few years older than I was, and he always had been one of my idols. None of us ever believed the Japs could destroy a guy as great as Joe, but they had knocked him down off Guadalcanal before they got me, and Joe Foss had last seen him swimming in the water. Yet no word about him, or his last fight, had come to us, and we simply could not believe that Indian Joe was killed.

So after my last caller, the general, had left my first night's interrogation, I asked Suyako if they had captured Colonel Bauer. After deliberating for some time he answered: "No, I'm certain we haven't. Every prisoner has to come through Rabaul. This is our area headquarters."

This Hawaiian-Japanese interpreter then suddenly turned on me, realizing that I had gotten some information from him.

"Say," he demanded, "who the hell is doing this interrogating, me or you?"

He seemed to be so annoyed at what he had done that, to change the subject, I quietly asked for a cigarette in answer. The trick worked. But I would have liked to ask questions concerning members of my Black Sheep and their possible whereabouts.

Only two cigarettes were left in his package and he looked at me and scowled as he said: "I might as well. Where you are going you're not going to need any more cigarettes."

Of course I thought he knew what he was talking about. I thought I was going to be lobbed off the next day maybe. So with that I reached over and took out both cigarettes and said: "Well, in that case, I'll just take them both."

Suyako just looked at me, didn't try to stop me or even ask for one back.

Early in the morning, still in the darkness, I was blindfolded again and put in the truck and driven some painful ten miles or so. I do not know where they took me. All those roads were so rough I just ached and pained in my wounds. Finally the truck stopped. I was taken out, the blindfold was removed, and there in front of me stood a swarthy-looking gent in a breechcloth and one of those funny little hats. He spoke to me in pidgin English. "The boys call me Captain here. You tell me the whole story tomorrow." At this point I was just so tired and exhausted that all I wanted, in addition to learning something, anything, about Joe and the others, was some sleep. And I kept thinking: "Oh God, I don't give a damn if they shoot me, burn me at the stake, or anything else tomorrow. All I want for the rest of the night is some sleep." I would have traded anything I knew in the world for sleep that minute. This shows how relative one's values are to things you want in this world.

The captain was a Nip Navy chief, as I found out in later

days. He took me to the door of a long cell block, rapped on the door, and said: "Roker, Roker."

Soon a tall, rangy fellow with long hair and gaunt frame came to the door and said: "Yes, Captain, what is it?"

The captain said: "I got company for you, I got company for you." The captain kept saying something to Crocker in half English and half Japanese, and I got the essence of what sounded like "No speako, no speako," or something.

Of course, I didn't quite get the idea, so I started to talk to Crocker. I knew he was one of the American pilots, and later found out that it was his white chute that I saw blossom out amid dark explosions on our first fight over Ballale. He had been transported to Rabaul by Nip destroyer.

But the next thing I knew the captain had clunked me over the side of my face and was literally foaming at the mouth.

Crocker said: "He means to say that you shouldn't speak to anybody, not even me."

I was taken down a long line of cells in this little building and was tossed on a kind of wooden crate affair; no blankets, nothing but a couple of gunny sacks.

This was to be my home for the next six weeks. The Japanese didn't permit anybody to come near me, wash me or anything, for ten days. When infection set in my wounds, I began to smell like a dead horse. I smelled so horrible I couldn't see how the guards could even stand to throw me in a truck to take me to the interrogating room each and every day.

Anyone in his right mind, not to mention a cartoonist, would think I could fall asleep, or just plain pass out from exhaustion, in what remained of my first night with the Nips, but obviously, my mind wasn't running along normal channels. And one would believe that I had sufficient trouble where I was at present to keep me occupied, but no, I was thinking of the base I had flown from. If only I could have a couple of those two-ounce bottles of brandy, then maybe I would be able to sleep in these two burlap bags and keep the mosquitoes from bothering me.

And Colonel Lard was worrying me, for I could see his ugly, smirking face as I closed my eyes in the darkness. Crime must pay off, after all, because Lard had certainly gotten the last laugh on me. Besides, he was losing no sleep where he was now located, protected by a veritable fortress.

I had counted upon his being inconvenienced when he was moved up to the forward area. But instead, he had made himself right at home as usual, for he had the troops fill sandbags and place them about the operations building, in which he lived. My guess is that this structure could have resisted anything but a direct hit from a two-thousand-pound bomb. My imagination led me to believe that Lard had been taunting me, deliberately, when he had invited me to a cocktail party in his fortress not long before I was shot down.

There had been other squadron commanders invited to Lard's party, but I considered it personal. I wouldn't have known about anyone else, as I was probably the only one who consumed enough of his good whisky to get drunk. But if only I could have one minute to be in Lard's quarters, just to take a couple of belts of his whisky, while he lay happily asleep.

Even thoughts of Lard could not keep me awake forever, and I finally fell asleep on the board bunk in my cell. In my sleep I somehow gathered an impression that I must have been dreaming all this.

CHAPTER **25**

DAYLIGHT BROUGHT ME to my senses: this was real, all right, and I had not dreamed about being shot down. The harsh commands, which I could not understand, appeared to be getting the Japanese and prisoners alike into two formations outside of the buildings. Judging by the expressions on the faces of the prisoners I was able to see through my window, I felt that this had all the prospects of becoming a permanent nightmare.

I remained seated upon the edge of my bunk, waiting for something to happen to me, whatever it might be, because I had no idea of what came next. The joker in the breechcloth entered my building, jabbering like a parrot, the same one who had pounded me for talking the night before. Part of his pidgin-English conversation was referring to me, I was positive, and the reference was: "Number Ten Man this, and Number Ten Man that."

Trying to figure just how I came to be linked up with the numeral ten had me licked. And I don't mean maybe, for no matter how I counted, after first edging my way over to the open door of the cell and counting in every direction I could think of, neither the cells nor the prisoners added up to ten from where I was situated.

Number Ten Man, I soon discovered, was to be my new name

for the time being, and was used by the guards and other prisoners while they were talking about me. Suyako finally enlightened me: everything in pidgin English is graded from one to ten; one is the very best, on down to ten, which is no good. The degree with which one was incapacitated, or banged up, stamped me as a Number Ten Man, just in case I didn't already know. This was quite a twist, I thought, because, although I had made a number of people's lists in my day, never had I made one without casting the main reference to my character in some way.

From here on in I was to feel the daily and nightly force of Allied bombs only too many times. In the daytime we could see our own aircraft dive-bombing, but during the night we were only able to listen and hope.

After ten days the Japanese finally permitted someone to clean me up and take care of my wounds for the first time. This was done by Hugh Wheatley, a doctor who had been captured at Munda when the Japanese had occupied New Georgia. The doctor was a half-caste who had been educated in the islands. He knew his medicine, I am positive, but he had little or nothing to work with as far as medical supplies. Hughie, as we called him, had to draw out infection by the application of steaming, salt-water compresses made of rags.

The Japanese always confiscated all the prisoners' medical gear when they captured them. They had taken mine too. And we were not allowed so much as a drop of iodine to place on our wounds.

Before the six weeks I was to spend at Rabaul were over, I had lost a great deal of my numerical seniority, as some of the newer captives brought into camp were in horrible condition. About the only way a person could maintain seniority was to go on living. If one were to go past Number Ten, they buried him. I had dropped down to Number Five Man before long, and for this drop I was damn happy, believe me.

Each day for this six weeks I was called into the interrogating room, tied and blindfolded, driven in by truck, and they asked some of the doggonedest questions. Of course, the others had gone through the same thing, but I didn't fully realize that at this time the Japs thought I was important.

The questions would go on and on like this:

"Have you ever been in San Francisco?"

"Yes."

"When were you in San Francisco?"

"1941."

"How many ships were there in the harbor?"

"I don't know."

"You must have some idea. Make an estimate of how many."

So I would guess. Of course, I didn't tell them I spent two weeks in bars while waiting for a ship to take us to the Flying Tigers, and never went near the damn docks in the meanwhile. But I plumb neglected to tell them anything about this part of my life, for I felt that it would be legal for them to kill me if they found out I had been a man fighting without a uniform.

Then came the joker of all jokers.

"Who were the commanding officers of these ships?"

They asked me questions about our wings and groups and squadrons, but these had become so mixed up by that time that even our own high command couldn't possibly keep them straight. I have mentioned previously that the job of straightening out the paper work for a series of squadrons had almost driven me nuts, even when I had all the necessary data for figuring things. Anyhow, the Japs kept insisting that I would think of the answers sometime. But I haven't to date.

Man, oh man, I was told so many times by the interpreter, and by those who were interrogating me through the interpreter, that I was awfully stupid for a major. And I felt at times like saying: "What's more, sport, there are those back at my base, who will agree with you, too."

While lying in this infested cell I came down with malaria. During the daytime I was not allowed to close my eyes, even though wounded and suffering from malaria. I had to sit up on this boardlike affair in my cell. Every time a guard came by and saw me closing my eyes, he would come in, grab me by the hair, and hit me in the face with his fist.

During the night they put handcuffs on me, which made it

almost impossible to sleep. But I soon was able to take care of this situation okay, for I bent a nail in my teeth that would lock and unlock them. The only trouble I had was when I failed to awaken in time one morning, and do you know, I had one hell of a time convincing that stupid guard that there must have been something wrong with the way he closed the cuffs the night before. He finally believed he had made an error somehow, but he ended up kicking hell out of me to save face. A guy just couldn't seem to get ahead in this league.

There was a jealousy that existed between their army and navy that was beyond all competition. This was carried right down to the lowliest man in each service, or even to the *horio* (a special prisoner, not a prisoner of war, the lowest form of life in their book), and I happened by chance to fall in that category.

This *horio* category was one I had hopes of graduating from, becoming a prisoner of war at a later date, so that the Red Cross would notify my family that I was living. But my hopes were never fulfilled, for I was to remain a *horio* until the bitter end, along with a few others.

But the Japanese army was more powerful than their navy politically, so I was lent, as many others before me, to the army interrogators for one week. Their army kept me in a cell downtown for the silly questions, which continued day and night. It seemed that the army wanted to get their money's worth in the short time they had been allotted. True, I got beaten up a bit, but things didn't seem too bad, for the army didn't begrudge one's lying to them a little.

Our diet, which I turned down for the first few days, became damn tasty all of a sudden, and as my appetite developed I began to eat everything I was offered and was looking for more. We were fed the leftovers from their officers' mess; soup, rice, and a multitude of things all mixed together. We called it chop suey.

After ten days or so, when the Japs were permitting Hugh Wheatley to treat my wounds, I thought I had a greater problem than my wounds or the war, and said so:

"Say, Doc, I've got a problem."

"What is it?" The little fellow smiled.

"No, I'm serious, Hughie. I haven't had a crap for ten days or more, and I'm just beginning to get a bit concerned about it. Have you got any physic handy?"

"I have, but I'd prefer not to give it to you."

"How's that?"

"Because I have nothing to stop diarrhea. The reason I hesitate is that we have lost a few fellows from this but none from constipation."

Maybe this condition added to my orneriness, I don't know, but one day, when they had me in town questioning me, something happened. Suyako came running into the interrogating room, out of breath, and said: "You are going to *have* to recall the commanding officer's name at your base, or the commanding general is going to have all of you shot."

"How come, Suyako?"

"Last night one of your bombers hit the entrance of the old man's private shelter with a bomb, not more than a second or so after he'd crawled into it. You never saw anybody so mad before."

"What in hell good will a name do him?"

"He also wants to know where he sleeps."

I had not lied when I told Suyako I didn't recall, for the C.O. of Vella Lavella was a brigadier general in the New Zealand forces, and I had forgotten the name. I hadn't even had the pleasure of meeting the man, for that matter, and he had nothing to do with aviation in the true sense. Previously I had evaded all conversation pertaining to him and his job, because I knew he was located down the coast from the Vella strip in the middle of thousands of gallons of one-hundred-octane gasoline. Although the dump was hidden in the jungle, it was a thing I didn't dare talk about.

But Suyako had given me a break, so I thought I should pretend to return the favor, in a way, so nobody would get hurt in the bargain. I said: "Suyako, I finally remembered the C.O.'s name."

"Great, great, what is it?" He seemed very excited and looked as if a heavy load had been removed from his shoulders.

"It's funny, I don't know why I never thought of it before, Colonel Living Lard."

"Good, now where does he sleep?"

"Will you get that aerial photo you were showing me the other day? And a very sharp pencil, please?"

I was thinking of the clear picture that must have been shot on a cloudless day from forty thousand feet or better, showing every little detail on our field with remarkable clarity. Of course I knew that one of their night bombers had about one in a thousand chances of ever getting past my pal, Gus Woodhelm, and his night fighters. But if it were possible, the Japs might just as well throw a scare into the right person without doing any serious damage.

Suyako dug out the photo, and stood there beside me sharpening a pencil, as I pretended to be studying the picture in great detail. The object I was looking for, at the foot of the hill and in the center of the strip, showed up like a sore thumb, Lard's fortress. I thought that perhaps there was a small chance of getting a laugh from my side of the fence, so I said: "I know a little bit about dive-bombing myself, you know. So if you can't get through——"

"Don't you worry, we'll get through."

"Okay, okay," for he didn't realize I was for him in this, "then lob one off about halfway down this hill. Sort of skip-bombing, if you understand what I'm driving at."

Suyako could be contained no longer and rushed out of the shack, so I smiled to myself, thinking: "I would love to see that no-good son of a bitch's face if it is at all possible for them to get through."

I never did find out whether they had been able to drop this bomb near Lard, and I'm afraid to ask now.

One evening in the middle of February, Suyako came out to our camp and told six of us prisoners that we were leaving by air the following morning for Tokyo. He didn't mention what kind of plane or where our stops en route were to be.

My five traveling companions, whom I had met in prison camp in Rabaul for the first time, were to be stuck with me for the duration of the war. There were two Australians, Brian

Stacy, pilot, and Brown, radioman; Air Corps P-38 pilot Captain Charles Taylor; PBY pilot Commander John Arbuckle; and Major Donald Boyle, another Corsair pilot.

It is an amazing thing, now that I look back on it, how you can practically read each other's minds under circumstances such as these. I know I could. And I found others could read mine, at least as far as recognizing pure insanity.

For a long time to come I was to feel a deep regret over something we possibly could have done after taking off in "Betty," one of their famous twin-engine bombers.

This doesn't refer to the first time we took off, but to the second, for the first time they put us into the Betty and took off, we got I don't know how high when we heard air fire coming around us. The next thing I knew, we landed very abruptly on some airstrip close by. I don't know where it was. We were taken out of the plane, our blindfolds removed, and were herded into the woods. It seems that our own boys had come over early this morning and found a few planes in the air. But this Betty we were in had gotten away from them.

The next morning the bomber, with us six prisoners back in it, tried again. According to the time by the sun, which we hazily could estimate even through our blindfolds, we appeared to have flown long enough to reach the island of Truk. And this estimation later proved to be correct.

But what still made me so disappointed until recent years— and I could wake up at night and get mad about it all over—is the disappointment in not having had five of my own Black Sheep with me there as captives in that plane instead of the boys I did have. For during that plane ride in that Betty from Rabaul on up to Truk, our Black Sheep would have had the opportunity of a lifetime. And later, while sitting in some bar daydreaming, I yearned and dreamed over what we could have done. Perhaps all of us have regrets like this, regrets over "what we could have done" at sometime in the past. But my regrets, in this instance, were, I felt sure, the biggest.

After we had been put into the Betty and had taken off the second time, we found out that there was only the pilot, co-pilot, Suyako, a guard, and one rear gunner. They were the only ones in the plane besides ourselves.

The music of the engines in a plane makes everybody drowsy, and I noticed that all except the pilot and co-pilot were practically asleep, and this started me thinking. I also had the bonds on my hands so loose that I could have pulled my hands free in a second's notice if I desired. But one of my six mates must have read my thoughts, or maybe he heard me mumble them, because he whispered: "Greg, I pray you, don't try to make an escape and take over this plane."

None of my Black Sheep would have talked like that, and everything would have been so damned easy if *only* I had had five of them there with me. All we would have had to do was knock over this guard. He was the only one with a gun handy.

We then could have taken this plane over and have manned it ourselves. I always did believe it, and this is why I still kept getting mad with disappointment later. But a person just can't do such things alone. But with five little helpers, five Black Sheep, we could have done it. I *know* we could have done it. We could have knocked out all the crew, or have killed all the crew, and have come flying this Betty back into our own territory.

We could have brought in that planeful of Japanese bodies and made a water landing just outside our own field's gunfire. Of course, that is, if our own side didn't shoot us down first. But I want you to forget it as I have, and get on with my arrival in Truk, which I experienced in February 1944, and again and again on television in later years.

It is not that I am necessarily camera-shy, because I doubt that I am, but these days I almost convince myself when, as I watch television, somebody once again happens to show that excellent Navy carrier picture *The Fighting Lady*. The sequence in this film that always interests me the most (because I am in it, though on the ground) is that big raid by our carrier planes on Truk. And during the showing there is just enough ham in me to want to point out "where I am." But the pit in which I am trying to seek cover shows up much better than I do. It is far more photogenic. But just the same, should my wife be sitting next to me, I can always point to the contents of that pit and say: "Honey, there's daddy-oh. Give him a hand. What an actor."

It seemed that this bomber in which the Japanese were carrying us prisoners just could not keep out of trouble.

After being flown from Rabaul to Truk we landed on a field at Truk but did not merely come to a stop. It happened to be the roughest, shortest of landings, intentionally I know now, I have ever experienced or ever hope to. Immediately we were all thrown out of the plane, practically on our heads. We thought it was just some more roughstuff but, because we had edged our blindfolds, we could see that down the runway came a Navy F6F, spraying .50-calibers all through the Nip aircraft standing there in front of us. The piece of transportation we had just crawled out of went up before our eyes in flame and smoke, and so did nearly every other plane we could see around there. It was one of the best Navy Day programs I ever expect to see, the first task-force raid on the island of Truk.

Suyako and the Nips in the plane with us booted us along the ground down the airstrip until we came to this shallow pit I mentioned, and there they threw us into it. I had been stumbling all over everything because of my blindfold, which, owing to the low bridge on my nose, pressed right against my eyeballs, and until I wiggled the blindfold free a little I couldn't see a thing. I envied those boys with the big hooknoses. They could walk right along and see about two feet in front of themselves when they were blindfolded.

At this time, though, I must say that Suyako used some of what he must have learned while being educated in the Hawaiian Islands. If we had arrived at Truk before the raid, and the raid had happened a few minutes later, we would have had to stand out in this field blindfolded and tied up during the whole thing, which lasted the better part of two days. But during the confusion (he told us all about this later) he was able to throw us into this pit without being hampered by the Japanese on the field. In other words, Suyako saved our lives.

From this small pit, after wiggling our bandages so we could see, we got a worm's-eye view of a real air show. I could not keep my eyes below the pit level. I just had to look and see what was going on. There was so much excitement I couldn't do any differently. I just had to see those Nip planes, some of the light planes like the Zeros, jump off the ground from the explosion of our bombs and come down "cl-l-l-l-ang," just like a sack of bolts and nuts.

The planes caught on fire and the ammunition in them began going off. There were twenty-millimeter cannon shells and 7.7s bouncing and ricocheting all around this pit. Some of these hot pieces we tossed back out of the pit with our hands. All of this, or a lot of this, is shown in the motion picture, too, but obviously from an angle much different from ours. The picture also shows how one of the two-thousand-pound bombs had its center of impact only fifteen feet from the pit we were in, and shows the crater there after the explosion.

But what *The Fighting Lady* cannot include, unfortunately, is the close-up dialogue of which we were participants there in the pit. Things happened that would have gone well on the sound track, I think, little scenes that seemed to have no specific rhyme or reason and yet were all a part of it—the raid on Truk—as seen from the ground.

During a momentary lull, for instance, a Japanese pilot came down and landed his Zero, jumped out and started running over to the edge of the field where the Nips had a lot of caves. On the way across he happened to glance in this pit the six of us were in, and he stopped and looked in at us.

He was wearing one of those fuzzy helmets with the ear flaps turned up, and he looked in at us, as surprised as we were, then composed himself and said in English: "I am a Japanese pilot."

During this time we stayed huddled down in the pit because we were not supposed to be able to see him through our blindfolds. "Buck" Arbuckle whispered: "Who does he think he's kiddin'?"

Then he repeated himself: "I am a Japanese pilot. You bomb here, you die," and patted the leather of the case containing his Luger.

I couldn't take any more; it all seemed both so funny and hysterical at the same time that I could contain myself no longer. I stuck my elbow into the rugged chap next to me, Don Boyle, of New York City, who was in the same predicament I was. I said something to him that later he laughed about and repeated to me. While glancing back up at the Nip pilot I had said: "With all the God damn trouble we got, *ain't* you the cheerful son of a bitch, though."

Whether this lug was serious we never knew, for he didn't even get another chance to talk to us. The last we saw of him his short legs were busy hopping over obstructions, the ear flaps of his fur helmet wobbling up and down so that he gave the appearance of a jack rabbit getting off the highway. His conversation and threats had been rudely interrupted by the death rattle caused by another Navy F6F's .50-calibers, crackling down the runway as it came just a matter of a few feet from our pit.

Meanwhile something else happened that was not quite so funny, and I figured it was up to me to do something about it. One of the boys in the pit was praying out loud: "Oh, dear God, oh, dear God, I know we'll never get out of this . . ." and so on.

I couldn't take any more of that, either, so I shook the boy and said: "Jesus Christ, Brownie, won't you shut up? I know we're all praying, but you don't need to do it so God damn loud in that direction, do you?" And then, remembering how lucky I had always been, I added in a quieter voice: "Brownie, crawl over to me, and stay next to me. I know *I'm* still lucky enough to get out of this mess."

Around late afternoon Suyako and the guard who had accompanied us in the plane came over and looked in the pit. I guess they were as amazed as at anything they ever had seen. They expected to see six mangled bodies in the pit, yet there were six people in there without a scratch on them other than the wounds they already carried up from Rabaul. They took us out of the pit and said that we would have to stay over in a wrecked building at the edge of the field until darkness. Suyako said: "Don't pay any attention to anybody who comes near you or kicks you or throws anything at you. We'll get you through this all right." It was a great feeling to hear him say that.

After darkness they led us, all six of us tied together, across the field. They told us they would have to take the blindfolds

261

off because, with the place so torn up, they couldn't drag us through. There were huge pieces of concrete upended, plane parts scattered all over, and the place was a shambles.

They put us in little boats to take us across to another, small island. They told us not to look around or we'd be struck. We were struck, because it was too hard to resist the sight of four ships still burning out in the harbor. When we landed we were put in some kind of a bus and taken to a navy camp, and there all six of us were put in a tiny cell about the size of a small half bathroom. We could not lie down. We stayed in there all hunched up, which was the best we could do. But the main point of all this, anyhow, was the raid on Truk and the part we "played" in it. In the film we are, I suppose, what would be called extras.

CHAPTER **26**

OUR QUARTERS AT TRUK were unique, I thought. The cell was neat and clean, and looked as if it had been built recently by a carpenter who knew his business, for there wasn't a single joint through which we were able to see light from out of doors. Of course, I had no way of knowing but I rather imagined that the builder had merely one prisoner in mind when he measured the boards, not six.

There were three openings through which fresh air had the slightest chance of entering while the door remained closed and locked. One barred window was in the door, but this was always covered by a tightly woven matting on the outside, so the sunlight could not enter the interior. There was another opening in the bottom of the door where the Japs shoved in our food, but this was also covered by matting. The only other hole looked as if the carpenter had omitted a six-inch board in the floor. The missing portion of our deck was no accident; it was omitted for a purpose and was meant to be used as a toilet by the occupant.

Throughout the following day until midafternoon our Navy planes came back, again and again, and on several occasions bomb fragments struck the building we were in. When we heard a really close one coming our way, it was fantastic to see six men get flat on their bellies in such a confined space so quickly. The first time we accomplished this spectacular feat Arbuckle laughed and said: "I knew six could lie down in this much space, but I thought half of them had to be female."

As welcome as that carrier raid had been, I, for one, was a completely content individual when they finally ceased coming over. Naturally, the six of us were making book on various aspects of the situation, odds being good for the United States to win the war, but the odds for surviving our own bombs were slim.

The heat was almost unbearable in this closed-off cell, for after all the Truk atolls are located practically on the equator. We peeled off what few clothes we had in an effort to cool down a little. The odor from our own filth and sweat was bad enough, but the slippery, slimy contact when we had to move, rubbing against each other, was even more unbearable.

The islands of Truk are a good example of those that get slight rainfall during the course of the year. Because of this we found that thirst, the same as others have found through thousands of years, is far worse than starvation. All the time we were confined in this cell, sixteen days, because water was very scarce in the vicinity of Truk, each of us prisoners was rationed to three small cups of water per day. Our lips became swollen, so had our tongues, and our mouths felt so stuffed full of cotton that we could hardly make an articulate sound out of them.

The guards in this prison camp didn't beat us, because Suyako and the guard who had come along with us told them we were very old prisoners and had been captured a long time ago. Suyako probably didn't have a difficult task selling them this because of our long hair, beards, and emaciated bodies. For this reason they never struck any of the six or hauled us out of the cell to beat us.

The third morning a Nip we had never seen before pulled back the bamboo matting from our door window and looked in at us, smiling with friendliness. There was more gold in that toothy grin than I had ever seen in any mouth. "Too bad," I thought, "Chiang Kai-shek's gang isn't here, because those gold-mad bastards would go crazy if they saw this guy."

264

Then gold-mouth said in what sounded like English: "Ohio," and smiled again.

Figuring the guy spoke our language, I said: "No, Idaho, I'm from Idaho."

He just kept smiling and said: "Ohio," several more times. I later found out he didn't know a damn word of English, but that *ohio* means good morning in Japanese.

Apparently there was no food shortage at Truk, for the Nips passed so many rice balls and salty dicon pickles under the door we couldn't eat them all. Not even Boyle. But Don did eat until he became swollen up like a horse that had access to an unlimited oat supply.

Then we had a new friend, diarrhea. This is when the six-inch-wide rectangle in the floor came into full play. The person occupying the rectangle couldn't sit down, he had to straddle, bending his knees and leaning his body forward to balance himself.

In these crowded circumstances where one couldn't move his face more than a couple of feet from somebody's hairy old thing to begin with, privacy was a forgotten word. Don had our new friend real bad. We didn't have a watch, but at the time I would have bet a sizable sum that Don muscled his way to our lower ventilator every fifteen minutes. He would let fly, time after time, until it was getting on the others' nerves. In the daytime there was just enough light to see this almost constant stream of slightly used rice, so we could keep from getting splashed too much, but during darkness it was impossible to get away by merely the use of one's ears and nose. Somehow, I was reminded of half-melted gold nuggets being poured out of a ladle.

I can never forget Brownie, or his accent, and what he did in these trying times. He was unusually neat. He became so frustrated after one of Boyle's bowel explosions he began to lecture him. At the same time he was lecturing he was busy scraping some of the nuggets that had overshot their mark with his bare hands. The rest of us started laughing as we watched Brownie pushing this stuff into the hole while he talked on. He said: "For goodness sake, Boyle, why don't you stop overeating for

265

just a little while? You're not getting much good out of this food; can't you see for yourself?"

Two other American prisoners were brought into camp two nights after that task-force raid on Truk. They had been picked up on some coral reefs where they had been able to conceal themselves for a couple of days after being shot down in the raid. One of these new prisoners was out of his head, delirious, and they beat him. They beat him many times and then finally packed him out. I imagine they shoved him in a hole somewhere and covered him up.

But the other American prisoner was placed alone in the cell next to ours and we whispered to him through a crack in the adjoining wall many times. We could also hear the guards beat him unmercifully outside his cell several times. At night we could peek through the bamboo matting against the lanterns out of doors and saw he was a big redheaded guy, and the Nips were whacking him with clubs approximately two inches thick. Of course we finally learned his name through the crack in the wall, without the guards ever knowing. And we heard him tell the guards who were beating him: "Why should I tell you anything? You are going to kill me anyhow."

When we communicated through the crack in the wall, I suggested a few things I knew would make it a lot easier for the poor guy. I suggested: "You might try talking to them, Red. You don't have to tell them any secrets. Just feed them a good line of bullshit, it works just as well. But stick as close to the truth as you think wise, so you can remember what you said, because they will keep on questioning you."

"Is that what you fellows did?"

"They will beat you to death if you don't pass the time of day with them. I found out they're funny that way."

"Who are you?"

"Boyington, 214."

"Pappy?"

"That's what they call me. What's your name and outfit, Red?"

"Now ain't this something. Everybody thinks you're dead, and I have to go to all this trouble to find you alive. I'm George

266

Bullard. I was Butch O'Hare's exec until he was killed, then I took over his squadron."

"Gosh, I never heard about that, what happened?"

"It was an accident. He was joining up on some TBFs at night. One of the rear gunners thought he was a Jap and shot him down. We never found him."

I knew Butch, he was my kind of guy, and I was truly sorry to learn about him. I recalled at least one occasion that fate had seen fit to change her mind. She had dealt a lousy hand to start with but smiled when she saw the guy had the guts to draw to it, leaving him a royal flush for his nerve.

He had been unable to take off with the rest of the carrier fighters because of engine trouble, and the others had gone on without him. Later, after they were out of sight, he had gotten his engine going and took off, intending to join up on the others when he located them. But instead of finding his own planes he found five Nip torpedo planes shortly after taking off, and he joined up on these. He was able to shoot down all five; he just barely nailed the last one as it was making its final approach on his own carrier. Naturally, everybody aboard the carrier loved the guy, and along with it he became the first American to become ace on a single hop.

There were some sour-grape versions made by pilots who didn't happen to be around at the time, concerning the spectacular achievement, but I discounted these completely, for I knew what kind of a person Butch was. As a matter of fact, I have heard derogatory remarks made, whether there was any basis for them or not, about every pilot who ever did anything important.

However, there is really only one case about which I can speak with authority, and that one is my own. I will have to admit that there is a sound basis in what they say about me. There was a particular crack I had heard in a Navy bar out in the islands before I was shot down, and it came from an officer who was obviously more drunk than I was at the time. Not knowing that I happened to be standing in this crowded island club, or even what I looked like, he said:

"I have searched the seven seas, but never have I been fortunate enough to run into one enemy plane. How is it that some drunk like Boyington decides he feels well enough to even go on a mission, and without even looking runs into all the luck? He is surrounded by Japs, and has to shoot his way out to get back to the free brandy to cure his hangover."

As a general rule it had been my habit of clobbering a gent for such a remark. I believe the only reason I let this guy off the hook was that he was drunk and I felt sorry for the dumb bastard. Besides, I couldn't take the time out because these clubs didn't serve more than a couple of hours.

Suyako came out to see us twice during our stay at Truk. One time a few clouds begrudgingly released a few drops of moisture while he was at the prison, and he talked the guards into permitting the six of us out in this light rain.

How relative things appear cannot be repeated too often, as far as I am concerned. If you could have witnessed the delighted faces, the laughing, and cavorting around by the six of us in this light sprinkle. How we scrubbed the moisture into our naked bodies. How we pointed our swollen, opened lips heavenward, cupping our filthy hands around them to try and receive more moisture in our parched mouths.

At last Suyako came with good news: we were to leave Truk, and probably the most uncomfortable existence I have ever experienced. The reason for the lengthy stay, as he explained, was that the task force had destroyed every piece of available transportation, and we had to wait for some to come in from the north. What a job they must have done, we thought, without trying to show any outward emotion.

Again we were blindfolded and our hands tied loosely together for a change. We were riding in a regular twin-engine passenger plane, a DC-3, or somebody had stolen the blueprints.

Should ever I return to Japan any of these days or years, one of my biggest novelties would be in knowing just how I was going to get there, or exactly where I was day by day while traveling. For on that first trip, while being flown from island to island, we were not told anything. All we could do was try to guess where we were and try to remember our geography.

Our first stop was overnight at what we presumed to be the island of Saipan, and I still think it was. After landing we were taken away from the airstrip about four or five miles and put into a chicken coop. Here we were kept overnight with several guards with bayonets guarding us in the chicken coop. During my brief stay at Saipan life began to take on a new look. I was served my first civilized meal in over two months. The fact that the last of the booze had been sweated out of me at Truk might have had a great deal to do with this good feeling.

The farmhouse adjoining our chicken coop was occupied by a Japanese warrant officer and his family. He was a kind, gentle person who insisted that we were fed properly. I know this because we were introduced to him by Suyako, who interpreted this man's words of friendliness. He said: "I would like to have you meet the man who is responsible for all this. He says he would like to explain a few things to you."

"Okay with us, anything after a meal like this."

"I'm not able to translate the exact words, but I will give you the message as best I can. He says he would like to have you know the majority of the Japanese are ashamed of the way you are being treated, but to have faith, because the horrible war shall be over before too long. Then we shall all be friends again."

For some reason I believed this man, I was satisfied that he was sincere and honest. As I watched the stars in the universe above me that night, as long as I could remain awake, I felt calm and comparatively happy. It was truly a heavenly sleep I had, among the leavings of the barnyard fowl, and I didn't begrudge the henhouse folk a single thing. Prior to this point in my life I never dreamed it possible to feel that a Japanese could be a true friend, a friend of mankind. So I was not saying good-by with my tongue in my cheek. For my money the warrant officer and his wife and children, who waved good-by to us as we left the farm, were a swell family in anybody's world. Even Suyako was so touched he forgot the blindfolds until we were driving on the airstrip. When he suddenly noticed this, he said: "For gosh sakes, put on your blindfolds or I'll be the one that's in hot water." We complied with grins.

His attitude had changed gradually since leaving Rabaul,

and by that time we regarded him much the same as a drill sergeant, because he yapped only when he thought somebody was looking our way. I had the feeling he must have thought we were his permanent wards after saving our lives and keeping the Japs from beating us up. Under these circumstances he had done his best to see that we were watered and fed.

The night after Saipan we spent at—well, I was not to learn the name of the island until after the war. Then, while being flown home, I happened to recognize a picture of the island while thumbing through a magazine. The island was Iwo Jima. In the picture I recognized Mount Suribachi. We had been kept in an open board-covered lean-to overnight at its foot, and anybody who ever has seen the volcanic cone that is Mount Suribachi will never forget it.

The place felt so quiet, so forlorn, so desolate, while I was there. Why anybody was on it in the first place was beyond my comprehension. So you can imagine how I must have felt when later I read and saw the picture of the Marines who had taken this desolate rock. And the Marines must have thought it worth over nine hundred per cent in casualties.

We were free as the cold breeze during this evening in the little board lean-to. The guards shared their food with us, and side by side—guard and prisoner alike—we ate from some cans of plums they had opened. I remember how cold it was, and we huddled together next to a large rock that was helping to hold the lean-to off the ground. These guards also shared their cigarettes and matches with us prisoners. We smoked plenty. We didn't stop to realize how scarce cigarettes were for them.

On the next leg of the trip Suyako didn't insist that we wear the blindfolds, which didn't make me unhappy in the least. As we were waiting to take off in our DC-3, there were any number of Japanese peering through the glass windows into the plane. They were ragged, not dressed exactly like the soldiers or sailors, at least no insignia of any nature. In peering in through the windows they plastered their noses flat against the panes and just stared and stared, much the same as a little waif at home would look into a department-store window filled with toys. I asked Suyako: "What are they looking at? And who are they?"

Suyako, for lack of better words—and I'm certain he meant no insult—said: "They are workers. Same as your Seabees. We call them Hee."

"What does Hee mean?" I asked curiously after I had seen him go to the windows and shoo these lookers away, several times, but more always came back in their places.

"Hee means flies in Japanese."

I felt that this expression was quite appropriate for these people, but somehow I had the feeling that the already-industrious Seabees would double their efforts if they could have heard Suyako make the comparison to them.

That afternoon we were flown into an airport in near Yokohama. I never will know just which one it was. Then we were walked to a junction on the outskirts of the city. From there we were taken some distance by truck and part of the way by streetcar.

Now that we were on the mainland of Japan, I rather imagine they felt that it was safe to remove our blindfolds for good. I never did learn of a white man escaping, once he was on the mainland. The people in the streets and on the streetcar just gawked and gawked at us. They couldn't seem to tear their eyes away. Come to think of it, we were such a mess that people back in the United States would have gawked at us too.

During our streetcar ride we put a multitude of questions to our host, Suyako, some of which I doubted he could have answered if he had wanted to. I asked: "Where in the hell are you taking us?"

"A navy camp, Ofuna, it's a suburb of Yokohama, the same as your Hollywood in Los Angeles, where they make motion pictures in Japan." And my hopes began to rise.

After we left the streetcar we sort of marched loosely back into the hills on a dirt road. The scenery was beautiful, like being out in the wooded countryside back home. We passed one of their ancient shrines, and Suyako explained about this as best he could. And nearby we were able to listen to the tinkle of prayer sticks, a sound that went on endlessly in the clear air,

271

coming from somewhere outside of our prison stockade at all hours. Finally we approached a wooden stockade, which, except for its fragileness, reminded me of those used by early Americans to keep out the Indians. Suyako said: "Well, boys, this is it, at last. This is going to be your new home."

We all had looked forward to this, for we had been told how nicely we would be treated once we were on the mainland. I guess we rather imagined we would be back to living the way we were accustomed, like please-pass-the-salt-and-pepper, and all that sort of thing. We could see other prisoners about the courtyard. I tried to see if I could recognize any, and I was able to see just one fellow I knew when I was on the *Yorktown* prior to the war. So I yelled at him: "Hey, Junior," but he didn't return my greeting.

Suyako said: "You're not allowed to speak until you have been in camp for a while, and then the haitisons [guards] will give you permission."

"Oh no, not more of that no-speako routine?"

"Just be patient, don't get upset, they will let you talk in due time."

I never did see Suyako again, and didn't know his real name, but after I had been home a few months I received a letter from the War Crimes Commission personnel in Tokyo, and they told me that an interpreter had claimed I had given him a watch; they described it, asking me if I had given it to him. It was a pleasure to be able to write back and say:

"Yes, I gave him the watch. It was broken, so I had no more use for it, and told him he could fix it up and keep it." And I had added, "He is a good gent, treat him right, and please wish him the Season's Greetings, most sincerely, for me."

I found that Ofuna was a special camp, out here away from everything in these country foothills. This was a naval camp, the only one, and it was even unknown to their civilian population. The Japanese Navy kept about seventy to ninety prisoners there all the time. The idea was to try to make you miserable enough so that they could pry military information out of you. This went on for a year to eighteen months for each prisoner. Not every prisoner went through Ofuna, but people they thought had some special value to them were sent here. There were submarine survivors, pilots, and technicians of various kinds, besides anyone with any rank they were able to get hold of. Fortunately for us, or I should say for the rank, they never were able to obtain many of them to my knowledge.

The manner in which the health and morale in the prisoners stood up, except for odd cases, was directly proportionate to their ages. The younger seemed to take it easier without too much consequence, while the older took it much harder with a great many aftereffects. Most of the older ones died off shortly after the war was over.

I wasn't exactly a spring chicken, but there were several reasons, in spite of my wounds, why my health took an upsurge under these circumstances. One of the main reasons, and I knew it then, was that I was finally placed on the water wagon whether I liked it or not. My health has always been remarkable when I leave the booze alone.

Another reason, I know now, despite my age then, was that I possessed the emotional growth of a child. So, barring no one, I was about as young-acting as anyone Camp Ofuna ever held.

CHAPTER **27**

MERELY THE CHANGE of scene was relief enough for
me, for all my life I counted upon some new geographical location as a solution. But in a very short time, I recall, Ofuna
turned out to be the same as any other locale I had ever been
in. It wasn't until the last couple of years that I came to the conclusion that every place had to be the same.

My previous opinions of the Japanese people, gathered from
propaganda, stories, and my own imagination, were changing
gradually. One item: I had thought that the Japs were a filthy
lot, but they turned out to be the cleanest race of people I have
ever run into. They saw that our living quarters were clean and
sanitary. Of course we prisoners did the physical effort in this
idea of theirs. They even made the prisoners keep their persons
clean when they saw no good reason for doing so. Truly amazing, it was, to see uneducated Nip guards have to shame some
of our American boys into cleanliness. Soap was about as precious as gold, and just about as scarce, and when a guard on
his own handed you a piece of soap, which they did on many
an occasion, you knew he was either a generous person or he
wanted to help you to remain clean.

Thank God, the chill of the winter was about over when we
arrived, for it was a process of months before one inherited

274

sufficient clothing to keep halfway warm. Our wooden cell block was unheated but served to protect us from the wind and rain and snow. We rolled up in the cotton blankets the Japanese issued us and slept on straw mats. As a matter of record, it became quite a healthy way of life for me and others; I never had a cold during the entire twenty months without heated quarters, or shoes most of the time.

Our particular little detachment of six arrived in the latter part of March 1944 and was not transferred out of Ofuna until the following year, April 1945. Very few prisoners died in this camp. The few that did had internal injuries of some nature when they were captured, and of course the Japanese would do nothing about such cases. A man with an internal injury was just sunk, that's all there was to it.

I tried to explain briefly earlier because I realized I would be using later a couple of words freely. The words "prisoner" and "captive" have different meanings, especially in Japan at this time, but it was not until we reached Ofuna that we became fully conscious of our status—or the difference in status. We were all warned that we were special captives of the Japanese, and that we were not prisoners of war, and that we would not be entitled to the privileges of prisoners of war. We were to be held strictly off the books, the sort of thing the Bureau of Internal Revenue dislikes so much. In other words, the Japanese did not notify our government through the Swiss that we were alive. To our people back home or anyone else we remained missing in action or dead. This is the reason nobody knew about my existence until fourteen days after the war was over.

One of the most aggravating things about this special category was the rule governing our food rationing: we were allowed a three-quarter portion of that assigned to a prisoner of war. As time went on, the other so-called benefits that a prisoner of war received became minor to us in comparison to this differential in food.

I realize that books about the war may be considered old stuff now, and I further realize that war books may once again come into their own after the customary lapse of time following any war. But my point in all this is not to put out just

275

another war book, for, God knows, I realize as well as anyone else how people on all sides hate war, and it is an ugly word. But in regard to this secret camp of Ofuna, suburb of Yokohama and formerly a film colony similar to our Hollywood, I would not be doing my duty to the all-around records of war if I didn't tell about it. Nor is it my fault, nor the fault of any of the other Americans who were held in secret there, that we did not through some miracle get out in time to let our story be known to the country when such stories were considered "hot." It was not our fault that we did not get out of Japan, or were rescued, or some such thing, before the war was over. Even now I hear it said again and again to me (and I am getting a little weary of the same old disc): "But, Boyington, the whole trouble with you is you're so late." It is almost as if I, or some of the other American captives there, were now being accused of not having had our Japanese guards furnish us with carrier pigeons or radio sending sets. But, be as it may, I haven't seen anything a ghost writer has written that has taken care of my memories, or I damn sure wouldn't bother you.

My main point is beyond all this: it is to show, in describing Ofuna, how people, any people, Japanese or Americans, behave under certain circumstances, and how any people, Americans or anybody else, may be expected to behave again in the wars coming up.

In this camp we called Ofuna none of the Japanese personnel of the camp was supposed to be able to speak English. They didn't want any Japanese around there who spoke English because they were afraid they might tell us how the war was going and therefore get less information out of us captives. The only Japanese who spoke English were the visiting intelligence officers who came out two or three times a week to call the boys into the interrogating room to ask them questions. I went through this routine thirteen months.

I thought that the prime requisite of being a guard there was to pass a minus-one-hundred in an I.Q. test, because these guards surely were some of the dumbest scoundrels on the face of this earth. We never were able to get any written rules from them. All the rules were in oral Japanese, and if the guards felt like beating us up or anything, all they had to do was talk fast, so fast that we couldn't understand what was being said, and then, because we couldn't we were accused of one thing or another and then punished by being struck in the face while standing at attention, usually until the guard got tired. If the guard thought the offense was bad enough, he would haul us out in the courtyard and have all the other captives line up and then he would get what was the equivalent of a baseball bat. You would be ordered to stand there with your feet apart, your hands raised in the air as in a stick-up, and then he would swing at your backside with this baseball bat and, believe me, one would gather the impression that he didn't give a damn whether he struck out or not.

I believe I got the worst beating I ever had just about one week after I was able to stand up on my feet without the aid of a crutch. Because of my infected wounds I spent my first six months as a captive lying in a heap of my own stinking bandages in the corner of my cell. But after I was out of this, and still using one crutch, I was taken out in a circle and beaten with a baseball bat. Baseball bat is a descriptive term, but the only difference actually was that these bats did not have "Spaulding" on them.

The guard who had accused me of the rule infraction had selected a club that was too long and too heavy for him to swing, so he tired quickly. He had also consumed a considerable amount of energy in his explosive fit of rage, much the same as a boxer who loses his temper in the ring. Because of the combination of errors I had counted on Lady Luck letting me off easy, but another guard noticed his mistakes, and after selecting a bat he could swing more readily he spelled his friend off. And the fresh recruit with the smaller bat and the even temper really and truly made old Daddy-oh feel like pulling leather. Of course, it is true that I didn't feel physical pain like some of the other prisoners. Mental worry had always been the painful thing in my odd make-up.

During the latter portion of the beating the only thing I could think of doing was to keep giving a sort of prayer to God for the power to keep standing on my feet. I had seen many boys

277

fall down unconscious and I did not want to let this particular
Nip guard think he could make me fall. When they were
through pounding me, my accuser drew a small circle in the
dirt, about two feet in diameter, and told me in Japanese to
stand at attention in this circle until nightfall. Then for the
additional benefit of the other guards, and prisoners who were
forced to witness this, "Swivel Neck," the guard, went on
screaming at the top of his lungs in Japanese:

"Now, now, do you understand that you have to obey the
Nippon Rules? You fool. You idiot. Don't you understand Nip-
pon is all-powerful? Do you understand? Do you understand?
Do you understand?"

I recall looking down, as I was standing at rigid attention,
into this infuriated guard's evil face, oblivious of the faces of
my fellow-prisoners. I had apparently answered this jerk because he had been so insistent upon screaming: "Do you understand," that saliva from his mouth had flown into my face and
I couldn't wipe it off while remaining at attention.

I wasn't to learn until several days after this beating, when
"Prune Face" Flynn, an Australian pilot, came near me and
talked out of the corner of his mouth to avoid being spotted by
the guards. Even the Allies were given nicknames we figured
befitted their appearance or actions. He said: "You know something, Pappy? I had you Americans figured out all wrong because I hated you for running around with our women."

"So . . . why the change of heart, Prune Face?"

"I'd like to take it all back after the way you answered Swivel
Neck when he asked you: 'Do you understand.' "

"I don't recall. What did I say?" For I had said part of it in
Japanese and part in English.

"You said, watashi wackaru, watashi wackaru, now go f——k
yourself, little man."

Then I realized that I had used a very common word in the
Australian vocabulary, and the only reason I had used it—I
was aware that Swivel Neck did not appreciate its meaning—was
merely what I had wished him to do.

So there I stood, in my confined circle.

But every time Swivel Neck wasn't looking I couldn't resist

glancing over my shoulder, as if something else was back there bothering me, almost disconnected from me, and it was my own old butt sticking out there about a foot. All the blood in your body rushes to the crushed portion.

In this camp every time one of us wanted to go to the latrine we had to look up a guard and bow from the waist and ask him in polite Japanese for permission to go to the latrine. On the diet we had there we often had to go many times a day. When we got through with the latrine, we had to look up the guard, bow politely from the waist again, and thank him in polite Japanese.

I have often thought what a pity it was that neither Lard nor Chennault could see the obstinate Boyington being subjected to some real discipline for a change. Somehow I thought they might enjoy it.

The first thing each morning all the captives were routed out and we had to stand in a long formation in the courtyard and turn to the direction of Tokyo, the Emperor's palace. The guard spewed the command and we would all bow as one to the Emperor. But if the poor Emperor only could have heard some of the comments we mumbled about him. Or if the guards had heard, they never would have asked us to bow again. They would have slaughtered us all instead, no doubt.

These formations, though, taught me something about ducks, or at least something about a certain duck. I had not known before that ducks are imitative creatures. Maybe all ducks are not, but this one I have in mind certainly was a mimic.

Outside of our cell block was a pool of water to be used in case of fire, and the duck swam around in it. The guards called the duck Gaga, and gave it quite a rough time. They threw it around and kicked it. Some of the guards even masturbated with it on occasions. One of its legs had been broken, and some captive had patched it up with splints. So the duck itself walked with a limp, the same as so many of the rest of us did who had been shot down.

Every morning when we had to fall out in formation to bow to the Emperor, this duck would limp along with us limping captives, and would get in the formation too, and always at the end of the line. And when we bowed, the duck would watch us and then bob its head too. Morning after morning of this, and it seemed almost unbelievable to all of us.

As I sit here writing, in the year of our Lord, 1957, my thoughts cannot help wonder how some other human beings are faring right at this moment. I know there are still some Americans, as well as many others who are forced to bow against their wills. Many are held in plain captivity, the same as I was in Japan. I wonder if they have a duck, or something that is ordinarily thought of as being unimportant, with which to rest their tortured brains a moment while they are praying and worrying if anyone will ever free them. I wonder if there are sufficient good people among the bad that are cracking the whip of submission over their heads.

No, I am not telling you how to think. But I know what happiness means to me at last. And it's not being satisfied by living within myself. I could never find true happiness until I made an honest attempt to help others. So, it is little wonder that I came to the conclusion that the world will never stand a chance of being happy until the last human being is taken out of captivity.

The years have taught me something I should have known in the beginning: never to generalize authoritatively about races or peoples. Even today some lecturers and some writers who should know better still do this sort of thing. They will imply such thoughts as: "All Russians are . . ." or "All Frenchmen are . . ." or "All Englishmen are . . ." or even "The Japanese are . . ."

Whenever people ask me today about the Japanese, I rather suppose I am expected to hate them, all of them, and largely because of what was done to us captives there in the camp of Ofuna. I know I am expected to brand them as primitive and brutal and stupid. But we can find right here in the United States, almost in any city in the United States, almost in any city block in the United States, people who at heart are as primitive and as brutal and as stupid as those guards with all their baseball bats. All that this type person needs to assert himself is an opportunity. Maybe the opportunity of numbers, or maybe the opportunity of getting away with it. But such people are here, nevertheless. They are all around us.

I have even generalized about the guards at Ofuna, and this is a mistake too. For finally, after we had been there a long time, four new guards came into camp and they happened to be college boys. They got into this camp through an error, I believe, because two of them could speak English: one of them quite well.

The one who spoke good English had worked for an English law firm. He passed me one day and he was covering something in his pocket. I looked and noticed a pocket Bible. I merely nodded my head that I understood, because in that league it was unlawful to admit you were a Christian. Maybe the Japanese high command didn't realize it, but their ranks were fairly well saturated with a fifth column, Christians.

This guard and the other college boys were finally transferred from the camp because they absolutely refused to beat any of us captives. Not only that, but this one guard who spoke such good English used to be beaten by his superiors at night, and partly because he would not beat us. I witnessed many of those beatings he received because at the time I was working in the kitchen and went to bed long after the rest of the captives did. So, while walking back from the kitchen, I could see some of the beatings.

One night this guard came down to the cell block, woke me up, looked up and down the aisle to see if any of the other guards were around, and then said he wanted to talk to me.

I answered: "Why, sure, it's all right with me."

Then he said: "You know, I never have told you boys anything about the war, have I?"

I answered: "No, you haven't."

He asked: "But you know that I am being beaten for it?"

I said: "Yes," that I knew and "I'm very sorry about it."

"Well," he continued, "the way I look at it, it doesn't make a damn bit of difference if I tell what is going on in this war. As long as they won't believe I am just trying to better my English by talking to you, I might just as well go ahead and tell you the whole story."

From then on he was the best source of military information we ever had hoped for. Even after he was transferred from the camp he used to come back and visit. He would come into the kitchen, where I was tending one of the fires. He would sit down on his heels, and if anybody came by, he would pretend to be lighting a cigarette. If nobody came by, he would have a stick going in the dust on the cement floor, showing me all the front lines in Germany, just what was being taken. He would tell me all about what was going on in the Pacific, and in April 1945, just before I was transferred from the camp, and the last time I ever saw him, he told me that our own forces would be on the main islands by September.

I said: "What about your navy? Can't it stop them?"

He answered: "No. Our navy is shot. There is practically nothing left of it."

It was a strange thing that when I used to talk with him I never thought of him as a Jap, as I thought of the other guards. He was one of the sweetest and nicest fellows I ever have known. He told me once that he hated to sleep in the guardhouse.

He said: "I don't have anything more in common with the guards in there than the man in the moon. I like it much better being with you boys."

He had been an orphan, he told me, and had been raised by some missionaries, he and his sister.

We had another reason for nicknaming most of the guards because they were hesitant to give out their real names. In fact, when we asked them, several of them said that they were not supposed to tell us. This Christian guard was one of the three guards in Japan who ever told me his full name. And although I had an occasion to correspond with him, among others who should not have been involved in the war-crimes procedure, I hesitate to mention this swell fellow's name for fear that some of his own people might not understand.

Some of the guards, as I mentioned before, we nicknamed after their characteristics. For example, the one who forever was beating us we called "The Slugger." Another one we called "Indian Joe" because he had all the appearances of a cigar-store

Indian. Another one we called "Flange Face" because his face had all the appearances of a flange, expressionless. And then there were some names that, God knows, I would consider too repulsive to put into a book.

One of the four college boys we called "Little Lester." We named him this after the character in a comic strip, for Little Lester was a shriveled-up, sawed-off runt. He could not have been more than four foot six. He was one of the boys who never struck any of the captives and was finally taken out of the camp. He had gotten me to one side one day and we had a little heart-to-heart chat. His English was not too good, so we mixed up a little Japanese in the conversation. He told me that the four of them were going to leave the camp, and I said: "Well, gosh, I am very sorry," for it was such a pleasure to have someone around who would not slug you all the time.

He said: "I will tell you why I don't believe in beatings."

"How is that?" I asked.

"Well," he began, "the four of us college boys don't believe in striking people to begin with. In addition to that, I look at it another way, too. I can't see any reason why I should strike you boys because in a short time I am going to be a prisoner and you boys are going to be the guards. So I would be an absolute fool should I strike any of you."

CHAPTER **28**

GOOD NEWS AND BAD NEWS seem to accompany each other so closely that we almost could imagine that they get together on their tricks ahead of time.

Good News to Bad News: "I'll go first today, and you come immediately afterward and give the wallop."

Bad News to Good News: "Okay. And don't worry how far you build him up, because you know I can carry him to the depths again."

This still seems to be the way of it, even here at Burbank, only it doesn't bother me any longer. One phone call may be something pleasant, and the next phone call what I used to term a smash in the face. The phone not ringing at all used to bother me, but that is no longer a problem with me. Now I am able to appreciate that everything has a definite purpose, whether I am momentarily pleased the instant it is thrown at me or not.

Looking back over my life, I wanted so many things, and I struggled so hard, always in spurts, to achieve my so-called desires, which weren't what I wanted at all.

I suppose, for instance, a fellow should feel happy when being informed that he has been awarded the Congressional Medal of Honor. But under the circumstances in which I first

284

was informed the announcement could have meant my death warrant. Nor did I realize that I wouldn't even appreciate later on this so-called honor in the slightest, and it would remain in the dust in our garage along with other things I don't know what to do with—or where else to put them.

In this secret intimidation camp of Ofuna I must repeat that the idea there was to make you feel miserable enough so that you would give military information on your own country. That was the sole purpose of the camp. With the "Quiz Kids," as we called our visiting interrogators, I thought I had been getting along all right because of the original lies I had told about my past. When first captured I had been unable to give a phony name because my own, "Major G. Boyington, USMC," was stenciled too plainly in yellow letters on the back pack brought aboard the submarine. So I had told my right name, hoping desperately that the Nips would not be able to connect it up in any way. Everything went on fine, and they finally stopped beating me in Rabaul for information. Also, I had given them this story: That I was an operations officer and merely gone along for the ride. Due to my inexperience and inability as a flyer, unfortunately, I was shot down, and that I had no Nip planes to my credit.

But now here in this camp of Ofuna I suddenly was summoned once again into the "Quiz Kids' Room," and saw a new interrogator facing me. He turned out to be a Princeton graduate, a captain in the Japanese Navy, and he told me to be seated. He was cordial—far too cordial, I thought.

He fumbled around in his brief case, hauled out a typewritten sheet of paper, and then went on shuffling around in his brief case as though he had misplaced something.

After a pause he said to me: "I thought this might be of interest to you, Major."

I looked at what he was showing me, and saw emblazoned in ink: "Major Gregory Boyington, United States Marine Corps, awarded the Congressional Medal of Honor . . ." and so on, and so on, along with the number of Japanese planes I had been credited with before being shot down and lost for keeps, and altogether far too much about my past. I always had

285

guarded my conversation about China, knowing that the Japanese would consider it more than legal to shoot me if they ever discovered I had once been a Flying Tiger.

So now, with all this evidence confronting me, I could not look up from the desk. I merely sat there staring at the paper.

Finally this intelligence officer, graduate from Princeton, looked up and said: "Well, Major, what have you to say about this? Is this true? Or is it false? Your story that you have been giving us and this radio broadcast from the United States do not exactly jibe, Major."

Finally I came up with a feeble answer: "There must be some mistake. That couldn't be me."

In the meanwhile the captain had located his other piece of paper in the brief case and said: "Then, do you happen to know a Mrs. Grace Hallenbeck from—I can't pronounce it . . ."

"Okanogan, Washington," I rather blurted out without thinking, for he was talking about my mother, and, needless to say, Mom had been in my thoughts more than once.

"Thank you for the kind assistance. Now, who is the woman?"

"She is my mother. Is she well, or has something happened to her?"

"Quite well, Major. As a matter of fact it states here that she has christened a new carrier in your honor, and wishes it Godspeed, to hurry up and end the war."

I thought, of course, that I would be beaten to death out in the courtyard, or face a firing squad, or whatever they had in mind. And I had resigned myself after hearing this, so I smiled and said: "You'll never know how nice it is to hear about Mom. It's great to learn that my gal is still working, even if her dumb son is hors de combat, forever."

Then this intelligence officer said: "You know, you don't have to lie to us. There are a lot of us around here who know just what the score is. I've spent many years in the United States personally. I was in the Japanese Embassy in Washington, D.C.

"But do you know something else?" he added: "Do you know that we appreciate a hero here in Japan even though he's from another country?" Then he offered me a cigarette, which I gathered up with shaking fingers.

After that I was dismissed from the Quiz Kids' Room, but only temporarily. And I still did not know what was being cooked up on my behalf or what their game finally would be. A few days later I learned from one of the Japanese non-commissioned officers in the camp just exactly what they did know about me, that the radio broadcast had been true, even though it was hard for me to believe. This Nip non-commissioned officer, strictly against his orders, further told me on the sly: "They've got a stack of papers"—and he motioned off the ground—"about three feet high. They've got your pictures, everything about you, magazines and everything."

While I was busy thinking: "Oh, Lord!"

This Nip chief laughed and said: "Your pictures look a lot different than you do now." With this he blew up the cheeks of his face to try to show me what I used to look like, and giggled again.

I must say, though (and I could take what confidence I could get out of it), that heretofore I had not been treated badly by any Japanese who spoke good English. And in my case this turned out to be true all during my captivity. Practically without exception everyone of these people who spoke English, especially the ones educated in America, all treated us well. They did not go out of their way to do us a lot of favors, and perhaps they could not. But, as far as I know, they were against having any of us beaten if they could help it.

And the navy captain, the intelligence officer, turned out to be one of these. When next he called me into the Quiz Kids' Room, he asked whether I knew that he spoke the truth when he said that he knew every admiral. I thought that he did because he described their appearances, but he didn't really know them. He wanted to know what I knew about each one. He asked me to write it down, but I told him that I couldn't. I said: "I've only met one personally and didn't talk to him for any length of time."

He wanted to know which admiral that was. I said that was Admiral Halsey. His face lighted up. He was very interested.

He said: "Please write down all you know about Admiral Halsey."

I said: "It wouldn't use up much paper, writing down all about what I learned during my conversation with Admiral Halsey. He's a man's man, that's about all I could write."

The intelligence officer's face dropped in disgust and he answered: "Well, skip it, then. That we know."

So for the time being that sort of ended that.

Another thing we heard from practically everyone we talked with over there was that after the war was over things would be different; we would all be allowed to go home; they really had nothing against any of us. We were all right, but there were some things that had to be done when this war was over: Roosevelt had to be hanged, MacArthur had to be hanged, and Halsey had to be hanged. And little did I realize that the reverse, as far as executions were concerned, was going to take place in time, sparing only the Emperor, whom we bowed to for diplomatic reasons.

Today, as I continue seeing more and more evidence of the United States being sold short not only to the world but also to her own people, I keep thinking of some of our own American kids back there in the camp of Ofuna and wish they had more say in today's matters. For those boys, ragged and starved though they were, would still do anything for a laugh or a joke, even if they were beaten afterward for the joke or for laughing. They are the types of kids who make Americans seem great people; they are such a contrast to the ambitious sourpusses who, during the war, held down so many of the bureau jobs here at home, and are still holding them down, and will want to continue holding them—even if it means the continuation of bureaus we no longer need. Even if it means the continuation of all these paid people still making the personal judgments for us—what we should eat, when and how; what foreign countries we should be good to, when and how; what we should think and when we should think it.

But these people themselves, or at least most of them, have never been put on a physical spot for their country. And by physical spot, I mean just that, a predicament in which day by day they were hurt physically, pounded by clubs, and just simply because they were Americans. And that, after all, was the real hurting test put up to those kids. And when they came through it, or survived it, they would do what all good Americans are expected to do: they would try to save their own sanity by their own sense of humor.

And this is certainly not something being tried today by people in a position to try it. So ambitious are they to remain Little Caesars, the same as they remained Little Caesars at home throughout World War II and Korea, that today they have forgotten how to laugh. Or never did know how to laugh. But more than that, they give nobody else credit for knowing how to laugh, or even how to make up his own mind about his own things when these things happen to be bad.

Those starved, ragged kids back in camp had more individuality than that. And because they had it they are what Americans are supposed to be, and they are what I like to think *real* Americans still are: people who through the years were able to take it on the lam, laugh about it, then take it again—but always going forward on their own individual guts.

As captives, and not prisoners of war, we were not allowed issues of clothing or anything else. I knew that the boys were going half nuts with nothing to do, just trying to talk in small groups. But every time two or three of us got together in a group, we would be broken up. We were not allowed to talk to any new prisoners who came into camp. All equipment for whittling or anything like that had been taken away from us.

But, to show how the boys would still do anything for a joke, there was one ragged prisoner who had something that looked like a piece of shingle. He made a hole through it with a piece of glass and shoved a stick through the hole. By asking different guards the time throughout the day he had made what he called a sundial.

Any time any of us were busy doing anything, a guard would come up and give us the famous old expression, *"Nunda!"* which in our language means "What the hell's going on here?"

The boys would then try to explain to the Japanese what was going on. This boy with the shingle explained: "When you captured us, you took all our watches. We had nothing to tell time with, so I am making a sundial."

He demonstrated the thing. He put it down on the ground. "Here are the sun signs down here. See this mark I have here? It is such and such a time."

The guard was a very important person, but actually he was one of the most illiterate Japanese. But the watch and the sundial he understood. And we could just hear the machinery ticking around in his mind. He asked the prisoner in Japanese: "That is well enough—but what are you going to do when the sun isn't out?"

This gave the kid a good idea. He was, as I said, half starved, he had been beaten and was in rags, never knew what was going to happen afterward in Japan, whether he was ever going to get home. But nevertheless he couldn't resist what he did. He told the guard: "I am happy you brought that up, Haitison. If the sun isn't out, all you have to do is strike a matchee, understand?"

"Match" is approximately the same word in their language as in ours.

"Then," the kid continued, "you hold the matchee over the sundial and you can tell the time even in the dark."

The guard, a very savvy person, nodded judiciously and said: "*Ah so ka* [I understand]."

The rest of us small group of prisoners, who had been watching as the boy explained, now walked off to other parts of the courtyard and left the guard staring at this sundial. He stared at it for five minutes or so while we watched to see if he would realize that he had been duped. It wasn't difficult to read this guard's mind when he finally had come to a conclusion. He did not come back to the prisoner. He just walked away, because it would have been loss of face, as Madame Chiang would say, if he had jumped up and charged the prisoner at that time. He let it go until three or four days later, when he accused the boy of doing something he hadn't done, and then jumped him.

There is one thing I want to emphasize: I've seen American prisoners tortured, but I never have heard one cry out. I've heard them moan when they were knocked senseless or just about senseless, but I've never heard one of them cry out.

Yet if we supplied the guards with the entertainment of beating us, they in turn supplied us with some dilly entertainment of their own.

One of the guards we had in this camp was short, even for a Japanese. The average was around five feet two inches, but he was shorter than that. Anybody could tell when he came on duty that he had been given orders from his higher-ups that, because all of us were desperadoes, he would have to watch us with an eagle eye. When he came on duty he would walk back and forth before our cell blocks, and if we were allowed out on the grounds, he would come by us and just glare at us. He had a rifle with a shiny bayonet, and at any simple request we made he immediately would say: *"Domai,"* which is like "no dice" in our language. In other words, that was bad. And if a prisoner persisted in his request, such as going to the toilet, this guard would stomp his foot and threaten the prisoner with that bayonet and go through the whole procedure of saying no.

But then, as with so many of the guards, curiosity finally got the better of him. He couldn't resist it, and on coming on guard duty the third or fourth time he started to question one or two of us. The questions he asked went something like this: "Where are you from?" We would say: "From the United States." Then he would want to know if we had mothers and fathers, if we were married, if we had any babies.

To the Japanese it was very intriguing if we were married or had babies. They were amazed that a lot of our boys were only nineteen, married, and had babies. In their world they are over thirty before they are able to support a wife and have a piece of ground or have any children.

Conversations invariably ended up with our motion-picture industry. The guard would ask: "So you know So-and-So, and So-and-So?" Clark Gable, Betty Grable, and so forth. We knew some of them. Or, I should say, I knew some of them. Then the guard would mention a lot of names and ask if I knew *them,* and some I had not even seen on the screen or anywhere else. I bet I was knocked down on my hind end at least a dozen or more times because the guard would ask me about different movie actors and actresses I didn't know, and he would end up by saying: "Why, you stupid major!" And haul off and clunk me on the jaw.

I stood up and took all this stuff for many months, but finally I got wise and found out it was just as well to fall down the first time they hit you because ordinarily then they would leave you alone. They would not kick you. I guess they thought they were very powerful on one swing. As long as it made them happy to feel strong I was just as well off.

I remember another guard who had been of the most ferocious type. If we asked to go to the toilet, he would stomp at us like a bull, point his bayonet at us, and threaten us. But after we had ceased to ask for permission to go to the toilet, or whatever we wanted to do, he would take out a pocket mirror and admire his handsomeness. Every now and then he would make a face in the mirror, then he would look at you with this ferocious face he had just put on, and then put the mirror back in his pocket.

Another time in the prison courtyard, after one of them had shown great interest in the movies, he handed his rifle and shiny bayonet to one of our half-starved boys. We had watched this guard for hours oiling and polishing his rifle and bayonet, but now he handed the whole thing over to a prisoner and took out a handkerchief and made a mask out of it. Then he mounted a make-believe steed. The guard's legs, which never had been astride a horse, were bowed so badly by nature as to make it appear that he had ridden the range since birth. The horse he mounted must have been two hands shorter than any Shetland pony I ever have seen. He galloped down to the end of the courtyard, some two hundred feet away from the group of prisoners, including the prisoner holding the shiny rifle and bayonet, and then came galloping back. He mercilessly spurred his imaginary steed with a pair of ill-fitting military shoes with outboard sloping heels, slid to a halt in front of us, got off the imaginary horse, took five or six quick steps away from the crowd, and spun on both of his sloping heels. Then he drew out two imaginary six-shooters from the hip and fired in Wild

West fashion, then, pointing to his nose, he asked in Japanese: "Who am I?"

He really had us. We didn't know the vintage of the picture or anything else. We didn't know whether he was supposed to be William S. Hart, or who the hell he was.

So, when we couldn't answer, he took off his mask and put it back in his hip pocket. I guess he realized he had gone plumb "beyond the call of common guard duty" and started looking around to see if anybody superior to him was witnessing this act of his.

He went over and got his rifle and bayonet back from the prisoner, who was as weak from laughter as he was from lack of food, and then nodded curtly and thanked the prisoner for holding the rifle. With that he stomped off and left us about ten minutes of peace and quiet. And if we had been anywhere but Japan, we could have shot the poor fool with the rifle and gone over the hill.

We had a method of getting our kicks out of characters like the ones I just mentioned. They were daredevil tricks, a bit different from the flying daredevil tricks, but nevertheless with consequences that could have proven fatal, or damn rough on us, if we had been caught up with. There were several items that enabled us to do this, but the main one was that we could understand Japanese much better than they gave us credit for, while the majority of the Nips never bothered with English. Another reason for their not catching on to English is that they were rotated all the time. And when a new one came and we figured we could have some fun with him, we spared no horses.

We realized that the guards went by your tone of voice or actions, and couldn't tell from nothing if you weren't speaking their language. So we would mix up a combination of Japanese and English that, although given in a flattering tone of voice, was the foulest uncomplimentary language we could think up.

For example, one would say: *"Ohio gazemus, Haitison,"* bow to him, and be all smiles and friendliness. *"Anatawa itchie bon . . ."* This being the proper polite form of Japanese and manners, saying good morning, and that he was number-one, the best with you. A guard like the ones I have mentioned would smile in return, bow back, and say a few nice things to us in Japanese.

Then our speaker, without changing the tone of his voice or outward attitude, would go on in English: "You ape. I'll bet you're the biggest Nippon —— walloper, mother ——ing bastard I ever had the pleasure of knowing," and he would bow once again, while the guard would smile at us in an appreciative way.

While in prison camp, and for a long time afterward, I was very much in the dark, so to speak, concerning two words. I prided my ego on both of them, although I knew, even then, that my pride in one of them was not honest. These two words seem to fit in well at this point with the rest of my thoughts.

The first one is "bravery," for which I took many a phony bow, and I imagine to this day that many people still believe I was mighty brave. I mention this because I was beginning to learn the difference between daredevil and brave. In looking back over the years I wouldn't go so far as to say I have never been brave, but most of the things for which I had been given credit for bravery were nothing but daredevil stunts. I was trying to build up my own ego, trying to imitate the bravery of people I had read about or had been told about in the years gone by.

The second word, will-power, closely allied with bravery in my mind, was a thing in which I honestly prided myself, for too many years. And, needless to say, it was quite a spiritual revelation to finally get these two bothersome, ego-feeding expressions straightened out in my mind. The reason it had taken me so long a time, even though it happened to be nobody's fault but my own, was that my emotional maturity was very retarded.

Can you imagine how the air went out of me when I finally found the true meaning of will-power? Will-power means that one is going to do whatever he wants to do most at any particular time. So actually one of the things I prided myself for is really no accomplishment at all.

My definition of bravery is when a person does what he

honestly believes is the best thing for him to do at any particular time. So the majority of my life can be linked up with show-off, or daredevil. The bravest man in the world would be the man who acts as he honestly thinks best more particular times than anyone else. Little wonder, then, that so many of the true acts of bravery go unheralded, while the spectacular or daredevil antics are played up.

I'm not trying to change the world anymore—people can go on writing and thinking what they damn well please—but for my own peace of mind I have to realize the truth about myself, and not what somebody writes about me—good or bad.

CHAPTER **29**

S OME SUBJECTS ARE TIMELESS, and I would say that food is one of them. Yet only by comparing notes this way can We of the World Who Have Known Real Hunger actually get together and form our own sort of imaginary club.

Our members today would be from everywhere, from Africa, from Europe, from Asia, everywhere. But regardless of our assorted languages, regardless of our assorted politics, the members would have something far more in common than the members of most clubs do. We would at least know that the universal implement we all have, the stomach, usually behaves the same way under duress and causes us all to have much the same kinds of dreams.

Now the Japanese themselves had very little food. They had a mixture of rice and barley for their main diet. This meant even the military, who got the best food in the country. But prisoners, as we know, got far less. In Rabaul our food had been supplemented by mildewed rice that had been left in Rabaul by the Australians. Now, provided this rice had been brought in as recently as the day the war was started, it nevertheless would have been some two years old by the time I was captured. This accounted for the rice being mildewed, full of worms and everything else.

296

To go with this were odds and ends from the officers' mess. This would come to us in the form of a brew that was poured over the mildewed rice, and accounted for the reason we oftentimes found plum pits in the brew and rice. We knew that nobody had put a plum in there. Some Japanese had merely spat it out of his mouth into his plate or onto his table, and everything had been scraped off and put into a rusty can, brought out to our camp, warmed, and poured over the rice.

The food we later got in Japan consisted of a mixture of rice and barley, one of rice to twelve of barley. Then we got a hot watery soup with it, flavored with bean paste, a by-product of the soya bean. There were a few greens in it, and greens in that country consisted of carrot tops, potato peelings, and the like.

Ordinarily one would think that one heaping bowl of barley and a heaping bowl of soup, larger than any bowl of soup to be had in any restaurant, would be sufficient for any man three times a day. In bulk we actually were eating more on this diet than we would have eaten at home. But the food value just was not enough to keep a man more than alive, and he gradually lost weight, went down, down, down.

After nine months of this I weighed one hundred ten. Ordinarily I weighed one hundred eighty to ninety and had been at my normal weight when captured.

As the prisoners were going down, down in weight, it seemed to affect the minds of most of them. I know that I put myself to sleep each night by thinking of all the iceboxes I ever had seen. I thought, or tried to think, of every meal I had ever had. I would remember from my childhood, very vividly, each meal my mother cooked me that I liked. The funny part of it was that I never thought of extravagant foods, just the basic foods, anything that was simple and common. I never craved fancy desserts or anything like that, just simple food.

The other prisoners sat around, just the same as I did, and dreamed of all these foods, and then they started making recipes. This was something that always amused me.

In this camp was Louis Zamperini, the famous miler, now an evangelist, and he is of Italian descent. No doubt his mother is

297

an excellent Italian cook and knows how to make wonderful Italian foods. Some of the prisoners would show me recipes that Louie had written out, and he must have been drooling from the mouth when writing them.

The others would say of Zamperini's recipes: "I'm going to copy these things all down," and they would be busy scribbling them. We were not allowed to have pencil or paper, or be caught writing or reading, so very secretively they would write them down. They swore that when they got home they were going to have all those recipes cooked.

Once or twice I looked at these recipes and saw that Louie had put the tomatoes in at the same time as the potatoes. And anybody who has cooked at all knows that tomatoes should be left until the last. He would put butter in the first thing, and it struck me that good old Louie Zamperini had never cooked in his life. He was just the same as any of the rest of us. He merely must have remembered that his mother's Italian cooking was good, and he just dreamed that he had cooked all those things. He would swear to the high heavens, though, that he had cooked all of these dishes himself.

The meals we had were a dietitian's nightmare. Often we used to mention to each other: "Good Lord, if any dietitian ever tells me when I get back home what I should eat, I'll just say: 'Lady, or whoever you are, you are nuts!' "

Our most favored meal was a heaping dish of barley, which would be given us sometimes on special holidays, and a bowl of mashed potatoes without salt, pepper, or butter on them. Nothing but starch. Practically every meal we had was mostly starch. Later, when I got a job in the Japanese kitchen there and could see for myself, I learned for sure that the average prisoner didn't get one pound of grease, meat, or fish in a year's time.

Sometimes I was interested, far more than amused, in finding out how little it takes to keep the human body alive. All we wanted was a little more barley or a little more of this watery soup and we would have been, under those circumstances, what could be called comparatively content, I suppose. But we didn't get it.

Most people, especially in America, just simply do not know

298

what it means to spend one's days dreaming and thinking of food. It is not their fault that they do not know, and may they never have to know. But We of the World Who Have Known Real Hunger *know.* And that is why our imaginary club should be such an understanding one, between member and member.

As another idea of how hungry a human can get, once I had a soupbone as big as my fist and it took me only two days to devour all of it, completely.

Prior to being captured, if I had been told that a large hungry collie dog could have gotten away with all of a soupbone as large as this one, I would have considered the informant crazy. But I got away with it, every bit of it, within two days.

After nine months of capture—and with my weight down to almost a hundred pounds—I met one of my most unforgetable characters. She was a Japanese grandmother, and I called her "Auntie."

But the reason I am especially thinking of her this evening is, perhaps, that I have helped my wife set the table for supper. And it is always in regard to food somehow that I remember Auntie the most. The Japanese word for "Auntie" is *Obason,* and this is what I called her.

After all this time as a captive the Nips were finally through questioning me two or three times a week, and I was getting to be rather an old prisoner around the Ofuna camp. So I was given a job in the kitchen to work from four-thirty in the morning until nine o'clock at night. For my services I was allowed an extra bowl of barley and a bowl of soup a day. It happened that I was not able to get along even with this additional ration because I was lugging heavy barrels of water and sacks of rice around that weighed close to two hundred pounds. For strength to do this I had to resort to other methods.

I guess everybody is inherently dishonest in some shape or form, or manner, so I stole food. I never stole any of the prisoners' food, of course, but I stole the Japanese food, which was a great deal more nourishing, and more tasty.

I decided when I went into the kitchen after nine months of starvation that I was going to eat four times as much as any

299

Japanese guard got of the same kind of food. Many times I had to vomit it up and many times I had other troubles, such as a little diarrhea, but I maintained that diet during all the six months I was in the kitchen.

Now, due to the help of the little old civilian lady who worked there, by watching out the door to see that none of the guards was looking, and my own kleptomaniac ability, I went from my hundred or so pounds to my normal hundred ninety. I could determine my weight because in the kitchen we had some kilo scales, and the kilo is 2.2 pounds.

This little lady, who watched the door so carefully to see that no Japanese guards were around, was the only sweetheart I ever had in Japan. When I mentioned this in one of my War Bond lectures (years later in Phoenix, Arizona), with my wife in the audience, some jovial old boy said: "I bet he promised to marry her, too." He was merely keeping current with the newspapers that were busy printing the statements of some woman who said that I promised during the war to marry her, and then married someone else instead. The newspapers had a spicy story to add to my war publicity, I'll have to admit, because talking happened to be one of this girl's strong points. The trouble with me was that I had always been slightly under the influence while these conversations had been going on, so I wasn't capable of paying proper attention. But neither the newspapers nor I realized that getting sobered up in a prison camp helps one to see things in a different light, at least for a short period of time.

Well, it was all good humor, even though this little old sweetheart of mine was about sixty years old. She didn't know a word of English and she had never been outside of Japan. If any of you mothers have given things to any of the war prisoners in the United States here, you were in a way repaid, for this little old lady certainly did help me out. To her I was just a starving boy. The fact that I was from America, the outfit that was sinking her sons on land, air, and sea, had nothing to do with it.

Of course, in her conversations when the guards were around, she would damn all prisoners. The poor little old thing felt she had to do that. But when the guards were away, she would continue letting me sneak out the guards' food; although she would have been beaten too, like anybody else, if she had been caught doing this for me. So when the guards were away, she would let me walk over to their lard barrel, the stinkingest old stuff anyone could imagine. I would get some fish also. Naturally I would look around too, while doing all this, for I wasn't trusting too much on her tired old eyes, for if one of these guards had caught me it would have meant a beating session that might cost my life. I would scoop out a big handful of this stinking lard, shove it in my mouth, and gulp it down in a second. Even though it did stink, nevertheless to me it tasted like honey.

And occasionally, when very important persons were expected, they baked fish in the kitchen. To get one of these, Obason and I had to co-operate to the fullest, almost like a quarterback and a fullback on a football field. For we weren't allowed all the time we had had with the lard snatching. We had to fool a kitchen full of people. Much the same as a quarterback, Obason would nudge me, and say *"Gomen nasi, Boyingtonson,"* for the guard's benefit, which means: Pardon me, fellow, for bumping into you. I would then put a free hand down underneath a fairly high working table in the kitchen, and there in the spacious folds of Obason's apron was a hot baked fish.

The first time she ever handed me one of these hot fish I stuffed it immediately down my throat to avoid detection. The thing was so hot I had to grab the tail between my front teeth in a futile effort to stop it from sliding on down and burning my stomach. And there I stood—the tears running out of my eyes, a guard asking: *"Nunda"*—while I was pretending to blow my nose and still keep from choking on the hot fish.

The reason I needed this food of some sort was that, before I worked in the kitchen, all of us had to do compulsory athletics twice a day. And when we prisoners were bent over for our calisthenics we could hear these knee-joints, and ankle-joints and elbows snap, crackle, snap, just like a dry forest of twigs going off.

301

During those days in the kitchen we usually had a lull in the midmorning and midafternoon when the civilian cook and the guards were not there. This was when the little old lady would say to me in exceptionally polite Japanese: "Let's have a yesomai."

This meant she and I would have tea together, and in addition she would fix up a few Japanese pickles. She would get us a tiny amount of sugar, too, which was kept on hand only for those high-up naval officers who frequently visited the camp to quiz us. And she would steal a little bit of this sugar for our tea.

And it was during the winter months that I worked in the kitchen, from September to April, and it was cold, bitterly so. Yet these ovens are kind of Dutch-oven affairs, with big rice pots in them, and we would open up the oven doors. Of course, during the midmorning and midafternoon periods nothing was cooking in the ovens. The big pots merely were inside of them. So we would put a little stool in front of each oven and she would start to talk.

Only with her did I dare speak Japanese, for I never did around the guards, because we could get our war information better from them by pretending we knew nothing about their language. She was too old, or would forget, when talking to the guards about me, that I spoke practically perfect Japanese to her and understood it.

We would have this sweet tea and she would break out a little old pipe with some of this hair tobacco we had. The bowl of the pipe was about the size of the end of my little finger, and I would reach in my pocket and pull out a can and sort around for my selection of tobacco from it. My own selection of tobacco consisted of what the Japanese threw down in front of the guard stove. The tobacco consisted of snipes. But they were sanitary because I had made a cigarette holder from a piece of bamboo. I would adjust one of these snipes in the end of my bamboo holder, much like Freddie the Free-loader, and take a sliver of bamboo and reach it through the open doors that were warming us, getting a light for Obason and myself.

So we would sit there, Obason smoking her tiny pipe and

I smoking my snipe, and sipping this sweet tea. And as we sat there talking and smoking, Obason would tell me, oh, how bad that war was, and how she longed for the day when it would be over.

She would say: "You can't buy any candy, you can't get any cloth to make clothes out of." For all of these people were in rags, officers and everybody. There was hardly a person I saw in all Japan who was not dressed in rags.

On the first day, for instance, when any American was captured in the combat zone, and if these officers were without shoes, they took them. I cannot say that I blame them for that. If I didn't have a pair of shoes and captured some poor jerk, I would take his shoes too. We cannot blame each other for such things.

Anyhow, Obason said she longed for the days when the automobiles were going up and down the streets. For months before the war there was nothing but a few of those coke-burning trucks that have to be pushed up every hill, and they all carried a crew of about ten men, and every time they would come to a slight hill, they would have to shove the truck up the hill. They would go all right on the level provided they had practically no load.

Then she would ask me: "How is everything in Baykoko?" —Baykoko meaning the United States.

I was, of course, just like every other G.I. whether in England, France, Italy, Burma, or anyplace else. I liked to brag, so I said: "Oh gee, Obason, it's great. We have all the tires in the world, all the gas, everyone has an automobile he can just ride everywhere he wants, everybody has a big ranch."

I would kind of kid her because she seemed to enjoy the tales so much, so I said: "Well, how do you like that as far as you've heard? You come back and take care of my kids for me, as I don't have a wife."

Old Obason would giggle and answer: "Oh, I'm afraid you might change your mind and shove me off the boat on the way back." Wherewith she clasped her hands, dipped her knees quickly, and giggled—as she always did with a joke.

303

And this is the way we would talk over our tea and tobacco during the lulls when the guards were not around.

On several occasions two or three of Obason's daughters came around. One of them had a child strapped to her back. Her appearance was almost angelic, her actions the same. One could not believe that she was what we thought of as "Nips" or "Japs"—especially with the guards we knew in camp.

When nobody was around this daughter would say the one or two expressions she knew in English. They were "I love you," or something like that. Then she too would giggle. Of course, she didn't mean it that way, but she had heard it from motion pictures they had shown in Japan. And the baby with her, a little kid with bangs, had the appearance of an ivory doll. The complexions of the women and children are, I think, the nicest complexions in the world, nothing like our American women. The skins were as smooth as if they had just been covered with cream.

But one day I did an awful thing to Obason, and without meaning to.

The prison camp was to be visited again by some of those naval intelligence officers who came out to ply us with questions, with their $64 questions. My, how time progresses, for we now have a $64,000 question.

In preparing the meal in advance for these higher-ups Obason wanted everything just so. Her pride and joy was some China dishes, and on these dishes she carefully arranged pickles and everything, including the fish.

But the more I kept thinking of these higher-ups, and all their questions that once again might be thrown at me, the less I must have remembered Obason. These intelligence bastards would be out here in a little while trying to pump military information out of us, and so, feeling mad about it, I deliberately selected this moment to clean out the stoves, allowing the grit to go all over their food on those pretty dishes.

The old lady screamed: *"Boyingtonson, Boyingtonson. Yamai, yamai!"* which roughly means "Stop, stop!" And she screamed: *"You're getting toxon gomai!"* which roughly means "much dirt."

304

So I stopped, but it does show how, just as in all wars, the innocent must suffer just because somebody (in this case me) had a mad on.

She forgave me, but I haven't quite forgiven myself. So when I first got back to the United States and heard that some of my Black Sheep pilots were going out to Japan, I gave them Obason's address. At least, I gave the best address I knew and told them to be sure and give her some money and some candy.

Yet the most I could do—even now—would be but the smallest of tokens for her kindnesses to me.

In fact, while sitting here in the den awaiting supper, I cannot help imagine how it would be if the old lady, through some miracle, should suddenly arrive, as if out of the skies, for one of our old "teas" again. We would sit and talk and discuss and smoke. Only in my case it would not be snipes any more. And then, just when we were about to eat, she quickly would say: *"Boyingtonson, Boyingtonson, Haitison,"* which means "Look out, Boyington, the guards." Wherewith, at her joke, she would clasp her hands just as she used to do, dip her knees, and giggle.

And you can bet your hat and ass that there were many occasions when I sincerely wished I could be back sitting beside Obason in the cold in front of those Dutch ovens. Those too many times that I was pulling myself off a terrific drunk with a terrible hangover. The time that the Bureau of Internal Revenue placed liens upon all my earthly possessions until I paid the tax and interest they claimed I owed them, for the period of time I was overseas and an undeclared prisoner of war, on my service salary, which I unfortunately never received. I found that my drinking troubles amused the world on the front pages of newspapers and in magazines. Anything for a laugh, I thought, as I read my name connected with the disgrace and drinking of people I hadn't seen in years.

CHAPTER **30**

As THE YEARS GO ON, we are going to learn more and more from the Japanese, the same as they are going to learn from us—and want to learn from us. With the bars of hate and suspicion no longer existing we can regard ourselves not as nations but as people. As visitors to Japan in the future we will not be there as spies, as was thought before. All that has been cleansed away, washed off the boards, although it did take a terrible war to do it. But as visitors of the future in Japan I do hope we can show as much sportsmanship in our victory as the Japanese are in their defeat.

In our guards I was seeing the worst Japanese at their worst, and they in turn were seeing us American captives at our lowest ebb. But even so, there was always some little redeeming feature, some little laugh somewhere along with the pain, or some little new thing to be learned.

As I go through my experiences with the Japanese, I am not trying to build them up or run them down. All I am trying to do is to get across what I saw and what I know. And if some of these observations do appear to be that way, the reason is that the Japanese themselves were often contradictory—the same as we ourselves are often. We are not machines. People are not machines. But I have seen even machines be contradictory, too.

306

There was many a college professor, as well as American-educated Japanese, who had been inducted into the movement of Asia for the Asians, with the industrialized nation of Japan on top, of course. Many of this type individual were employed with a reserve military status as interpreter. And I believed the majority of them when they said they didn't have a thing to say about the matter. And were in a boat similar to ours. The Japs didn't trust them, either.

I also believed one who was educated in Chicago, and knew that he was sincere when he instructed some Chicago boys to contact certain professors in Chicago if he didn't happen to turn up after the war was over. Thank God for all these interpreters and their kindnesses.

Personally, I spent money with a lawyer here in the United States trying to help many of these people after the war. It appeared that almost all military-connected Japanese were thrown into one mass prosecuting bucket. They were tried jointly, to save time, with others who didn't belong to the same world.

One of these fellows, Jimmy, a Southern California graduate we called "Handsome Harry," did a great deal to help prisoners, especially the Americans. Many of us ex-prisoners tried to help him by writing depositions through our own lawyers to be used in his trial, but they were disregarded completely in Jimmy's case—he is still in prison in Japan.

While talking with a former American military prosecutor on the golf course here at Burbank recently, I endeavored to find the reason for their utter disregard for our statements. This fifty-year-old, self-styled playboy nauseated me, for he told about not having time to go over evidence because the prosecutors were busy with the geisha house they had built to entertain themselves while the trials were going on. He spent most of his time telling me about all the fun I missed, but added: "We went under the assumption that anybody who was educated in the United States deserved anything we could pin on him."

Anyhow, "Handsome Harry," as Jimmy was called by those who didn't know his real name, and I had many a delightful conversation during those brief intervals when we were certain we were alone. In fact, Jimmy told me right off the bat, at an intermission in my first interrogation at Ofuna: "I know you are lying like hell, Boyington, but stick to it, as it sounds like a good story. But, for heaven's sake, don't tell anyone I told you so."

"Okay, don't worry, I won't, and thanks." I thanked him even though, at first, I was certain that it was a trick of some kind. It didn't turn out to be one at all, but I might mention that I didn't trust very many people then, as one might have gathered by now. Jimmy said much the same to others in Ofuna, but for fear of his own safety he wasn't going about making such statements at random. His family was over there too, so he was more or less forced to use some discretion.

During one of our discussions when no regular officers had accompanied him to the camp we sat by ourselves, the two of us smoking and sipping tea in one of the interrogating rooms. Our conversations were different from what one might imagine —because we were laughing and joking. Jimmy once said: "Greg, I hope you don't hate the Japanese people after the war is over."

"If I don't, please believe me, it won't be because some of your goons aren't trying hard enough."

"Yes, I realize that, and I am sorry about it."

"But fantastic as it may sound, the Japs have made a habit of saving my life, almost since I can remember. When I was six years old a Jap farmer boy snatched me from the spring flood waters of the St. Joe River in Idaho. Well, the other times you know about."

"This does seem to be more than a coincidence, doesn't it?"

"In addition to all this you people, unbeknown to yourselves, have been the only ones to put me on the water wagon and make it stick. Friends, relatives, and commanding officers have tried it before without much success. I have even tried to do it myself, sincerely, but always fell off before the time was up."

Jimmy appeared astonished and said: "You certainly don't look like you ever had any trouble that way."

"No, truthfully, I would like to think I owed a debt of gratitude to the Japanese for shooting me down and capturing me. For I was slowly killing myself, I know. But let's talk about something interesting, for a change."

"Like what?"

"Like sex, for instance. How do you think the Americans and Japanese are going to make out when they intermarry after the war's over?"

He leaned back on the legs of his chair, placing his feet in anything but true Japanese fashion on top of the table between us, thought awhile, then started talking:

"I believe Japanese women would make wonderful mates for the American men, but I don't think that the American women could stand the Japanese men."

"Why do you think that way?" And what he told me made sense, and is just exactly the way it turned out after the war.

Jimmy said: "The Japanese woman is very affectionate, and is devoted to her husband. Yet she remains in the background, and doesn't try to run everything. But our men, I know, would never be able to keep up with the American women."

I knew he was serious and had put some thought into his statements, but I couldn't resist hamming things up a bit, so I laughed and said: "I don't know about your women, because I haven't been given the opportunity, but I think I know what you mean about the men not being able to satisfy American women."

"How's that?"

"Well, these guards stand around open-eyed while we are taking our bath. They point at us and say: 'Toxon, toxon,' so I would gather from this the girls back home really don't know how lucky they are."

Jimmy coughed, choking on cigarette smoke, and had to drop his feet from the table to catch his breath; afterward both of us laughed together.

Also, whether it seems contradictory to my previous reference to the cold, I want to tell about being able to take a hot Japanese bath each night after I finished my chores. This was after I had been transferred to kitchen duty, and when my hours of work were finished after nine at night, I was permitted

309

this luxury. During the cold winter months these baths were really a Godsend. Part of the reason I was allowed to take them could have been that the officers wanted their kitchen help clean.

We had watched how the Japanese took their baths, how they soaped down, sponged off in hot water, and then sit for twenty minutes or so in a tremendous tub of practically boiling-hot water. When we were first allowed to try it, we could not stay in more than a second, but gradually I got so I could take it just as hot as any Japanese. We captives who worked for the Japanese got into the tub after the Japanese were through, a large cement tub that a half-dozen people could immerse their entire bodies in at one time. If anybody had told me prior to my capture that I would relish sitting in a tub of water that the Japanese had been soaking in, I would have thought he was off his beat, but I thoroughly enjoyed it.

We captives who were permitted to take this bath at night got so heated up in the bath that when we walked to our cells to go to sleep, even when there was ice and snow on the ground, we could walk right on it barefoot and not feel it. In fact, one's body could become so heated up that if he wrapped himself up in his blankets the heat would not seem to go out of his body until the following morning. One would sleep warm all night long.

Each morning at four-thirty, while I was working in the kitchen, one of the guards awakened two prisoner helpers who had to start the fires and get everything going for the prisoners' food and the guards' rice. Naturally one is not very cheerful being awakened at four-thirty in the morning, before dawn. Every time, they gave us the little old pidgin-English expression, *"Speedo, speedo,"* which means, "hurry up, hurry up." Sometimes they added a few of their swear words to insult us a bit. The worst thing a Japanese can say to you is *"baka,"* or *"kanero,"* which means "you fool" or "foolish one." Many times a guard came in the kitchen and asked me to do something, adding *"Baka."* The tone of his voice as well as what he said would make me resent it, and I would say calmly: "Baka yourself, you son of a bitch!"

"Nunda?" he would ask.

"Nothing. How correct you are. How correct you are," and he would feel satisfied. Sometimes I would smile and bow and say very politely: "To your honor, you son of a bitch," then he would smile and nod back, just like we were old buddies.

I recall a rather nice young coolie-type guard I had a conversation with one morning, even though he didn't know a word of English. I kind of picked my guard. I was busy trying to get the fires started. I didn't get them going in the first three seconds, and he gave me this *"speedo, speedo"* business, which I rather imagined he thought was part of his duty. I ceased my activities on this particular occasion, turned around, pointed my finger and touched his shiny belt, and told him in his language: "You're a very good guard, do excellent guard duty."

He nodded and smiled at me, taking it as a compliment, and I continued: "You don't allow any unlawfulness or disobedience among the prisoners or anything. I compliment you on being a good guard."

He bowed to me again. Then I explained to him that I was in this kitchen to be a fire builder and take care of all the heavy duties around the kitchen. I explained to him that I was a very good fire builder. Then I said: "You tend to your guard duty and I'll tend to building the fires. As far as I'm concerned, everything that goes on every morning, this *'speedo, speedo'* business, whether the fire starts off in one minute or ten minutes, is making me tired. As a matter of fact, it gives me very much pain"—and I pointed to my tail—"very much pain right here."

This guard looked at me a few seconds. There must be no expression in their language that says "pain in the ass," because all of a sudden he started to laugh. It was about four-thirty in the morning and he ran, still laughing, into the guardhouse. I think he must have awakened every guard in the place and told them how I said *"speedo, speedo"* business gave me a big pain in the ass. Why it struck him as so funny I still don't know, but it was obvious that we had funny ways to them, and they slayed us with some of their idiosyncrasies.

The guards' cook in Ofuna was a civilian, Hata. He was the

only male I knew, outside of the interpreters, who wore his hair long. The military and us prisoners had their hair cropped off close. "Curley" was the name he was called by the prisoners. He was only about four and a half feet tall, a rather handsome face, and he took pride in keeping a wavy head of black hair well groomed. He had one of the most perfectly muscled bodies I ever saw on a man—a miniature Charles Atlas. He was forever looking up English words in a Japanese-English dictionary. He would ask George Whiting, an American submarine lieutenant who worked in the kitchen with me for a time, how to use these English words he would look up. Then he would proceed literally to wear out each word in broken English sentences for days.

One day George and I were lifting one of the hot, heavy cast-iron vats from the Dutch ovens to repair the firebox. In doing so we accidentally slopped a great deal of soup on the cement floor of the kitchen, making quite a mess. Hata was furious with us because it was just about time for lunch. He figured we were about the clumsiest pair in captivity, judging from his Nip mumbling. Then he quieted down and said in English: "In your language, I imagine what you call this is 'masterpiece.' " George and I laughed so hard it was a wonder we didn't spill what remained in the heavy vat. Hata's expression stuck with me, and I had many an occasion to use it after the war, especially upon myself. For every time I came off one of my periodic drunks, I chastized myself silently, sometimes out loud, and during these many times I invariably said: "Masterpiece, Boyington, masterpiece."

By Christmas I considered myself most fortunate. My wounds had finally healed. I was getting plenty of food for a change. My ankle was misshapen but I walked with only a slight limp. I was looking forward to this being my first sober Christmas, where neither I nor anybody around me had any liquor.

Junior, whom I mentioned earlier as the only prisoner I knew prior to my capture, and I were counting our blessings that Christmas. There was never a more thankful gang than the prisoners of Ofuna on Christmas of 1944. And we had nothing in comparison to now.

Junior Condant and his Navy TBF crew had been shot down on a raid over Marcus Island. I was to see and hear more about him after the war, and I was very happy with the company of a loyal and true friend at this time.

Whenever I see the movie *Fighting Lady*, I am also reminded of Junior, for it shows him and his plane taking off the carrier, and says: . . . "never to return again." The two of us had many things in common.

In recent years I have learned about a Commander Jim Condant from a Marine classmate of mine, long after I was through with the USMC. It seems there was a group of experimental test pilots from the various services gathered around a research table at a testing base in Maryland. My classmate said: "I had no idea that any of the officers at that critique had ever met you, Greg. Anyway, your name came up during the business at hand—I forget just how—and an officer I am sure had never even met you before said: 'Why, that no-good so-and-so. He did this and he did that.' As soon as he said this I realized there was somebody who knew you, besides myself, when Jim Condant said: 'I am positive you have never met Boyington, but I have. I spent two years in a prison camp with him. And I'm giving you just five seconds to apologize.'

"The officer said: 'I'll be damned if I will.'

"And believe me, Greg, the armed forces experimental critique was ended, because Condant waited just five seconds, then sailed across the top of the table and grabbed this guy by the throat, tipping his chair over backward and carrying him to the deck. As he was sitting on this guy's chest he was screaming: 'I'm going to beat your head on the deck till you apologize.' The rest of us had to pull him off, or he would have killed the guy."

Maybe this sounds egotistical. But the reason I mention it is that I don't have to bother any longer about who likes me and who doesn't. As long as I can face the gent in the mirror in the morning, I won't ever have to worry about my share of friends.

This classmate of mine never told me what the officer had said in a derogatory manner. But if he called me a drunken

313

bum, God bless Jim Condant. I'm afraid his efforts were for naught, because this is something I admit to quite honestly.

During my one and only Christmas at Ofuna, we prisoners asked the guards for permission to sing carols. The guards said okay, as they too enjoyed singing, even though they couldn't understand the words. And they knew good voices from mediocre or bad.

If I were only capable of writing an opera, this prison camp would be the greatest setting I know of. There were a few fellows with great voices. Frank Tinker, who had an obviously well-trained voice, and Brian Stacy, the Australian pilot, who had an untrained voice, were called upon to do most of the singing for the camp. Both of these fellows possessed a remarkable delivery.

We had started something the Japanese wouldn't let us stop. They would have either Tinker or Stacy, time after time, go out into the center of the courtyard to sing for them. Sometimes in the dark of the night. I couldn't help feel the utmost pity for these two fellows with their beautiful voices, as I watched them through the window of my cell while they were out in the courtyard singing. At times eddies of snowflakes would obliterate the lone singer from my vision, then he would seem to return mistily back again, and the sound would be loud or soft as the snow commanded. The buildings on two sides and steep hills on the other two sides formed a theater in which the acoustics were perfection itself.

As we sang through the days from Christmas to the New Year, I suddenly realized that in two more days I would complete a year without a single drink, my first year without liquor since I had started drinking. I don't know why I felt so proud of myself, but I did. I really had no reason to be, just because I happened to be someplace I couldn't help myself. I thought: "At last, I am finally going to last out a year without taking a drink."

New Year's Eve and the following day are quite some occasion in the lives of the Japanese, I was to find. All of their birthdays are believed to have some connection with the coming of the New Year. This was the all-important occasion, I gathered, while Christmas to them meant nothing other than our singing carols.

Curly and Obason labored all day in the kitchen, getting things prepared for a New Year's feast of some kind. They cooked all natures of Japanese delicacies and stored them away in the kitchen cupboards for whatever they would be doing that night and the following day. Curly and Obason would have tomorrow off with their families.

The chief petty officer in charge of the camp asked me if I would remain and tend fires in the kitchen until after midnight. The Japanese called him "Gocha," but we prisoners referred to him as the head goat. The goat was a rather plump individual, and not too bad a fellow, I thought. Anyhow, I informed the goat that I would be only too happy to help him out, because I had the stealing of some of those choice foods in the back of my mind.

The big doings were to take place in the guards' quarters. I couldn't see what was going on but had no desire to find out how things turned out. I remained alone most of the night in the semi-dark, blacked-out kitchen, huddled beside the guards' stove, smoking quietly by myself until about ten-thirty that evening.

Then the goat entered the kitchen with a case of bottles filled with some colorless liquid, and said in Japanese: "Boyington, will you keep a pot of hot water going on the stove?"

I asked: "Nunda?"

He said: "This is sake, and we have to warm it up for the New Year party. Understand sake, Boyington?"

"Yes, I understand sake," I replied. I knew sake was their drink, much the same as bourbon was an American drink. But this was no concern of mine because all that was required from me was the heating; the Japanese would do all the drinking. I didn't have the slightest desire for a drink; my mind was thinking about food and just how I was going to get it.

It came like a bolt from the blue when one of the guards entered the kitchen to pick up something for their party and asked: "Boyington, do you like sake?"

I lied: "Yes, I used to before I was captured. Why?"

"Then get your cup quickly, before anyone comes, and I'll give you a little."

Without giving the matter a second thought, or this guard an opportunity to change his mind, I started to go for my tea-cup. While standing there in the darkness, as I was about to pick up my cup, I could only think of how small a cup was. Then I momentarily thought of a rice bowl, which was considerably larger, but I ended up with a soup bowl, which was still larger.

When I came over into the light with the soup bowl where the slightly inebriated guard was waiting to pour, his eyes seemed to pop out as he exclaimed: *"Toxon, toxon!"*

"I can't find my cup, this will have to do," I lied again. Without the slightest intention of saying: "When" before he stopped pouring, I watched him. If it had been left up to me, I wouldn't have spoken until I saw that he was starting to overrun the bowl and waste some, but when the bowl was over half full he stopped, and as he left the kitchen, he cautioned: "Don't tell anybody I gave you sake."

I assured him: "Thank you, Haitison, don't worry, I won't." And he left me by myself.

I didn't know what their regulations were in regard to giving a prisoner a drink, but I rather imagined that the penalty for stealing sake, especially on such an occasion, was probably the double-handled sword. But the guard had given me this extra-large serving, so I felt like my hands were clean as I sat down to enjoy my drink. The two days that remained before I completed my first year of sobriety, for which I had been so thankful, passed quickly from my mind. I finished the bowl, smacked my lips, and lighted a whole cigarette, for a change, which the goat had presented to me, then I settled back on my stool beside the warm fire and waited for that wonderful glow to arrive. But the glow seemed so slow that I was thinking: "Maybe this junk isn't as powerful as bourbon."

I heard laughter coming from the guards' quarters until I became unaware that anyone but myself existed on this earth. Several more guards made trips to get sake, which they found properly warmed, and they complimented me for this. But that

316

first drink had done it, I threw caution to the wind, and I put the bum on every single guard who entered the kitchen.

I would be waiting for them with my soup bowl handy, and I would say: "I wouldn't think of stealing any of your sake, but I haven't had a drink for a year," and each guard would believe me, for he would fill at least a part of the bowl.

Finally the guards' trips for sake appeared to have stopped about the time I was just beginning to feel good; maybe they were getting filled up. So I decided to pour my own. And I did. Now I know that nothing, absolutely nothing, scares an alcoholic—not even death.

I had no idea what possessed me, or who was taking care of me, other than my Higher Power. But just before I started to black out in the dimly lighted kitchen, a thought came to me: "This is too good to spoil, somehow. I'd better get to my cell and roll up in my blankets."

Fortunately for me I made it to my cell, and whether I got the blankets around me properly I don't know. The goat had given me permission to sleep in that morning for tending the fires, so I don't know to this day just how many were wise to me. I do know that a couple were, but they remained silent— thank God.

CHAPTER **31**

AFTER THE NEW YEAR'S incident life seemed to go on much the same as before until the latter part of February 1945. Then all hell appeared to break loose over our peaceful country valley. It all started by hearing the distant wail of air-raid sirens, which we prisoners paid no attention to because we hadn't dreamed this could be anything but a drill. But in a matter of some twenty minutes everybody in Japan came to the realization that this was no drill. Just twelve miles from our camp the large Jap naval base of Yokosuka was taking a thumping something terrific.

Dive bomber after dive bomber started down, the hills between the target area and our camp momentarily chopping each bomber from view, making it appear as though they were diving into the hills. But in a few seconds we saw them pull out about the same time we heard the ka-lumph of the exploding bomb. Even at this distance the noise from so many engines sounded much the same as a gigantic waterfall—a steady roar. Obviously this was not a morale strike like the Doolittle raid; this was concentrated, and we knew that this carrier raid was the beginning of the end for Japan.

Prisoners were ordered by the guards to go to their cells, and to keep away from the windows or they would be beaten. This order was analogous to asking a person to stop breathing, one can stand it only so long. None of the guards bothered me, as I was in the kitchen, and I was able to get an eyeful.

What a sight, I thought, as I saw a Zero scooting low along the hilltops directly over our camp, being chased by a Navy F6F. An old familiar feeling came over me, causing a tingling to run through my body, as I watched the F6F pour his .50-caliber machine guns into the hapless Zero, which belched flame and crashed into a hillside as the F6F pulled skyward. I knew he was looking for new prey, for I felt close enough to the action, while standing there on the ground, almost to feel that I was thinking for that Navy F6F pilot.

I was thrilled by the sights of two more shoot-downs before one of the guards finally shooed me inside through the back door of the kitchen. As much as I wanted to remain and continue watching, I had seen enough, so I didn't mind.

Curly, the cook, was frightened half to death, and he was pleading: "What is the best thing to do? Where is the safest place?"

"Flat on your belly is the safest place I know of." I tried to console this excited and frightened man. Curly must have taken me as an authority when I spoke, for he was flat on his face before I had finished.

After the racket had subsided and nothing was visible but a huge column of smoke rising behind the hills in the direction of Yokosuka, Curly looked up from the deck like a little child and said: "Is it all right to stand up now, Major?" And this was the first, last, and only time the little cook ever addressed me by my rank.

I would have given plenty for the little fellow's thoughts during that carrier raid. I knew enough about him already, and that wasn't good. But I rather imagined, just briefly, that he was asking for forgiveness for his sins toward American naval prisoners.

Of course, we all had had our suspicions concerning Curly. But few of us were able to verify them. The Japanese Navy had actually allotted a sustaining diet for captives and prisoners of war, but fellows like Curly saw to it that their orders were only

319

partially carried out. This is reminiscent of how, in a larger way, tremendous donations to starving nations by the United States are sidetracked, black-marketed, and how a few American citizens make fabulous fortunes for themselves. These fortunes have a habit of coming back, after a period of time, to the good old U.S.A., where they are deposited safely, and they are not subject to federal income tax, either.

The only difference I can see is that Curly was a miserable cheap crook and is now spending life in jail, while some others very close to us have the titles of "Honorable" and other such high-sounding names.

However it may be, Curly carried on a booming business in a small way each night after supplies arrived from the naval base of Yokosuka. Then between shipments he would have to do some mighty sharp figuring in order to make what he had left stretch until the next load of supplies arrived. But I'll have to take my hat off to the little cook; he was a master mathematician, for he knew to the ounce of bean paste and barley what would keep a man barely alive.

This is apparently a world of people who think they are doing somebody else, and somebody else is thinking at the same time that he is the one who is doing the doing. We kitchen helpers would steal part of the guards' allotment of barley and bean paste in the dark of the morning and place it, as a compensation for Curly's thieving, into the prisoners' ration.

After this Navy raid we helpers became even more brazen in our thefts of the guards' supplies. As a matter of fact, I found that one can want so desperately to help people that he can kill them with kindness, for one morning in the darkness I stole so much of the guards' rich bean paste, which is protein, and camouflaged it in the prisoners' watery soup that all of them got diarrhea. I naturally assumed that it went unnoticed, as nobody accused me, but there was one hell of a to-do around camp because they couldn't track down the cause.

Finally, one day in April, eighteen of us were told that we were going to be moved from this intimidation camp of Ofuna to a prisoner-of-war camp. This information immediately aroused in all of us the hopeful prospect that at last our status

320

might be changed from that of captives to prisoners of war. This meant that, after all these months, our folks would be able to find out that we were not dead.

We had been in the intimidation camp for more than thirteen months, and before that in other camps or cells, but always as people who did not exist—except to the Japanese who were quizzing us or roughing us up. Naturally all eighteen of us had plenty of reasons for wanting the people at home to know we were still among the living. I am in no position to tell the case histories of all the others, but as an example I certainly can tell my own.

Not only did I want my parents to know that I was living, that I had not been killed when shot down during my last fight; I wanted my three children to know it too. I wanted them to know they still had an old man. Their mother and I had long been divorced, but the children had been placed in my custody. Obviously I had seen practically nothing of them since the war started; I had been in the Pacific and Asia so long.

That I would have given anything for word to be sent back to the United States that I was still alive goes without saying. It would be the same with any father or son.

I figured, too, that any geographical change would be better for me. For a few trying minutes I thought that this change was going to be just a day too late, because the day before I was to be transferred I found that Curly was wise to me. He had a heart-to-heart talk with me the day prior to my leaving Ofuna.

Curly said: "I want you to know that I knew you were spiking the prisoners' food from the guards' cupboard."

Because I had been so confident in thinking I had everybody fooled words nearly failed me, but I asked: "Why did you wait until the last day before turning me in?"

Then he floored me with: "I'm not going to turn you in."

I asked: "Why the sudden change of heart, Cookson?"

"I knew all along what you were doing. But also, I knew what else was going on, too. And I don't believe our military, either. I know the war will be over soon. I didn't turn you in because I would have only had you hurt for nothing. And it doesn't matter any more."

I thanked Curly and shook his hand good-by, but I looked back over my shoulder at the closed gates of Ofuna with no nostalgia as the eighteen of us were leaving. When we walked back the same road I came in on originally, I wasn't conscious of the quiet wooded scenery in the same way, for I saw no beauty in looking back anyplace.

We got on a streetcar and went, I should judge, about twenty-five miles, and then we had another long walk of some five miles before we arrived at the new camp. We took hope again when we understood from the guards that this was the headquarters camp for the whole area. I'm not sure about that, but I do know that, upon arrival, we were lined up in front of an administration building, and there they had us standing the whole day.

We stood there in the cold and were kept practically at attention, apparently because some Japanese big shot was expected to arrive to make an announcement to us. But if the announcement was what we hoped it would be, that no longer were we to be special prisoners or captives (the same thing) but were to be prisoners of war—well, all this cold and all this standing would seem to us very secondary indeed. So, while standing there, we whispered about our hopes as much as we dared, and prayed about them, and yet tried not to fidget too much for fear we still might do something wrong—before the announcement came—and thereby spoil everything.

Finally, toward evening, a Japanese colonel appeared. He turned out to be the commanding officer of this camp, Omouri. When he came out, there was a great deal of bowing and scraping going on. He came over and stood in front of us. Now would come the announcement.

It came.

An interpreter said—and we had already picked up enough from the colonel ourselves to sicken us—"You are to remain in this camp as 'special prisoners.' If any of you try to escape you will be killed."

I thought: "I wonder where in the hell this gray-haired old coot everybody is bowing to, and we waited so long to see, thinks we could escape to. A white man would show up like a boil on the end of his nose."

322

This was it. The colonel wheeled around and walked away, and the eighteen of us were taken into a small room that remained our sleeping cell until the end of the war.

The home stretch is not the easiest part of any endurance race, even though a popularization of the phrase has made it seem to be. Even though some of us were aware that the end of the war was in sight, a group of men who are starved, underweight, overworked, and out of touch with their families can do things that normally would seem crazy, for they are not getting their logic in some comfortable library at home reading philosophical books. They are not waiting for the war to end while listening comfortably to announcers on the radio.

Besides, during the last few months of the war, the bombings from the B-29s continued terrifically. Hardly a day or night went by in which we were not pounded. Though "The Music" meant our ultimate liberation, a lack of sleep night after night can also tell on starved men who for so many hours after hours had to do such hard work by day cleaning up debris and digging tunnels.

Because I was senior officer in this little group it was up to me to keep them living and sane if possible. As for me, I am fortunate in never having had trouble with the will to live. I always have wanted to keep on going, and still want to keep on going; some of us may be blessed with this gift more than others.

There were fights among some of my nerve-racked people, and I had to settle them, and I had to keep some of them from stealing each other's food, and I had to be the interpreter with the guards, translating when my boys got in trouble. Yet, strangely, I found that the biggest curse, or the biggest threat, I could give any of my group who were troublesome was to say: "Listen, when we get out of this and back to the States, I'll never speak to you again."

In one case I still have lived up to that threat, for the officer deserved it. I still do not want to see him or speak to him again. He did steal fellow-captives' food, and also let others be beaten up for something he himself had done.

Most of them kept on going somehow and became ashamed

immediately for something they had done. And once it was my turn to feel very sorry. It was a sorrow that came from my own inadequacy to keep one poor little fellow alive.

There is nothing of the chaplain about me, God knows, but a chaplain's duty became mine too. This was thrown in with the rest, and especially during those hard closing weeks of the war. The night I failed at this job, or at least the night I remember failing the most at this job, was when I just simply seemed unable to "will" one of my younger boys to stay alive.

I wanted him to pay attention to me long enough to hold on for one more month—just one more month. But he would not eat. I would scold him, but he still would not eat. The fight for survival had gone completely out of him in his weakness. So I tried to force food down this poor little soul's throat, and then I would scold him again for not trying.

Finally, after many attempts, he looked up at me and said: "Please, Greg, don't scold me."

That evening we posted a guard to stand by and watch him. I had told him, then, to try to get some sleep. I was to have the first watch over him. It was about seven o'clock when everyone turned in, and I was going to have a four-hour watch. About nine o'clock the little fellow died.

And yet just one month later it was all over, and he would have been free. But, of course I realize that it is not up to me to make such decisions, and therefore I should not worry about them.

Because in the next great war we are destined not to know what will hit us, and because in the next great war we are destined not to see or hear ahead of time whatever it is that will destroy us, this report about being on the receiving end of our own B-29s already seems obsolete and far away.

We prisoners in this new camp first heard about the B-29s from the guards, but they also told us that the planes were all being shot down as fast as they came over, or even before they reached the coast of Japan.

Not having seen a B-29, and not even having known of this new ship's existence, all I could do about these first rumors was to remain as baffled as the Japanese must have been. And then one day, a surprisingly short time later, I saw for myself, my first B-29s. There were four of them, all flying high, and from that moment on I had no doubts whatsoever that the Nips were really in for something.

I happened to be out working on a coal-dump when I saw these great ships. They were flying so fast and so high that the few Japanese planes sent up to intercept them were immediately out of sight. All I could see of them were their vapor streaks up there, but periodically I could hear some of the firing, and then down came the immense bombs.

From then on, day after day, as the B-29s kept coming over, we special prisoners were given a new type of work to do, but a work we really relished. Our work consisted of going out early each morning into the city streets on the outskirts of Tokyo and Yokohama and picking up what the B-29s had laid down. Where the bombs hit, everything was knocked or burned flat. We had to take the heavy pieces, like cement blocks and pieces of metal, and lay them in neat rows along the city streets. Then we burned up the wood and trash. Then we had to mattock the ground surface, which had not had anything planted in it for, I imagine, a thousand years. It was really rough work at that time, and I was back again to my original starvation weight.

But work, almost no matter what kind, was better than being made to sit in a cell doing nothing. And this is what had happened to us during the first month in Camp Omouri. We had not been able to do a thing, and every time any guard came in, we all had to jump to attention and bow.

When I was a little fellow, I was told a few things about the Japanese. One thing was how they would take off their shoes before entering a house. I found that to be very true. I was also told that they had advanced so far that they no longer used human excretions for fertilizer. But that is not so. It is not so because I had to carry many buckets, just like a coolie, of human crap and urine to put on this garden or that garden. We would have to go around to collect this fertilizer from the toilets of bombed-out houses. The buildings were completely gone, but the toilet-like affair is just kind of a cement bowl under the ground, and we dipped this human crap out of these old

325

toilets. I think that is what is wrong with my sense of smell now. I used to have a keen sense before the war, but now I can smell hardly anything, all of which was probably nature's way of taking care of me during those assignments. Not to forget some of the foul-smelling joints I sold beer to for over six years after the war.

The Japanese certainly must be the world's greatest gardeners, because some of this soil was practically half masonry and the rest volcanic ash. But with their means of fertilizing and watering we grew some beautiful vegetables with that prisoner work. The only trouble was we did not get enough of them to eat.

Some of the guards, of course, were better than others, and when the vegetables started growing, some of them let us steal the vegetables and cook them on fires in back lots. These good guards told us to be careful that none of the officers saw us do it, so we would keep boys posted, and when we saw an officer coming down the street—they usually came on bicycles—we would ditch the stewpot, which had nothing in it but green vegetables. An exceptional stew was one in which we put radishes or turnips or anything solid. Occasionally a good guard would get some fish from some of the civilians and let us throw that in. This was really Number One, as we called things out there.

During the last four and a half months we had B-29s coming over daily and nightly. We were not allowed to get into air-raid shelters because we were still "special prisoners." We would have to sweat it out on top, but, even so, each raid was just so much more good news to us. And even though not allowed the protection of an air-raid shelter, these ragged, starved prisoners had a hard time concealing their delight from the Japanese. We realized that we had to go through so much in order to get out of there. We knew that some of us would be killed, but that the majority of us would get out.

To prevent the Japanese from understanding what we were talking about, we called the B-29s coming over "The Music." We originated the term from the sound made by the siren warning. Also, the prisoners would bet a part of their meager rations of food that "The Music" would come before such and such a time. This meant we were betting mighty high stakes, in as much as we received only a three-quarter ration of what was received by the regular prisoners of war.

During one of these raids I was returning from the latrine to the room we were kept in, and a dive bomber hit the causeway between the sandspit our camp was constructed on and shore. A tremendous piece of concrete—it must have weighed a half ton—sank into the roadbed about twenty feet in front of me. There was nothing I could do, I was not allowed into any shelter, so I just had to walk calmly into where the rest of the prisoners were being held under guard at bayonet point. There I sat down and started talking with the rest of the prisoners in a low voice. For we did not want to show any signs of excitement when a raid was going on. Any time we were caught smiling, during one of these raids, we were hit with a rifle butt or called to attention and struck in the face. And sometimes we were just slugged because feelings were running a bit high.

CHAPTER **32**

M ONTHS OR WEEKS AFTERWARD, on being brought back
to the United States, I was to learn how much confusion had
been in the minds of the people here as both wars neared their
ferocious close. And so it was in Japan, too. Rumors were followed by denials, and then by rumors again.

I must say, though, that even if we prisoners were not allowed
any military information from the Japanese, we were nevertheless able to follow the war rather closely. We received some of
it from the new prisoners who came into the camp, men who
were just recently captured. We were not supposed to talk to
any of them but managed to do so now and then secretly. Our
main source of information was, of all things, the Japanese
newspaper.

During our almost two years of being captives we finally had
learned how to read a few printed characters in the Japanese
language. Some of the boys were better than others, and they
became more or less our official code breakers. They didn't de-
liver us the daily paper, or anything as easy as that. But when
we cleaned out the Japanese living quarters each day, we would
pick up the papers the officers had been reading. They were
one or two days old, and we would smuggle them out to some
secluded place, away from the guards, like in the toilets, and

there we would get our code-breaking staff together and pore over these papers.

We found, as a general rule, that the first paragraph or so in each article, whenever there was an Allied victory, was perfectly correct. Then the articles would go on at great length to say: "The great Japan will shove them back off into the sea; we will counterattack. . . ." and so forth. But during the next two or three days we would see nothing in the paper about anybody being shoved back into the sea, so we knew it was the same old story again. Our people had gotten on another piece of ground closer to Japan.

The articles the Japanese papers printed on Germany were always true. There was no camouflage whatsoever. The articles told the actual facts, naming the towns, showing all the fronts, having the casualty lists, even diagrams we could follow to show us what was going on in the German theater. We got the word when Germany went out of the war. In fact, we knew just about everything that was going on. We never were in the dark, even though the Japanese were not allowed to give us any military information. But some of the better-educated Japanese had secretly given us their own predictions. This had occurred at many points all along the line, even as far back as Truk. An educated interpreter told me then that if we survived our own bombs we would be free men in a year and a half. The time, of course, was a wee bit longer than that. But just the same, it seemed at the time a funny prediction for him to make because the campaign in the South Pacific was going slowly for us then. We were behind schedule in everything we did, and there had been no second front in Europe. We figured, well, at least three years of this.

In Camp Ofuna, the civilian cook, Curly, spoke to me the night before I was taken away to Camp Omouri. He was well educated but had not talked to me about the war during the whole six months I had worked in the kitchen with him. That night he told me that there would be a lot of war in the next four and half months, and he added: "It will be all over and you can go back to your mama and papa."

At another time, just one month before the end of the war,

another informed Japanese called me to one side and asked me how my morale was. I told him it was fine. He said: "Well, it will only be another month or so and the thing will be all over. I will be just as happy as anybody in the world, myself."

Meanwhile the final bombings of Japan were something to behold, great hordes of silver B-29s coming over in the daylight. They looked beautiful. Occasionally we would see some lone Japanese fighter plane try to tangle with them. It would come streaking down in flames, and we could hear it crash to the ground. Then the beautiful silver things would start releasing their eggs, and the ground would shake. The windows would tremble and shake, and the sills on the doors would creak back and forth. Yet this was not so bothersome as at night, when the B-29s came over low, at around four to six thousand feet. We could hear them swoop down and dive, the engines roaring. We didn't know where they were, didn't know when to duck. We could just put our faces down into our cotton blankets—and hope.

About a month before the end of the war we were taken off our garden work and the clearing of debris and were set to digging huge tunnels in the hillsides on the outskirts of Yokohama. We worked at this twelve hours a day, just like muckers in a mine. I was familiar with this sort of labor, for I had spent a summer vacation while going to college working in a gold mine in Golden, Idaho. These tunnels were two hundred feet under the surface of the earth. One of the guards told me that this was to be an air-raid shelter, but I couldn't imagine what kinds of bombs were going to be dropped to necessitate a tunnel two hundred feet underground.

Then one day a non-commissioned officer tried to tell me about the atomic bomb. He could speak no English, it was all in Japanese, and I couldn't fathom at first that it was only one bomb he was talking about. I thought it was just some more Japanese propaganda. But he said no, that his family had lived in the city of Nagasaki, and that only one bomb had been dropped on the city. He said that people were still dying there, and that he had not been allowed even within the city limits to look for his lost family.

I had no conception of what kind of bomb it might be, but I knew that it must be something horrible the way we were being rushed on digging those tunnels. I didn't fully believe this story about the atomic bomb, even though I was helping to dig the tunnel. I didn't fully believe it until after the war.

On my way from Japan by DC-4, after the surrender had been signed, I was thumbing through some current magazines left aboard the plane, and there it was—pictures and the works. The atomic bomb was no myth.

It has often puzzled me how I could figure out some things so easily, while others never dawned upon me with all the evidence apparently staring me right in the face. The truly master puzzler of mine was alcohol, but I have come to find that I am far from being alone in my past bewilderment, because approximately 5 per cent of the world's populace shouldn't drink at all. But this atomic puzzler was staring me in the face as well.

Shortly after the first bomb was dropped, we prisoners, old or fresh—it made no difference—seemed to have a lot of new company, for the Japanese moved about a hundred college-boy soldiers, a sort of Japanese F.B.I., into the camp. They were to be found everywhere, listening and watching us. No matter which direction we turned, no matter where we were, we could see them lurking around in the vicinity—day, night, toilets, mealtimes, everywhere.

They tried to conceal the fact that they could read, write, speak, and understand English fluently. But we got wise to them over something very simple, and they became dead giveaways, even though none of us had any more than the remotest knowledge of the existence of the bomb.

One of my boys had picked up a coil while working in the bombed-out city and had taken it back to our cell for an express purpose. He had bared the electric-light wires and arranged the coil so that when he made contact, the coil would heat up red-hot, thus providing an excellent cigarette lighter. He had gotten sick and tired of asking a guard for a *"matchee"* and being turned down. We had been using this coil for some time and thought nothing about it, although we hadn't advertised its use, naturally. But the first time one of these English-speaking F.B.I. fellows took a gander at our contraption he shouted for everybody in camp. This is when we knew how well they spoke and understood English. This poor jerk was positive that this innovation of ours, which looked like a Rube Goldberg affair, had some very definite connection with the atomic bomb. But even if it had, the Japanese had lost both secrecy and surprise in the battle royal that ensued over this petty contraption. Poor Mr. Kono, the prisoners' benefactor, our friend, could not talk everybody into any semblance of order this time.

Kono, the person who explained the singsong-sounding Japanese prayer I couldn't understand all those many months, was without a doubt one of the greatest men I ever met. He had been a wealthy importer, was around thirty years old, and had decided that the only way he could help matters was to act as an interpreter, or a referee of sorts. He wore a uniform but held no rank. I knew that he was a Christian, although he never told me so. Kono's heart was being torn out most of the time, a combination of pity for the ignorance and brutality of some of his own countrymen and a complete understanding of the suffering of the prisoners. But my admiration came, not from the way he felt, especially, but from the manner in which he handled himself with no outward fear of consequences—not even death. Yet he never violated the military ethics of his fellow-countrymen, as I saw it, while doing acts of kindness too numerable to mention. But if ever there was a man who could read between the lines in the Japanese orders and the Bible combined, it was Mr. Kono. This man's courage in saving lives and preventing hardship will apparently go unrewarded in the ordinary sense—like medals from either Japan or the United States. But I can assure you that he will stay in the hearts of many men—for there was a far braver man than I.

Because the people of our own American cities have been spared so far the cataclysm of aerial bombardment we can only guess how our own people will behave when the time comes. We know how the English behaved, the Italians and the Germans, the French, the Russians. We know how some of these nationalities behaved differently from others. But our own American cities, being composed of a composite of races and nationalities, may behave accordingly. Some racial sections may go completely crazy; other racial sections in the same city may be calm. But at most we can only guess. And at most we can only guess, too, how enemy prisoners will be treated immediately after being shot down during the heat of one of these catastrophes. People whose homes and families have just been destroyed will be wild then—and we can only guess what some Americans might do. Yes, we can only guess.

But we don't have to guess how the civilian population of Japan behaved. Or at least most of us prisoners who were there at the time don't have to guess. But, to keep all things clear, I will limit these observations to just what I myself saw or underwent.

While in this second and last camp I really got to know the population of Japan quite well. In our daily work of removing the destroyed homes of the Japanese civilians, and even when they had lost members of their families, relatives, or friends, I did not seem to notice any belligerence toward us. I walked by the crowds of civilians, within three or four feet of them, in rags and half starved, and never once did I have any occasion to fear them, before or after the B-29 raids.

Shortly after I was released, I read articles by correspondents who had gone into Japan, and they told about the surly mobs standing around. But I cannot understand this, the way I look at it, because, to the contrary, the majority of civilians were very good to us. We were not allowed to speak to them, and they were not allowed to help us in any way. Yet despite this order they risked beatings to help us out by giving us cigarettes and small pieces of food. I saw many of them punished for trying to help us. In fact, practically every day I saw at least two or three beaten by the guards who were standing on duty over us. Even the policemen had the right to strike civilians. If one were caught jaywalking, for example, the policeman ordered him over, the civilian would stand at attention, and the policeman would then strike his face, first with one fist and then with the other. When civilians came near us, one of them might say hello in their language, and the guard would call the civilian and have him stand at attention while hitting him repeatedly.

I never will forget one little old man with snow-white hair. I judged him to be about seventy. He came over to light his pipe in one of our trash fires. He had not spoken to any of us, yet the guard called him over. The little old man laid down his bundle and bowed three or four times, then the guard laid into him with his fists. He knocked the little fellow down, I would say, a half-dozen times. Finally the man's face was bloody, and then the guard, when he was through, said a few more words to the old man, who bowed two or three times, walked over and picked up his bundle, and went on down the street.

The civilian population going to and fro on the street never even looked up while this beating took place. They were used to it.

Unlike those few educated Japanese I have mentioned who seemed to have a savvy about the outcome of the war, the majority of civilians had no idea that Japan was not going to win. Yet they still were kind.

There was one lady who lived in back of a partly demolished store. She had two or three daughters and an elderly father. In this instance we happened to have one particularly good guard on duty whom we called "Limpy" because he had half of a foot shot off. Yet he was about one of the fairest and squarest guards I ever saw. He would permit this lady to cook up food for the eighteen of us when we were out working around where her store was.

Then one day the guard said that the lady, her girls, and the old man were going to leave. They had all their belongings packed up on a truck. I went over and in my politest Japanese bowed to her, just like old-home week, and told her how much we had appreciated the things she had done for us. She was all smiles and, speaking perfect Japanese, told me what nice boys she thought we were. Then, after they got all the kids and their belongings on the truck, the lady and the old man got on too, and as they started to drive off, the eighteen of us half-starved prisoners stood there waving good-by, just like you would wave at any friends back home going away on a train trip.

A few of the dried-fish peddlers around town occasionally would slip one of the boys a fish, and when we had these stews, cooking up the vegetables, we would throw in the fish to give the stew a little flavor. Any time the guards caught any of the civilians doing such things, or even talking to us, they invariably called them over and we had to witness the beatings.

One day while we were working out in a garden, a soldier came up to me and in perfect English asked me if I were an American or an Englishman. I told him, and he said: "You know that President Roosevelt died?" There was so much sincerity in his voice that I knew he was not joking with me. Then he told me that he was very sorry about it, and so forth. All of a sudden the guard with us came up and told me that I was not supposed to talk to any guards outside of our own camp, that I would be beaten the next time I was caught talking to any other guard. This meant, then, that I could not talk even to people in uniform from anyplace other than my own camp.

The women of Japan seemed to be especially kind. I never heard of any of them being ornery to the prisoners. As a matter of fact, even the people in bombed-out homes would give the prisoners, when nobody was looking, small portions of food salvaged from their own wreckage, or anything else they thought the prisoners could use—as long as the guards did not catch on.

Contrary to what people would think, the guards who gave us the most trouble on the whole were the young ones who never had left the mainland. Those who had been out to different parts of the world and had seen action, and even some of those who had been terribly wounded, seemed to be of much better nature than the young ones who had stayed in Japan. These were the fellows who administered most of the beatings.

Uniforms can do strange things to some people during their first weeks. Now I can appreciate even better why the Marine Corps wants to wear the newness off a boot's uniform by sending him through boot camp prior to turning him loose on the public at large.

CHAPTER **33**

AS LONG AS PEOPLE are still alive to talk about the end of this war, and before getting into the next one, each person no doubt will have his own version of where he was, what he thought, and what he did on the day hostilities ceased.

This was the case after the First World War, as we know; and, judging from our grandparents, it was the case after the Civil War; and so the whole thing must have continued this way right on back to Helen of Troy.

Under the circumstances, and because we *are* individuals, each person's version must remain somewhat different, how he received the news and what he did immediately afterward. The end of a war suddenly can become such a personal matter, and all at once, that the only way we can be honest in telling of our reactions is by merely sticking to our own and letting others stick to theirs.

So, even if this chapter does seem personal, too personal, that is all I can do about it, or should do about it. For, after all, I was only one of a billion who had his own feelings during those transforming hours.

The day hostilities ceased I was lying ill with yellow jaundice on my straw mat back at camp. The guard on duty called me over to him. He was one of the elderly guards and had never given us any trouble, so I believed, more or less, what he said, although I cannot say that it quite dawned on me.

He told me in Japanese that the war was over. I stared at him. He repeated himself, saying: "Yes, the war is over. It was over fifteen minutes ago. Don't tell anybody I told you, because if it is found out the officers will punish me."

I really did not believe that the war was over. I thought that maybe there was some sort of a peace parley going on. I knew definitely that something important had happened. The rest of my gang had been working in a mine shaft and came home early that afternoon, and said that they were told to bring out the light equipment and take home all the tools.

A party of Englishmen who used to go down daily and work on the railroad yards all came home that afternoon. It was different from any other day we had seen them come home because this time they were all singing.

Every night and every morning we had to stand in formation. I would stand at the head and give the command to attention and so forth, and salute the Japanese duty officer and his staff as they came by. But this evening, after I had given the final salute, I said to my own people: "Hey, fellows, we don't know whether this is over, but I would like to suggest something."

They said: "What is it?"

I said: "Let's stay in formation and all repeat the Lord's Prayer together."

We did, and after we got through one little prisoner said: "Oh, Greg, that sounds so wonderful, why didn't we include that with every one of these formations?"

Although I have had my share of nightmares in my day, the remainder of this night was about the largest and longest real nightmare I ever hope to have. I don't believe that I could stand a much longer one.

Looking back, in a different light, I am able to appreciate the utter disillusionment and hopelessness some of these poor Japanese guards must have felt. I can feel for them now but truthfully cannot say that I appreciated any part of it at the time it happened.

Resorting to alcohol to try to solve one's problems, or to try

337

to attain peace of mind, was thoroughly familiar to me. And I can understand why the majority of the guards proceeded to get drunk. Furthermore, had I been invited, I probably would have gladly joined them in their drinking—but for the opposite reasons. Any reason is a good one, though, if one happens to be an alcoholic, or emotionally immature.

All seventeen of us were awakened from sweet dreams, not by the drunken shouting coming from the various guard quarters at Omouri, but by the guard on duty at our doorway. He was trying to be calm and suppress his anxiety, saying: "The guards are getting very drunk. Some are threatening to kill all the American prisoners. Here is a hammer and some nails for you to nail your door closed. And don't worry, because I'll protect you with my life—because that is my duty." So we proceeded to put the hammer and nails to good use without delay.

Before long we could recognize the drunken shouting of a non-commissioned officer we had always considered to be a right guy, and he said: "Let me at the captives. I am going to kill all of them. I'll prove to them that Japan is greater than the United States. Let me at them."

Through the cracks and windows we were able to see this drunken character staggering around outside. Our guard was restraining the drunk as best he could, trying his utmost to pacify him. The drunk would break away occasionally, and take huge slashes at the air with his double-handled samurai sword, such huge slashes that he almost fell on his tail each time he swung. Then he would beat upon our door until I thought that he would surely break it down, when all he had to do was walk through one of the windows. But a drunk never does anything the easy way, I know.

This non-com would wear himself down with his antics, then sober up slightly from the physical exertion. He would disappear for a while, returning to the guards' quarters for more drink and confidence from his fellow-drunks. Several of these door-breaking attempts were so serious, in my estimation, that I stood to one side in back of our doorway, clutching the handle of the hammer our guard had given us. I fully intended to make the first swing upon this drunken non-com's head, regardless of any consequences, had he accidentally or otherwise bolted through the nailed-up door.

Thank God he didn't!

Our guard at the door talked to us in his free moments, informing us that several of the guards had vowed among themselves to commit hara-kiri before the night was over. He mentioned one whom all of us prisoners liked, an exceptionally large Japanese, and said that this fellow was then in the midst of his hara-kiri ceremony.

During the previous twenty months of my captivity I had listened to so many tales about hara-kiri and Kamikaze that I thought these were coming out of my ears. Bunk, I thought. Somebody would be capable of wanting to take as many of his enemies along with him as he could, but this junk, never.

No, I was wrong, the guard insisted, it was a tradition in Japan.

Then I thought of all the head-on runs I had made with Japanese fighter pilots in the past. In all cases I had had a more durable aircraft, and greater fire-power than these Japanese had. About the only method they could have used to beat me was to have flown head-on into my plane, killing us both. Yet, these pilots had chosen to give ground.

My point was verified the following morning, as we hadn't lost a single Japanese. The big fellow had only been able to cut his belly sufficiently deep, during his lengthy ceremony, so that the wound could be covered by a Band-aid. Another had cut one wrist slightly.

Not that these Japanese weren't suffering, because they most certainly were, something horrible, for this happened to be the largest number of hangovers in one place of one nationality that I ever witnessed in my life.

The following day it really dawned on us that something must be over, because the Japanese commanding officer, who never had given us even a nod of kindness, came through our barracks and wanted to know, through the interpreter, how the living conditions were and so forth. The old son of a bitch must have been awfully stupid, I thought, not to think we could understand all we wanted to without the aid of an interpreter.

The next thing we knew, we were all being issued new clothing, the only decent clothing we ever were given. Then the Japanese medical officer started sending in vitamin pills. It said on the bottles: "Take so many of these; take so many of these!" Each time more vitamin pills would come in. We had cod-liver-oil pills, multivitamin pills, and iron pills. Well, we tried to follow the directions and after about three days I was belching iron ore, cod-liver oil, and everything else. I had to quit.

After five days we were notified that we could go talk to the regular prisoners of war. This was a great day, one we had been looking forward to for a long, long time.

When we were finally released, I experienced something of which I had had a premonition a year and a half before. One day I was walking on my crutches out to the latrine, and on the way back I had stopped to talk to a couple of the boys. I had said to them: "Gee, I had the wildest dream last night."

"Yeah, what was it?"

"Well, I dreamed that I was in a building something like a schoolhouse, a very modern building, and I was reading a Japanese newspaper and I could read it just as plain as day. It was in the early fall and this newspaper said that the war was over."

Then I had continued limping down to my cell. The boys—I could see them as I looked over my shoulder—were all shaking their heads because, as I was sick with this infected leg, I guess they thought: "Well, what do you know, old Gramps has finally flipped his wicket."

Now, here it was fall, a year and a half later, and I did read in a Japanese newspaper (I had no idea a year and half previously that they printed one in English), in the *Nippon Times*, that the war was over!

The dream, or the premonition, had come true.

On the sixth day after the war they moved us to different quarters. According to my rank, I was now placed in a room with a Navy officer, a submarine commander, and then we had our first visit by the Red Cross, the Swiss.

There were a couple of ladies in the crowd and they, no doubt, had been there through the whole war and had known of our existence but apparently they could not get permission to visit us. Now they were coming by, smiling at each prisoner and wanting to know how he had been mistreated and this, that, and the other thing. They actually sickened me with their talk. The way I felt, there were many things they could have done for us. They could have smuggled out our names, even though we were special prisoners.

I think it is just as right for anybody with the Red Cross on his arm, whether Swiss or not, to fight for what that Red Cross represents as it is for a poor boy in khaki uniform to fight for what his cause is supposed to be. So I had nothing to say to these people.

On this subject, months later when I was in Washington to receive the Congressional Medal of Honor, in this line-up to receive the same honor was a young fellow who bore the Red Cross. He was a hospital corpsman, and as he stepped by I really got a big lump right in my throat. This man had one eye shot out as well as many other injuries. He had been a conscientious objector (before the war), but he had earned his medal by proving what he thought was right. He had received his injuries while picking up Marines on the fire-swept hills on Iwo Jima. He had then, in his own way, really fought for what he believed.

About ten days after the war, or the cessation of hostilities, I should say, our own planes, Navy and Air Corps, came over these camps and started dropping clothes and foodstuffs. The prisoners went wild. They were running all over the place, and when the B-29s started dropping fifty-gallon drums packed solid with concentrated foods by parachute, I took to an air-raid shelter.

One prisoner said: "Why don't you stay out here and get some of this stuff? You can watch these things come down and they won't hit you."

"Nuts to that," I answered. "After living through all I have, I'm damned if I'm going to be killed by being hit on the head by a crate of peaches."

There actually were three or four lives lost among the prisoners after the war was over by parcels dropped from our own planes.

Then, a few days later, some of the boys decided to paint my name on one of the buildings. What they used for paint was Japanese tooth powder. They mixed it with water and had a rag for a brush. They painted in big letters: "Pappy Boyington here!"

The following morning a Navy plane flew by. We could see that he was taking a look, because he dipped his wing, this being the usual way a pilot takes a look. Then he circled around and came back again, and we could see somebody in the rear seat grinding a motion-picture camera.

All these months I had been wondering what my reaction would be on being rescued. I could imagine myself crying, maybe laughing and jumping around, doing practically anything. As I looked around, all these prisoners were now doing these things. But for my own part I was numb. I just couldn't feel. I couldn't cry. I couldn't laugh.

As the Higgins boats docked, the sailors jumped out and stuck three flags into the sand on the beach. There was little wind, so the flags did not unfurl immediately. But I walked toward the nearest flagstaff, the one on my right, and slowly raised my eyes, letting them follow the flagstaff from the sand to the top. And there on top was a Dutch flag. I lowered my eyes then, and walked over to the second flagstaff, and did what I did before—letting my eyes move slowly up from the sand to the top. There I saw the flag of England. Then I walked over to the third flagstaff, and did the same thing all over again. And on top this time was the flag of the United States.

I had been a slave now for more than twenty months, and as I looked up at this flag now, which had released me, which had made me a free man, I did something which today may seem oversentimental. I did not have a hat on, and I knew that a Marine is not supposed to salute uncovered, but just right then and there I gave this flag the snappiest salute I have ever given her.

As I turned and walked away from the flags, a gentleman I had seen two years previously, when I had a short talk with

342

him, came up to me and stuck out his hand. God knows how he recognized me, because I didn't look anything like I had two years ago. But there stood Harold Stassen, former Governor of Minnesota.

He said: "God sakes, Pappy, we didn't know you were alive until we saw that picture the plane took this morning. We were out here on the cruiser *San Juan*. The official signing isn't going to be for five days, but we couldn't stay out there anchored just a thousand yards from you boys and let you stay here any longer."

The Japanese colonel in command of the camp did not want to turn the prisoners loose because there had not been an official signing, so our American visitors sent back to the ship and brought out a couple of platoons of Marines.

The camp commander asked what these people were for, and the answer was: "Oh, just to help things along, help get the boys out of camp."

So the commander permitted us to leave the camp. The dignified old Japanese colonel, I heard later, had lost his boots, sword, and collar insignia to some of the prisoners. He must have been awfully disgraced.

In the past I had been on many boats going ashore. They had been called liberty boats. But this was the first time I ever took the first one away from shore back to the ship. This Higgins boat took us aboard one of our beautiful hospital ships, the *Benevolence*.

I went up the gangway, and somebody told me to go down a certain ladder and turn to the right. As I went down the ladder I was almost bowled over by one of the cutest little nurses I ever have seen. I do not think it was altogether because I had been away from women all this time, for this little nurse was really cute. I did not have presence of mind to say "pardon me" or anything.

I had started to turn to the right, as we had been directed, and then I thought: "Oh no, I had better turn around." I turned around and said: "Hey you, baby."

She said: "Hello, big boy."

I said: "How about a smooch?"

She threw her arms around my neck and about the time we were in the middle of a clinch somebody tapped me on the shoulder and said: "This way, bub. Take your clothes off and take a disinfectant shower, and we will issue some new clothes."

After getting cleaned up we were sent down to the dining room. If I ever had prayed for a meal, we had just exactly what I would have asked for in our first meal that evening aboard the *Benevolence*. It was ham and eggs.

I had about five orders of ham and eggs, and some poor little starved B-29 pilot sitting across from me just shook his head sadly and said: "My God, Greg, I wish I could put all the stuff away that you do."

Many of the boys could not eat. I was lucky. I guess part of the reason I was always able to eat everything that was given to me in Japan was because I was raised on poor man's food, which consisted of a great many starches. I had very little dysentery all along the line. Most of the prisoners were troubled terribly with this.

After a short screening by the medical department, those of us who were permitted to travel were put off onto another ship. I immediately found an icebox next to my stateroom, and while I was looking at it a Navy chief walked up to me and told me that if I wanted anything just to help myself. So that is where I spent most of the next two days.

A couple of old chiefs came in there and were talking to me and one said: "We thought we had a new chief aboard." I guess I really made myself a member of their mess, twenty-four hours a day.

After the third day being aboard ship I was looking over the railing out to sea, and somebody tapped me on the shoulder. I turned around and there were about fifteen news correspondents staring me in the face. They had a microphone setup, shoved it in my teeth, and said: "Talk, brother."

I did not know what to say, but finally I managed to blurt out how happy I would be to go home and whatnot, and then I said hello to my eldest child and told him when I got home

344

I was going to take him hunting, for I remembered it was getting near the season, early fall, back home.

(Incidentally, after I did get home a long letter was waiting for me from some woman in New York. She had a cat monogram on her stationery, and after welcoming me home in one sentence she then went on at great length to write how horrible she thought I was to go hunting, as if "you haven't had your blood lust satisfied now.")

After being out in Tokyo Bay for four or five days watching our planes go by in review and formation over Tokyo, and this time they were not dropping bombs, I was taken to an airport outside of Yokohama, and I started for home in one of the first planes to go back to the United States.

On the flight from Tokyo to Guam the pilot of the DC-4 was an old friend of mine, and he asked me to stay in his quarters in Guam and not in the hospital. We got in his quarters and he, being real kind to me, fried up bacon and eggs, and also poured me a stiff drink of good old United States bourbon and soda. I got about halfway down this glass and said: "I'm awfully sorry to turn this down, I know it isn't like me, but I just can't seem to get it down."

I labeled it stupidity for a long time, but now I appreciate that it was pure insanity. This reaction, or aversion to bourbon, really made my mind tick, for I was thanking prison camp for finally making alcohol difficult to swallow. Never, for a second, facing the fact that my run-down condition was the most logical reason for my not wanting it. And as time went on, I didn't even thank prison camp or the Japanese for apparently removing my obsession to drink, as I was more than willing to accept all the credit for myself. My great will-power, that's what did it!

Then I politely asked that if I got hungry later on would it be all right if I used their icebox. They said: "Sure, take anything you want in there." About midnight I got hungry, and went out to this icebox and in it I saw three lovely steaks. I knew that there were three people who lived in this place and so I thought, rather than deprive just one of them of a steak, I might just as well fry all three. I fried all three steaks, ate them, and then I fried eggs, too.

Some of my old friends there on Guam took me around to all the supply places and outfitted me with adequate clothing, got me some snappy sunglasses, and so forth. Then one chap asked me: "Can you think of anything else you would like?"

I said: "I wish you would lend me a dime." I didn't have any American money.

He said: "What do you want it for?"

I answered: "Well, I would like to get three of those chocolate bars."

He laughed and said: "Why, sure thing."

But he stopped laughing a little while later because we had just finished lunch and I was about halfway down the third candy bar when I noticed that this chap was looking kind of sick around the gills. I said: "Oh, excuse me, Zack. I didn't stop to think how nauseating it was to watch someone eat three candy bars."

I was thinking back prior to being shot down, and recalled how the non-alcoholic jerks wolfed down ice cream or something sweet, not understanding how in hell they were able to enjoy such things.

Sometimes I wonder if anyone can blame me for stating earlier that my life should have been taken care of by some fiction writer, or a cartoonist, perhaps. Especially when one of the persons I ran into on my first stop out of Japan was none other than my old nemesis, just like he had been waiting for me all these months. He hadn't looked me up, though. We had run into one another, quite accidentally, during a staff lunch. A peculiar expression appeared on his ugly features, as I spoke first, saying: "Hi, Colonel, I'm back again!"

When he finally spoke, I thought I noticed a combination of coolness mixed with forced cordiality as he said: "Good to see you back again, Boyington."

I could imagine that Lard had thought that fate had double-crossed him again, throwing one of his problems back, after he had gone to all the trouble of patting himself on the back. In my mind Lard had become unimportant, for by then I had heard so many compliments on my so-called greatness that I mentally shoved him out of my mind as any further source of hardship.

After spending a couple of days on Guam our DC-4 flew us to Kwajalein, remaining there only about an hour or so for fuel, then we were off for Pearl Harbor.

The meeting I shall never forget, and I don't mean all the cameras and newspapermen, was when I stepped out of the plane at Pearl Harbor. For *all this* was not sufficient for a man who just wanted to be *wanted,* and for some reason or another had felt that he never had been since childhood.

Here at Pearl Harbor was where millions of Americans as well as their opponents had seen the beginning of a four-year stretch that was to send them far and wide, some never to return. And here, standing in the background for his station in affairs, more or less, letting the cameramen and newspapermen shove ahead, was an old friend.

The moment I saw him I started elbowing my way to him, and forgot all the others for a brief period. I was oblivious to cameras and newsmen as my old friend threw his arms about my shoulders, hugging me tight. And I did the same in return. My friend said: "I blamed myself for your getting shot down, and felt like I had killed you. You don't know how wonderful it is to see you alive."

I said: "Forget it, it was all part of the game. But, believe me, I am glad that it turned out this way."

He said: "So am I, so happy for you, my boy."

And as he backed away from his embrace, I thought there was *something* different about the wild eyes looking at me from beneath the thick bushy brows. I was correct, for I could see the eyes had glazed a bit, squeezing out a couple of tears upon those wrinkled and tanned cheeks.

I was happy as we walked along in an unmilitary manner, and I could see that my friend was too, for he was smiling and swinging his unnecessary cane. He was Major General Nuts Moore.

CHAPTER **34**

AFTER REACHING HONOLULU I had my future all mapped out to perfection, part of which I falsely believed, and part of which I was willing to assume. This plan had grown gradually since my release, and seemed very logical because I had been reading a lot of stories that were quite flattering indeed. At first I thought there must be some mistake, somewhere, but no, there were my photographs with my name. It was almost too good to be true, I thought.

But I decided that I would smarten myself up a bit, so I might be in accord with the public's conception. It was during the week layover at Honolulu that on Moore's advice I decided to become this person they were writing about, because I definitely was pleased with the change in attitude. I was going to forget my past. I planned on accepting my newly found position in life graciously, modestly, and with dignity.

This character part had been growing in my mind since the end of the war, approximately the same length of time as the hair of my dapper mustache. Having never worn a mustache previously, I suppose I was trying to hide or change my appearance—therefore the bush.

During the layover the general talked to me like a father, giving all the help and advice he could think of. Before leaving to take care of his marine-aviation business, he turned his quarters over for my use, also his car and chauffeur, and just about everything with the possible exception of his command.

Giving an alcoholic power isn't exactly the proper thing to do, but I doubt that the dear general was well versed on the subject, or probably had no idea that I was one. His only motive, I am certain, was to see that a Marine got a few breaks he thought he was entitled to. As he was leaving, he said: "Son, they have a habit of forgetting too soon. As long as you are a demand product, remain here an extra week, and we will get a few of the things they promised before you are forgotten. I am many years older than you are, and I've seen it all happen before."

I promised my friend that I would remember to do exactly as he suggested. Considering that an alcoholic has difficulty keeping any promise, I have often wondered how on earth I was able to carry out everything he had suggested.

There was no question that Moore knew he was in the twilight of his career and could take liberties no ordinary officer would dare to. He cabled Washington and demanded that my regular commission be forwarded to the Hawaiian Islands prior to my returning to the United States. My regular status had been guaranteed through typewritten error (no regular officer was to have gone on the Flying Tiger mission). A special act was put through Congress in my case, because now that the war was over I was being billed as "The White Hope" of Marine Aviation publicity.

It was truly fantastic; the legend of bravery and idealism that had been concocted during those twenty months since I had last been seen going down in a ball of flames. And, on top of it all, the majority of all this had been released from Marine Corps Public Relations. There was no question in their minds that my watery grave would hold me, and that I would never return to disgrace them or haunt them, or, one thing for certain, they would never have let those releases out of their hands.

Actually, they did hold out for many months, using their better judgment. That is until three months after I was last seen, and the more stable characters would have held out longer, if it hadn't been for pressure from the Executive Department.

As the story was told to me, the Executive Department had gotten a bit shaken by a certain editorial by a New York columnist. And I'm certain—because I have heard congressmen say: "The only way I know about what's going on is to read the newspapers."—that it was the only reason the Executive Department took notice. For over two years of war, and all overseas, I hadn't been recommended for so much as a Purple Heart and I was supposed to be dead.

Anyhow, the columnist wrote an article titled "Two Soldiers and a Marine," which caused the leveler heads in the Corps to act against their better judgment, in place of waiting until six months after the war to make dead sure. Of course, I believe they would have still remained firm if the Executive Department hadn't gone in and said: "Who is in charge around here?"

The article stated: "To the best of my research, there have been over 200,000 medals of various types dealt out since the war began some two years ago. But here are two soldiers and a Marine who have done this, and have done that, and have been dead for a certain length of time. Yet, none of their families have been awarded so much as a Purple Heart, which, I am of the understanding, is the least that a fellow can receive for giving his life."

Nuts Moore had used his influence or rank on his Navy medical staff, I was soon to learn, as they rather begrudged passing me for the promotion I should have had before I was shot down. One of the medicos caused considerable pain when he pressed upon my swollen spleen, asking: "What is this lump?" Another one said: "Good grief, I'm glad I'm not a regular officer—if we get caught for overlooking all this—our names are going to be mud."

Anyhow, they passed me.

A former C.O. of mine was flown from the United States with the findings of a promotion board that had been assembled rather hastily for the purpose. He told me about the board members, although he wasn't supposed to divulge this information. Half the board had argued that they couldn't possibly recommend me because there weren't any fitness reports on me for two years, and the last one Colonel Lard had filled out was nothing they could promote anybody with.

But the senior member, whom I was talking to, had had his orders unbeknown to the others, so I was a lieutenant colonel in the regulars again when I boarded a Martin Clipper for San Francisco.

At San Francisco I was given a most fantastic reception by the American public and press. More fantastic than I had ever dreamed possible, even in my drunken dreams. Now I appreciated the full meaning of General Moore's advice. And how happy I was that I'd decided to be a dignified character behind a mustache, and how fortunate I was that liquor was no longer an obsession, so I wouldn't louse up the act.

But I was soon to find that carrying on with this act wasn't going to run as smoothly as I had planned, for I found that my drinking past was waiting back home, to pick up where I left off, whether I wanted to or not.

And I do not know what Lazarus found when he returned from the dead, but as for me I found myself and my earthly affairs in one hell of a state of confusion, and maybe Lazarus had found them that way too. Naturally, mine happened to be all of my own making, I know.

Anyhow, while honors were being pitched at me from one direction, and faster than I could receive them, from the other direction came flying equally as fast confusion and my past drunken dealings. To return from the dead, then, and to be back among mortal folks, may not always be the sporting thing for any of us to do.

Three years are a lot of years for any of us to be out of touch with what we have left behind "in case of death" or for any other reason. And it might be more graceful for us, or more sporting of us, if we could just return as some other person. I certainly had planned, but I should have known that it would not work out.

So, of all the banquets, dinners, and the like, which were showered by the bucketful, only one reception of the lot do I hold really glorious. And this was because of its sincerity, my own and that of the people in it. For these people were not out for anything, and neither was I upon this particular occasion. They were not out for monetary showmanship, or to parade me around for their own ends, or to have me raising money for this cause or that cause. No, these people were *my* people. They were twenty of my old squadron mates, twenty of my old Black Sheep.

Previous to my being shot down and lost I had said this to the squadron, for morale effect more than anything else: "Don't worry if I'm ever missing, because I'll see you in Dago and we'll throw a party six months after the war is over." And the reason I had used this six-months business, as I mentioned before, is that if one doen't show up six months after the war is over he is officially declared dead.

But, after leaving the Hawaiian Islands, I certainly had not expected to see twenty of these old squadron mates already waiting for me at the airport in Oakland. Oh, that was a wonderful feeling. They tossed me around on their shoulders, and they sang the "Baa-Baa Black Sheep" squadron song, and we had a great reunion.

Then one of the boys asked: "When are we going to have that party in Dago you promised?"

I laughed and said: "It may be a long time before we all hit San Diego. So, will you let me off the hook for throwing one in San Francisco instead?"

They all cheerfully replied: "Okay by us, Gramps. Dago is too long a time to wait for a drink anyhow."

We had the party that evening in the St. Francis Hotel, and it *was* a party. But fortunately, after having been in the prison camps so long, I couldn't seem to drink, and after trying my damnedest for a few hours I left the party with a few of the pilots, which was unusual for me. A few of us went on up to another floor and took a steam bath and got it out of our systems. I went to sleep on one of the cots in the steam room for the rest of the night.

But I must mention, too, that, of all the keys-to-cities and other junk that come the way of anybody being put on momentary exhibition, the only gift I truly value after having gotten back is what these boys themselves gave me. They gave it to me at the dinner that evening of the party. And it is a gold watch with the inscription on the back: "To Gramps from his Black Sheep." When I asked the fellows how they had gotten the watch engraved so soon, they told me. They explained to me that they had taken the watch into a jewelry shop and had told the jeweler what they wanted engraved on it. The jeweler had answered in customary procedure: "On account of the war that will take me about a month, fellows."

The gang had answered: "Bud, we got news for you. The war happens to be over. We won't go into who won it, right now, but you're going to engrave the watch right now. And we're going to stand here while you do it."

So that is how the watch came to be engraved in one day, the same day as my return to the States, and in time for dinner.

All of which made just one more reason for a long time to come why I wished that all my own Black Sheep could have flown wing for me through all the problems that followed. Now I know that even my Black Sheep could not have helped.

During the day of the party, among the multitude of reporters were a couple of reserved gents who impressed me right off as nice guys. One said: "We understand you boys are having that party tonight. The one that was supposed to be in San Diego."

"Yes, that's right. By the way, if you're not doing anything, drop over, and I'll see you get a few drinks."

The two men thanked me and left, and one of the Marine Corps Public Relations officers said: "Just how naïve can you be, Pappy? Don't you know who those two guys are?"

"What difference does that make? How nice do you want me to be? I invited them to our party, didn't I? By the way, who are they?"

"Stupid, those are *Life* magazine representatives. Don't you know you can't buy or even ask for mention in their coverage?"

"Okay, I'm sorry," I said to this P.R. officer. "But how was I supposed to know? I'll know better next time."

"You mean, if there ever is a next time."

It had completely left my mind, even when these two *Life*

men showed up at the party, for I didn't see any cameras. I figured they were just two nice guys who had accepted my invitation. I believed them when they volunteered to cover the party, but *Life* had never covered a drinking party since its beginning.

And that was that!

I found myself on the beginning of a scheduled but seemingly endless bond-tour drive that was to last for three months. I was to make appearances several times a day, going to most of the major cities in the United States. Our government wanted to sell bonds, and the Marine Corps wanted the publicity. So my squadron intelligence officer, Major Frank Walton, and I were to accompany one another about the country.

It was a couple of weeks after the Black Sheep party, which was by now a pleasant memory to me, when Frank and I got off a TWA plane in Denver for a breather. We noticed a woman pointing in our direction and looking back into a *Life* magazine. So, there was nothing to do but buy one ourselves and take a look.

Unbeknown to us, one of the fellows from *Life* had come to the party with a candid camera. There were over six pages of unposed pictures of our gang, which are about the only kind *Life* takes, I found out later. But it was a surprise to us, for we hadn't seen him. I thought the pictures very cute.

Then *Life* had thought so much of the Black Sheep that they had gone against their rules and printed their first pictures of a drinking party of any kind. Not that I could have done anything about it, but I have often wondered if they were sorry they had, because the end for the leader of the Black Sheep turned out pretty sad in most people's estimation. They were right the first time, and should have stuck by their rules, the way things turned out. But then, how dull life would become if we knew all the answers.

A number of other people besides my traveling mate Frank, some of whom I didn't know, assumed charge of me and appeared to have the authority for doing so. I was going crazy trying to figure out a way to take care of some of my personal affairs, but I didn't have a chance.

I would ask how long I could sleep and they would look at their watches and say: "Well, you've got just fifteen or twenty minutes." And I would take off my shoes and lie down on the bed and then they would shake me and say: "It's time to go."

I seemed to be talking every place under the sun, over the radio or at some luncheon or dinner or public square. I was so groggy with this new life, and needed sleep so much, that there were times when I didn't recognize friends I had known for years. The faces I recognized, but for the life of me I couldn't think of their names. These talks were not for me. I got nothing out of them. I was still broke. These talks were mostly for War Bonds or other causes.

The reason I had not received any money or back pay is that before going away in the Pacific I had all my wages put into a trusteeship for my three children. I had done it through a reputable law firm and a bank in San Diego. But arrangements like this take more than a reputable law firm and bank, for they can't do anything about an alcoholic's friends. Anyhow, my friend (female) had taken care of things until her alcoholic buddy was missing in action, then things ceased being carried out as planned.

Please don't get me wrong, because I am not trying to pass the buck to anyone, let alone a woman. I know that nobody was to blame for my being incapable of managing my own affairs prior to the war. It was caused by alcohol alone, by the alcohol that I myself drank, not the alcohol that anyone else drank.

But in regard to women whose company I chose prior to the war they all seemed to have one thing in common, and this one thing above many of their other varying qualities that I apparently liked, because it gave me an excuse to drink. Most of these gals didn't drink like I did, but nevertheless they were drinking partners as far as I was concerned. This one thing in common was that all of them could talk on for hours on end about how noble they were for the particular quality they had least of. Honesty was the forte of the kleptomaniac; virtue was the stand of the nymphomaniac; learning was the blabber of the illiterate; social drinking was the soapbox trail of the dipso-maniac; and I seemed to cherish all of these different types equally well at one time or another. I cherished them because their endless conversations about qualities they didn't have gave me an ideal excuse to get drunk while I listened to them. So I cannot honestly place a particle of blame for my mismanaged affairs on any of these poor sick females. But because I was gradually getting my health back, and because I was unable to have the opportunity to take care of the females I was mixed up with financially, I automatically returned to drink for the answers.

Frank must have recognized some of my old patterns because he looked worried. Finally he said: "The Marine Corps was terribly worried about you before we started this bond tour."

"Like hell they are, or they wouldn't have sent me on this rat-race, letting all these publicity seekers wear me out."

"Some of them back in Headquarters, knowing how you used to drink, were hoping that you wouldn't start again."

I laughed this off, saying: "Don't worry, old boy, I am forced to take a few on this tour to be polite like you are. But after it is over, I'm going to quit."

Frank looked relieved and said: "Well, I wasn't worried, but I'm sure glad to hear it, because you have too much to lose. And I know you're going to do it."

It wasn't that I was trying to kid Frank, for I think that was the furthest thing from my mind. I really meant what I said. Just like I meant what I said many times afterward.

Our itinerary took us to Washington, D.C., and Admiral Nimitz Day, where the nation was going to pay homage to our great Navy and its heroes. I was scheduled there too, for I was to pick up the Medal of Honor from our President, Harry Truman, and a Navy Cross from the Commandant of the Marine Corps, General Vandergrift.

The Navy Cross took but a brief moment of Vandergrift's time. He shook my hand, pinned the Cross on my blouse, and his chief of staff gave me the piece of paper to go with it on the way out—all of two minutes.

After leaving the Commandant's office I read the citation, then I couldn't help likening myself to some guy who was being buried on "boot hill." The only reason dirt was thrown in one's face was to keep the odor from offending those who remained. By their standards I should have picked up at least a dozen medals of various denominations, but it was apparent that not one of my combats had ever been cited, even in this lone booby prize I had just received. Someone had composed this citation at Washington from an old newspaper version. It stated briefly, gallantry in action, shooting down one enemy plane, and then being lost in action on January 3, 1944.

Not that I thought a Navy Cross meant anything, for I was certain that it meant very little. I recalled two very affable colonels in the Guadalcanal days; both were aviators and had been buddies since their academy graduation. These two colonels thought they were heroes for ducking bombs by going in and out of an operations bomb shelter, so they each wrote the other up for a Navy Cross, which happens to be the top award the Navy gives. And do you know, both of them received their Crosses.

Then I thought back about the three-page night letter I had wired over the heads of everybody, and the little cutthroat who sat in the office of the director of Marine Corps Aviation's most of his career. A great many things became clear in my mind. They were intending to squeeze the last drop of publicity out of me for the Corps, then somebody was going to cut me from ear to ear—and I knew who my executioner was going to be.

Receiving the Medal of Honor turned out to be quite a lengthy process. Not that its presentation takes long, for this honor has a loop they throw around your neck, thus obviating the chance of sticking one's fingers like some of the lesser medals that are pinned on.

Our group of sailors and Marines had to wait in formation on the White House lawn so damn long they became faint. I thought Harry Truman took his damn sweet time coming out. We were in two rows standing at attention, one row facing the other, sailors facing the Marines.

Owing to the delay, one of the official party waiting on the lawn walked over behind me to kill some time. He was an old acquaintance, a brigadier general now, and the last I had heard of him he had been sent over to England on some kind of mission as an observer.

He addressed me by an old nickname: "Hey, Rats?"

"What do you want, General?" This was out of the corner of my mouth, because I couldn't break ranks or turn my head.

He laughed and said: "There are those who never counted upon your showing up again, don't you know?"

"Yeah, they say a lot of nice things about you when you're dead that they wouldn't say when you're alive. But I sure screwed 'em, didn't I, Dad?"

"I wonder what's holding up the show. Maybe Harry has to check first and see that you guys are all democrats."

"The way I feel, I might get this thing posthumously after all."

"Rats, your case reminds me of a deal I saw in England."

"How's that, General?"

"Their head man was out pinning on medals one day, and it was quite a chore for him. He had a hell of a time with one fellow in particular.

"He started out: 'Sergeant F-f-f-f-lanagan you have been awarded the Distinguished F-f-f-f-lying Cross f-f-f-f-or shooting down f-f-f-f-our F-f-f-f-olke-Wulf f-f-f-f-ighters.'

"Then this sergeant interrupted: 'But, Your Majesty, I shot down *five* Folke-Wulf fighters!'

"So the head boy gave it another try: 'Oh, very well then, Sergeant, f-f-f-f-or shooting down f-f-f-f-fuh-fuh-fuh—shooting down f-f-f-f-fuh-fuh-fuh—it doesn't make a damn bit of difference how many—you are only going to get one f-f-f-f-fuh-fuh, ——ing medal.' "

Of this group of sailors and Marines I was the first to march up to the President, as I was senior in rank. Truman was brief. A handshake apiece, followed by these words: "Congratulations, I would rather have this honor than be President of the United States."

This line sounded awfully corny to me and I wondered who had written it, because they hadn't even trusted him to pronounce our names. As I said before, the only man I really felt for was the hospital corpsman who refused to kill anyone but got shot all to hell saving Marines on Mount Suribachi.

Now that this was all over, the picture couldn't be complete without New York giving a hero's welcome home, as only New York can. From the world's tallest buildings they throw torn up telephone books and used ticker tape, a gigantic display, regardless of who is being welcomed.

I had finished riding up the New York streets on the back seat of a Cadillac convertible like many before me, waving, nodding, and watching torn pieces of paper come down like snow. The police were busy holding back a mob of well-wishers. A middle-aged man with a thin face and graying at the temples broke through the line and grabbed me by the arm. A policeman grabbed him and started to put him behind the line, but I said: "Wait a minute. I think he wants to tell me something."

He did: "Enjoy it today, my boy, because they won't give you a job cleaning up the streets tomorrow."

CHAPTER **35**

In NEW YORK I was housed in the most pretentious quarters I ever hope to be in. Yet, I was able to enjoy these only for the time when I was sleeping. *Look* magazine had graciously supplied the Prince Edward Suite in the towers of the Waldorf-Astoria Hotel for two weeks, while Frank and I commuted in and out of the area surrounding the city making talks.

As closely as I can remember, for I would have been as well off in a basement room in the Y.M.C.A., the few brief glances were out of this world. Seven rooms, fancy chandeliers, master bathtub one could swim in, and all the other luxuries too numerous to mention were at our disposal. Yet we had barely enough time to complete a full-course meal in privacy.

Oh, how sick I was of the celebrity business! All places seemed the same to me. All people responded the same to me. My reactions and feelings can best be explained in telling about the famous Mayor Kelly of Chicago fame.

More than once during publicized "Boyington Day," in this city or that town, I was given my own clue in this regard. Perhaps the sharpest clue occurred in Chicago, where I stayed two days, was invited into the great Mayor Kelly's office, and was presented with a key to the city. While our photographs were being taken together, and so on, I couldn't help notice the writing inscribed on the key. It had been presented to some joker back in 1937.

Also, while the place was lined with pressmen, Mayor Kelly started to ask me a few questions. First: "Well, where were you shot down?"

"It was in the St. George Channel," I answered. "It was between New Britain and New Ireland."

The dear old mayor had not been paying much attention, but at the mention of Ireland his old eyes brightened: "Oh, they got you in Ireland, eh?"

"Oh no, Mr. Mayor, not in Ireland—but off New Ireland in the South Pacific."

"Well, go on, son, tell me all about it."

I started explaining how I was swimming around in the water, being strafed, and finally had to take off all my clothes to keep afloat—but before I could finish, his eyes brightened again: "Oh, they caught you while you were in swimming, eh?"

What was the use? I just gave up and began wondering when I could leave the place.

As a sort of paradox, though, I must say that I did not mind, and still don't, addressing audiences, once I got used to it. I do like my audiences to be somewhat open-minded, though, and sometimes I found them that way, and sometimes I didn't. For at that time I felt that I had something to say to Americans that was useful.

The audience would be disappointed at first, or at least puzzled at first, why I—all banged up by beatings, wounds, and so on—didn't hate the Japanese. Sure, I hated the little guards who made me miserable when I was a captive. But the best analogy I could make to my audiences was as if some little kid were making you miserable if you were tied up on a davenport. You would hate the little devil, but, after you got loose and turned him over to the authorities or sent him to a detention school, you would not hate him any more. You would realize that he had to have education.

I explained to my audiences that I couldn't hold any hate in my heart for the masses of the Japanese population. I had read recent articles on how the Japanese actions over there might be termed facetious in their love for America because we won the war and they want to work their way out the easiest possible way. But I saw enough in the war, and before the Japanese knew they were going to lose it, to know that the Japanese gave Americans better breaks than they did other nations.

When asked to give information on Japanese war criminals, I answered that anybody who was named by any of our fellows who had been prisoners would be looked up by the Japanese themselves. All we would have to do was ask the Japanese where these had been, give their descriptions, and the Japanese themselves would be only too happy to look up these people. This proved itself out. Everyone they looked for who had not committed suicide was found with ease.

The occupational forces we had in Japan were small, and yet we had little trouble, and I explained why. I explained that the Japanese would co-operate to the fullest extent, which they had done and were doing. By handling the situation properly we had gained complete control of the Pacific.

I made the analogy that the Japanese islands are comparable to the Philippine Islands, and I reminded people that not many years ago we waged a bitter war with the Filipinos, who are now our bosom friends, buddies, and allies. I tried to make the analogy that the Japanese people are far more industrious, and that in time we will have a much better asset in Japan than we have in the Philippine Islands, because the Japanese have proved themselves, even in being an enemy, far more co-operative and industrious than the Filipinos in trying to rebuild their country and get things straightened around.

And in closing most of my talks I would remind the audiences again that Japan has followed us and copied us in everything we did, and that they liked our way of doing things since the day we forced trade upon them. And that in twenty or so years from now, or even less, Japan would be one of our greatest assets, an American-thinking Japan right off the coast of Russia!

At the height of my luxurious living, I didn't have time to enjoy it, and I realized that I never would—even with time.

Once again in my life another milestone, another location, turned out to be just another millstone around my neck.

So I indeed welcomed a long-distance call from the Marine Corps Headquarters in Washington. It was from one of my first squadron commanders, now a major general in Headquarters—old "Skeeter" McKittrick.

"Hello, Rats," the general chuckled over the phone, "this is McKittrick."

"Well, hello, General. It is nice to hear from you." But I was thinking: "I wonder what's wrong now. If there were any complaints, then, what right have they to complain, after all I've done for them. It isn't fair for anybody to criticize me for the wonderful job I'm doing, educating the public."

He continued: "Just received a hostile letter from the Bureau of Medicine and Surgery, giving us hell for using a guy who has too many things wrong with him. The way they describe the guy, I don't think he's alive."

"Is that so, then, who is he, sir?"

"I'll read the letter, because I believe you know more about this fellow than I do."

Then the general went on reading this lengthy, damning letter addressed to Marine Corps Headquarters. It stated ailments too numerous to mention, such as beriberi, liver, and some high-sounding medical terms for something radically wrong with a leg, and various other diseases caused by malnutrition, and wound up by ordering them to have this individual turn himself in to a naval hospital of his choosing, immediately.

Yes, it was difficult to believe, but they were referring to me.

How happy I was for an excuse to wind up this madhouse I had found myself in. But I just had to pretend that I was gallant, so I said: "General, I only have one more week scheduled, which winds me up in Portland, Oregon. So, with your permission, I will do my duty on the way back, then turn into a hospital near Los Angeles."

"Okay, Rats, that will be all right, I guess. Good luck, let us hear from you." General "Skeeter" closed out, little realizing that they were not only going to hear, but they were going to see an avalanche of unfavorable crap plastered all over the front pages of every newspaper in the country as a result of my drinking past. I knew that all this was on its way even though I pretended otherwise, for I just simply couldn't face facts. And my drinking pattern was coming back again, worse than ever. I was able to get by with the talks and in some very fancy places because I was smart enough not to take a drink until the occasion was almost over, consequently, a great many people were spared embarrassment. That is, all the people except those who attended a talk in the last city on my itinerary, which happened to be Portland, Oregon. Once again I had counted upon completing a job before casting it to one side as useless; but no, fate, as I termed it—fate later became alcohol as far as I was concerned—was to rear its ugly head. And with my lecture tour in the bag, so to speak, it happened again.

After getting out of the car in Portland we were taken up to a large suite. There was a grand piano, along with many other things I had no use for. However, I soon spotted one item that could be of some use, a scotch-and-soda setup on the table. The committee said: "Go ahead, take your time. Rest, get cleaned up and take a shower and shave. We won't have this informal dinner for a couple of hours."

"But I'm not expected to go to any dinner tonight," I answered. "The program's supposed to start tomorrow, not today."

"But this is just a little dinner," the committee said. "Only a few of us will be there. You'll not even have to talk. Just relax, take a few drinks, you'll have plenty of time to get cleaned up later."

All my life I seemed to have difficulty saying no to anything, especially when I was drinking. But my biggest problem was that I could never say no to liquor—and mean it. I suppose the only reason for the war record is that I couldn't stop myself from volunteering. When I didn't have to say no, all I had to do in most cases was to remain silent. But silence wasn't one of my virtues either.

The committee hung around. I poured drinks for them, and they poured drinks for me. They began to feel good, but I am certain that I felt better. One of the more jovial said: "Pappy, I've heard that you can give a hell of a good talk, but that you're always sober. I'd love to hear you after you've had a few drinks, so you could feel free to cut loose, giving us the real lowdown."

Frank could stand no more and said: "Man, you don't know what you're asking for. Please believe me, and let well enough alone. Why don't you all leave and let Greg get some sleep? I know what I'm talking about."

With a few drinks in me I resented this, but I laughed for the benefit of the straggling committee and said: "Oh, Frank is just the worrying type. Thank God he is, or I'd never been able to complete this trip. But come on, fellows, I love good company, so let's have another drink."

Frank left us, saying: "I'm going to catch an hour's rest. But don't ever say that I didn't warn you people."

The shower, shave, and rest I had looked forward to slowly slipped out of my mind. We drank right up until somebody said: "My, how the time flies; it's time for dinner."

I was escorted down to a lower floor where the informal dinner, or whatever it was, was to take place, and I found that this informal affair included about two hundred of the city's leading citizens, all dressed formally for the occasion. Leading, I might add, as far as making money was concerned.

A combination of shock and scotch made these guests go out of focus, much as if they were standing behind the heat waves coming off from a hot radiator. I had been tricked. I had to talk, and there was no way out of it. In order to get by I realized I was going to have to eat and then drink a lot of black coffee before it came time for me to speak.

I had every intention of sobering up, and I was trying my damnedest by gulping down a few cups of coffee. My audience was beginning to get into focus a bit better, when one of my drinking friends in the committee said: "Too bad you can't talk like Patton. Have you ever read one of Patton's speeches, Pappy?"

I answered: "No, I haven't, but that is a man I really admire."

He laughed and handed me a sheet of typewritten paper, and he said: "This is a copy of one of Patton's speeches. Go ahead, read it. I'll bet you wish you could talk like he does."

365

The coffee had cleared my vision enough to enable me to struggle through a speech that had a wonderful selection of four-letter words. This had been given to a completely different kind of audience from the one I had facing me, but the committeeman had started my ego rolling.

In an attempt to get sober I hadn't so much as touched any of the drinks lined up in front of me. They just stood there waiting until my talk was over. I was going to be announced any minute. But by now I was desperate. Forgetting the fact that my audience was a group of men and women, and all of them swells, I was going to try to top Patton's talk, which had gotten his troops so fired up. In order to do this I needed something, and something in a hurry, too.

The answer was staring me right in the face, five or six glasses full of scotch and soda (heavy on the scotch and light on the soda). I downed the lot of these glasses about as rapidly as I would have downed water on Truk, if the Japs had given it to me. The stage was set. My lengthy and fantastic introduction was at an end, at last.

With General Patton's speech before me to help remind me just how far to go, I started out:

"Good evening, ladies and gentlemen. I compliment you all, for I have never seen more beautiful gowns or handsome dress clothes. And how thoughtful of you to invite me to this little surprise. I wish to thank you for gathering here tonight, because I realize that it must be quite a sacrifice on your part.

"But I will assure you that I will get right to the meat of this occasion. I shall not keep you long.

"You came here to be entertained by some side-show freak, I know. You want to hear about the time when my foot was bleeding so badly that I had to roll my Corsair onto its back to make my blood last longer. How I continued shooting down Japs upside-down against overwhelming odds. Yes, you'd love to have me dramatize the race between running out of ammu- nition and running out of life's blood.

"But I know the only reason I should be here tonight. And I would like to inform you of the only reason you should be here.

"It is not to pay homage to a so-called war hero, because he would have been helpless without the financial assistance of slobs like you. So, in closing, I'm going to remind all of you slobs to continue to invest in War Bonds.

"Thank you for your time. Good night."

Then I sat down. There wasn't one single clap of hands. The guests filed out of the private dining hall with bewildered expressions on their faces. None of them ganged up at the speaker's table to shove and shake my hand as they usually did.

The committee members were dumfounded and probably hoped that the whole thing was nothing but a bad dream. I recall saying: "This serves me right. I shouldn't talk over people's heads."

Then someone put his arm around my shoulders and said: "Come on, Greg, forget it. I love you. You're just at the wrong address tonight, so let's go to a night club where we're wanted, then we'll have a little fun."

This man took me to a night club. I have often wished that I had some way of repaying him for some of the kindness and thoughtfulness he has displayed throughout the years. He happened to be my uncle, Guy Boyington, and I am positive that he would do the same for any poor soul.

But the bond tour was over, at last. It was loused up at its completion like everything else in my life. Frank and I headed for Los Angeles, and his home.

One of the things I have never been able to figure out is how lucky a person can be, especially one who has a knack for always getting into trouble. Others have wondered too. Some have said so—to my face.

A few years prior to the war a classmate who was killed later while dive-bombing at Guantánamo Bay, Cuba, gave a toast one night. His name was Ray Emerson, and a great person. Ray and I started out in the Marine Corps together, so he knew me well enough to wonder about some of the luck I had.

My drinking had not progressed to the point where it seemed to bother me in the slightest, but some things were happening that most people pass off as bad luck, things actually caused by neglect and by forgetting what seemed to be a part of me, leading to forced landings and car accidents. Although none of these incidents was pinned down as my fault, I am certain most of them could have been avoided if I hadn't been drinking.

One evening when we fellows were drinking toasts to this, that, and the other thing Ray said: "I would like to give a toast."

"Okay, what to?"

"I would like to toast to the luckiest unlucky man I know. Here's to Rats, may his luck continue forever."

We all drank; I did too, even though they were toasting me. Most people miss all the fun, for they just take everything at face value, or would probably know why somebody gave them a toast. But I had to wonder. I asked: "What do you mean, Ray?"

"Simple," he said. "You are forever losing your wallet, somebody takes your car and bangs it up, and the C.O.s always seem to choose you when they have a mad on and want to chew somebody out. We feel sorry for you and stick up for you. But I sometimes wonder why, because, if anything important happens—like a wing coming off or your car rolling over a dozen times—you seem to always fall into the proverbial backhouse—and come out smelling like a rose."

Maybe the same thing Ray spoke about was the reason I had decided to end up in Los Angeles instead of somewhere else. For here is where I met the right girl for me, although it was doubtful whether it was vice versa for a long, long time. This lucky thing happened while I was in the naval hospital.

As a patient I was granted special permission to go within a certain radius of the hospital as long as I kept in touch. And this is the time my friends and I drove down to Rosarita Beach, about eighteen miles below the border. We went down for the evening for dinner.

Our little party consisted of Frank Walton, who had been with me on the tour, his wife, her sister and her husband, and a beautiful friend of theirs to whom they previously had introduced me. I had not known her before the war, or even for very long, as measured by weeks. But for some reason, whenever we had been together in the group, she of all persons seemed to make me forget that there were troubles in this world of ours.

So again this evening, while at Rosarita, and with Mexican

music going on, I suddenly felt happier than I had felt for years and years.

The word "love" has been thrown around so carelessly in songs and stories that it has come to mean very little any more. In fact, it is almost better to avoid the word. But whatever the feeling is, or whatever word it has come to be known by, all I can say is this: that while we were talking or just listening to the Mexican music, I knew now for sure that this girl, with her slightly pug nose, and blue eyes with blond hair, her quick little way of laughing—I now knew for sure that she was the one somebody I should have known from the very beginning. I wanted to tell her so, but I didn't know how, and I didn't dare, although ordinarily I am not particularly reticent around women. But this seemed—for the first time in my life—altogether too right and too real.

Anyhow, rather than risk shooting off my mouth about what I was thinking, I guided her over to the bar and ordered two drinks from the little Mexican bartender, who, without my knowing it, had been watching us all the time. For what he did right then is the reason the girl is now my wife. And he did it all so simply. With laughing eyes he merely said: "For two people who have the look you two have, I'll break out the crystal glasses." And immediately that little bartender, with all the wisdom of the Latins, began to polish up two of his most beautiful glasses. With his words and his gesture he broke down what seemed a barrier, and Franny and I both suddenly found ourselves sort of crying and laughing at the same time, and we found ourselves suddenly telling each other about each other, and we were on Cloud Thirty-six, and the little bartender had put us there.

Further to celebrate the occasion, this sudden new feeling, I immediately changed the order to champagne, and the little bartender happily drank with us. And there were no troubles anywhere in the world any more. There was no other world. There was only Rosarita, and it was the world.

Home from roaming the globe, I had at last found my mate, but I had yet to ask that all-important question. It is not an

369

easy matter to ask a girl to take, not only a husband, but three children in the bargain—nice children, as I know they are.

To add to my dilemma, as I sat squashing out cigarette butts in an already-overflowing ash tray, listening to the radio, my friends, the press, were telling the whole world about me. Everything except that it was all caused by my own personal drinking past. No question but what Franny was listening, I was positive.

It sounded to me like the Voice of America. Naturally it wasn't, but it was just as loud as far as I was concerned. I happened to be newspaper copy, the war was over, and they were short of news. So they were spicing up every utterance that came from the lips of a woman who wanted her next husband waiting outside the doors of a divorce court while she shed the one she already had.

I couldn't say that I hadn't been warned, because I had—in no uncertain words. Also, I knew that this party would stop at nothing, and counted upon my being in such a position that I wouldn't take a chance with the threat of bad publicity. But my tour in prison camp had sobered me sufficiently to decide upon the correct move, and to hell with the threats.

The press didn't know the real reason, and didn't give a damn, but it was money. My old drinking buddy somehow figured that the Medal of Honor brought in a good deal of loot, and under no circumstances wished to have anything like that taken away. This is understandable, however, because very few people know that this honor brings in ten dollars per month, but the catch is—you have to reach your sixty-fifth birthday before it starts coming in.

Anyhow, they didn't ask me my side for two reasons: the stories wouldn't have been nearly so interesting, and besides I was too hard to locate. But somebody had dared me, and apparently no one has ever had much success choosing this method on me. Switching off my radio tormentor, I decided to take the bull by the horns.

"Operator. Please get me Hempstead 0872—in Los Angeles. Hello. Hello. Franny—is that you?

370

"Now that you know all the gory details, I want to ask you a question. Will you marry me?

"Oh, Franny, say it once again. I want to be certain that my ears aren't just ringing, Honey. Pack your bag, because we're leaving on the plane in two hours for Las Vegas."

The connections by plane were rough, but there we were in Las Vegas in the bare cold room of the justice of the peace, which seemed to grow warm and bright in its wintry surroundings. A Western-appearing gent in cowboy boots was on hand to stand up as best man.

There are weddings and weddings, but when it is your own, well, it is just your own. We know things only by our own feelings and experiences, as I have mentioned before. But a sense of rightness and sincereness took place about our wedding, as though it were being held in a huge cathedral filled with white roses instead of in the tiny office of the justice of the peace in Las Vegas—in the desert.

My bride wore one lone orchid in bright shining hair. No other flowers were needed, for indeed we had all the happiness any two people were entitled to.

As the amiable little justice congratulated us after the ceremony, he told us how he would like to be in for another term, as business was great. He had no idea that Franny and I were eloping, for both of us were past that tender age. But we were eloping—from the press.

And as time has gone on, I can see more and more evidence of what Ray Emerson was toasting to: "The luckiest, unlucky man I know."

CHAPTER 36

SHORTLY AFTER THE WAR the glamour was gone and there was nothing in my life but turbulence for nearly ten years.

To start with, the Medical Department of the Navy recommended that I be retired because of injuries received during the war. For this, I was thankful; it saved the Marine Corps the trouble. Or, I probably should say, a few people in the Corps were robbed of the pleasure.

The outlook ahead appeared to be getting darker instead of lighter, and somehow I sensed that I was eventually going to get "socked" in tight and run out of gas. For as time went on I seemed to be on some one-way street on which the buildings were becoming closer and closer together as I moved along.

To add to my problems, I found that it was next to impossible to obtain employment. Nobody seemed to want any part of me. There had been so much notoriety printed about me that I can hardly blame anyone for not wanting to hire me. Any hopes that had been entertained at intervals were always smashed just about the time I thought I was going to work for some top-notch company. I was lucky to get any kind of a job.

But one can always do something, and so did I. For four years I had one job after another, but I remained with each until it

372

became evident that I couldn't make my salt. These were all selling something, and the things I tried to sell varied from soup to nuts: air freight, clothing, jewelry, stamps, and insurance. Every one of these companies had one thing in common, though, in that they were having so much difficulty in selling their different specialties that they would have hired Satan himself if there had been the slightest possibility that he could sell their particular lines. All except one had something else in common too: they have been out of business for a long time.

If it hadn't been for a money-making hobby of mine, my family would have had some mighty slim pickings, the way things were going. This hobby took very little of my time, maybe two nights a week, sometimes three. These nights were spent inside of a squared circle surrounded by a pack of howling idiots who fouled up the air with smoke and words while I was busy refereeing professional wrestling.

There were any number of occasions during these ten years when the newspapers carried my name far and wide—just like the war publicity—but none of it was good. Sometimes I had the feeling that nobody was ever going to print anything about me again—unless it happened to be bad.

On these occasions either the sheriff's boys in tan or the chief of police's boys in blue would meet me coming out of some bar, first. Then, I would be driven to their place of business, where I would be booked, photographed, and fingerprinted for their records. Then they would leave me to sit behind barred doors and windows for the mandatory five hours. While I was cooling my heels someone on the force invariably was thoughtful enough to call the press and to inform them that I had been picked up.

The pattern was always the same; first I would pay my twenty-dollar bail, which I had no intention of fighting for, then I would see the story appear in the local papers the following day; after a week or so I would receive press releases on the same thing from disinterested parties in other cities, and finally I would get honorable mention in both *Time* and *Newsweek*.

While waiting one night at a sheriff's substation, it took the photographer quite a while to get there, so they decided to hold me until he arrived. When he finally did and they let me out, this photographer asked: "Now, then, where are the two arresting officers?"

A deputy said: "They have both gone home, probably in bed by now."

The photographer said: "That's too bad, but I have to have somebody. Would a couple of you fellows mind standing in for a picture?"

Before the guy snapped the picture, seven deputy sheriffs were standing around me. One would have thought that these boys were all necessary to capture Public Enemy Number One.

As for refereeing, there were many occasions when I entered the dressing rooms half blind from vodka just before the first match. I told myself that I had to get this way so the crowd wouldn't bother me, but before the night was over I usually had the crowd screaming for my blood.

During the first match I usually had some difficulty in keeping out of the way of the wrestlers. But as each match would come along I would be sweating it out, so by the time the main event arrived I was in rare form. The shows were regulated so that the preliminaries were dull, gradually working up to a climax in the main event. My actions fitted the program perfectly.

In case I forget it, or anybody wonders how on earth I arrived at these arenas that were spread all over Southern California, my wife usually drove me. My troubles were mild compared to what they could have been without her help.

On several occasions when I couldn't even stagger into the ring one of the wrestlers had to referee the first match—and sometimes the second match—to protect me. The wrestlers were all big, good-natured fellows who wouldn't hurt a fly, and they must have liked me because they did their best to help keep me out of trouble. The State Athletic Commission had its hands full checking on fixed boxing and crooked promoters without having to carry me—and they did look the other way. I might add that infuriating crowds is not healthy, for they can become uncontrollable, even though they are only watching an exhibition. The referee's duty is to see that the hero-villain act doesn't get too gruesome. It was small wonder that I wasn't hurt or even killed, the way I conducted myself a few times. I imagine that a psychiatrist would claim this form of amusement took the place of my combat flying.

Wrestling, as well as other professions, has a language all its own. In fact, even if people heard us talking above the clamor, they weren't able to understand what we were talking about. For examples: wrestle is "work"; fall is "going over"; "finish" is the routine just before the deciding fall; hero is "baby-face"; villain is "heel"; and building a hysterical crowd up to a climax is called "heat."

But to get back to my darling and very capable wife, and the part she played in my wrestling career. Sometimes help arrives from sources where one would least expect it. The fact that Franny has always been an outdoor girl, and remains in good physical condition by playing golf several times a week, came in right handy one night while we were putting on a show at Southgate, where there was usually a rough crowd. Some of these audiences were rough, some were gentle, but we thought we knew just how far to go with each before they became violent.

As I mentioned, it was up to the referee to control the "heat," but I had disregarded this, as I had on other occasions. This time I had made up my mind to wait for a particular wrestler to make the decision himself. In the past he had repeatedly coaxed me to permit the "heat" to build up a little longer. The idea behind all this was to excite the cash-paying customers sufficiently so that they would pay for a ticket the following week. When this wrestler realized that I wasn't going to say anything if the fans tore the place apart, he became worried and said: "Pappy, we'd better turn off the heat, this crowd is going crazy."

Then I needled him: "Oh, come on, let's build it up just a little bit more."

He said: "To hell with you, there isn't a cop in the joint, we're going to 'finish' right now."

So the main event and the evening were wound up, I thought. It was just another tag-team match with two baby-faces against two heels. The baby-faces (guys with hair and youth) were beaten by every piece of foul play and skulduggery known to man. The heels (balding men with fat bellies) had triumphed. The arena was a holocaust—a bedlam. Wadded-up paper cups, because the fans aren't permitted to keep bottles for obvious reasons, women's shoes, and other non-lethal weapons came sailing into the ring.

The heels were going up an aisle to the dressing room back to back, so that the fans who were now a mob couldn't jump them from behind. The baby-faces who pretended to be demolished and would never speak to the heels again were not far behind them—to protect their play-acting buddies in case things got too rough for them.

The referee was waiting in the falling debris in the ring, as usual, waiting for the wrestlers to open a path in the aisle leading to the dressing room. Prior to my reaching the dressing-room door my path became blocked by some oversized fan who had enough to drink to make him brave. In trying to work my way around this gent I soon found that I was surrounded by an infuriated mob, and the wrestlers were out of sight.

The safest thing to do was to get through as diplomatically as possible, I knew; I was an old hand at this. I had no fear of this big jerk and was itching to belt him, but I was also smart enough to know that if I didn't flatten him with one punch I would really be in trouble.

Whatever I did, it would have to be quick!

This big fellow seemed to know what I had in mind—and he wanted my blood. He wasn't going to attempt this with his own capable hands. He wasn't that type of hero. He was going to give the mob a chance to jump me by delaying my exit. I sensed all this.

The mob would do the job if he could stall me a few seconds. They would release all their pent-up hatred for every crooked public official they had ever known, such as mayors, policemen, congressmen, and what have you. So I said: "Come on, be a good guy, and get out of my way."

He answered: "Come on by, I'm not going to stop you."

I said: "Thanks," and started to pass. But instead of permitting me to pass he grabbed me, and I was forced to give him the knee to shake him loose.

This was all the encouragement the mob needed, and I felt someone trying to jump on my back. The same thoughts I had when I was shot down in the South Pacific came through my mind: "Wise guy, you finally got it, didn't you?"

My wife screamed: "Turn around, Greg!"

She had jerked some man from my back. I started a swing going as I wheeled about and planted it flush on the button of this man, who dropped like a steer in a slaughterhouse line.

It was only a matter of a few seconds before Franny and I were standing in the center of a circle of fallen fans. About that time the eight wrestlers came back to help. After all this commotion there wasn't a scratch on my body other than a few skinned knuckles, but Franny had lost a couple of her precious fingernails, and some dame had sunk her teeth into a wrestler's arm while he was pulling me off the guy who had stopped me.

One might gather that all the fans were alike, but this is far from true. However, it was obvious that most of them used these matches for emotional releases, or believed that the purchase of a ticket entitled them to act along with the paid performers. Outside of a few people who seemed to laugh throughout the entire program, no matter how we acted, the bulk of the fans were mousy-looking people who appeared henpecked. They looked like they spent five or six days each week saying to their boss, or to a mate, yes sir and no sir. The type of people who felt like they had to laugh at a joke whether it was funny or not, just because somebody told it. But these people changed once the matches started; they were different persons completely. They would yell what they were going to do to the referee and the heels after the matches, just like they were sure of themselves for the first time in their lives. Some of these milquetoast creatures would take off their glasses and pull off their coats, shaking their fists in anger. Yet they were confident that their threats, swearing, and actions were never going beyond the ring ropes.

One night, out of a clear blue sky, one of the wrestlers started another one of our conversations that had nothing to do with wrestling. As a matter of fact, very few of them did. He said:

"Pappy, did you realize that wrestling fans had such stupid faces before you started refereeing?"

"No, I didn't. It's a pity my psychiatrist couldn't work in my place some night."

"How's that, Pappy?"

"My God, he'd find enough customers in one arena to last him a lifetime."

"I have a more horrible thought than yours."

I asked: "Yeah, what is it?"

"Look at them again. Then stop and think that each one has a vote, and that it counts as much as yours or mine."

"I see what you mean. Nauseating, isn't it?"

Sometimes one of the wrestlers would get to laughing when he was supposed to be registering pain or anger, so his opponent would cover his face with his body somehow. He would have to pretend he had some kind of new hold, or something, until the laughter died down.

The largest part of our audience was out of sight, the television fan. However, many of these would send in complaints to various addresses. The Athletic Commission would answer some of this mail, but the majority was unsigned for obvious reasons, or needed no answer. But when some of the more persistent folks got a letter into the governor's office—now, then, that was a horse of a different color.

To begin with, a governor usually doesn't give one Nippon Rising Sun about anything but votes. He weighs everything in his mind against so many votes—a unit of measure with a man in that position. The fact that some voters are crazy doesn't make a particle of difference; it is his vote that counts.

Because it was mandatory that all wrestling had to be announced several times as an exhibition during every television show, about all the governor's office had to do was send a mimeographed letter emphasizing this to some stupe. But no, the votes. The commission secretary gets the bright idea of having the referees answer these crackpots whose important-sounding letterheads had reached the governor's office—to take any "heat" off His Lordship.

The few I did answer were much the same, with a copy

mailed to the Athletic Commission, and an extra copy marked for the governor's office. Being a "patsy" in the ring was of my own choosing, but I have always balked when somebody else tried to make one out of me. Perhaps the few letters I did answer were sufficient, I don't know, because there never was any response from any address.

The commission stopped passing the buck to me when they read their copies. Whether they ever forwarded the governor his copies, I don't know, and care less. But the most amazing thing about these letters and their personal slurs is that not one of these mentioned a single word about my drinking, which was no doubt the most damning thing in my character.

My wife dreaded this hobby of mine, and pleaded with me to referee differently or to quit. But I couldn't seem to stop this part of my life any more than I could drinking. They went hand in glove. Refereeing doesn't affect some people the way it did me, but, by the same token, neither does alcohol. Perhaps, because I wasn't capable of controlling my own immature emotions, I was taking sadistic delight in fooling around with thousands of other human beings' emotions—such as violence, fear, hatred, and even passion—but violence seemed to be my pet.

About four years ago I was forced to give up my hobby, but not because anyone asked me to leave. The most powerful thing that I had run into up to date, alcohol, had made up my mind for me.

I had reached the point where I knew that I could work the entire card and not even sober up for the main event. This is the only reason I stopped refereeing.

CHAPTER **37**

GREEK LEGEND IS very applicable to my past, for it was as though a Minotaur was gradually taking possession of my mind and body. The tales of my black-outs that my friends told about after some of my drunks were so horrible that I had to believe that they were fables in order to consider myself sane.

Another vent was the sympathetic feeling I had for the so-called minority groups. Rooting for the underdog is more or less prevalent in us all, I guess. But whether these minority groups were large or small made no difference, I was attached to them all. And they seemed attached to me—more or less—in common bond. For I have been taken home, or taken care of, by the very rich, the very poor, the Catholic, the Jew, black men, brown men, yellow men, and red men. And invariably, in so many words, I recalled their self-pity for being what they were. It is logical to assume that my company brought some of this out.

My case was different from any of theirs, I thought. In fact, I didn't see how any of them had a right to indulge in feeling sorry for themselves. But they were probably helped somewhat by taking care of me—if nothing other than by comparison. I didn't have to be born into any minority group because I was the kind of a person who made his own. Some people might

380

term my actions as an effort to be exclusive—but I don't. Unless, of course, exclusiveness is synonymous with unhappiness. I never found peace of mind in whatever I was seeking for forty-two years.

It seemed to be inevitable that, when I finally found steady employment, it would be in the alcoholic beverage business. It was, and I became a draught-beer salesman.

During those six years with the brewery I had to force myself to sober up countless times by sheer determination, so I would not lose this special job. If I had used the same amount of effort in flying, I would have been the first man to fly to the moon.

During the brief spells when I was sober I had better-than-average sales, so my employers held me on in the hope that someday I might see the light. They raised my salary three times, gave me special assignments, in fact, they did everything except the right thing—they should have fired me.

While I was employed by the brewery I had a lengthy session with a competent psychiatrist who called in consultants much as though I had the first head ever to have been pickled in alcohol. But they found no answer for me.

Many an early morning when I arrived home by taxicab I discovered that somebody had slipped religious literature into my pockets while I was blacked out. But I wanted no part of religion. I feared that religion would make me so pure if it cured my drinking that I would never want to do anything I considered pleasant.

Somewhere in the back of my mind I had hopes that science would someday develop a pill, or something, to make me a social drinker like other people. Finally I came to the conclusion that I had about as much chance of becoming a social drinker as I would in starting a new political party in the Kremlin. I resigned from the brewery in the spring of 1955 because I was sick and tired of drinking, and everything that goes with it.

A few days after this two well-known men whom I knew only by names and pictures dropped over to my home and had a long chat with me. They had had problems with alcohol at one time, but both of them had been sober and happy for years. I

listened to their stories and somehow thought that they had
lived part of my life.

For several months I remained sober by merely talking to
these two gentlemen occasionally, then for some reason I felt
so good that I thought I would try a drink just to see if it
would bother me.

This time I awakened in some unfamiliar room, so ghastly
ill that I felt I couldn't sit up. I must have looked like death
warmed over because I was flat on my back on a bed with nothing over me but a sheet. The lights were on, and I hoped that
this would turn out to be a bad dream. As soon as I heard foot-
steps and voices and somebody opening the door to this room, I
knew that it was no dream. A man and a woman were talking,
but I couldn't recognize either one, so I closed my eyes in a
futile attempt to hide from my visitors.

The woman said: "What gives with this?"

The man answered: "Damned if I know. But he looks like
he's left this world some time ago."

The woman pulled back my sheet and tried to feel my pulse,
dropping some hot cigarette ashes on my arm, but I didn't
flinch because I didn't have enough strength to. There was considerable alarm in her voice when she repeated: "Speak to me,
speak to me."

"Hello," I said, and slowly opened my eyes.

"Thank God, he's alive."

Why all the concern for me was beyond me because I had not
the slightest idea who she was, but I blubbered out: "Gosh,
you're so *nice* to me—and I hardly *know* you."

Just how nutty can you get? This was it! As soon as I could
get some coffee down, I was back to my sober-drunk friends,
willing to do business their way. I asked: "How can I stay sober
and happy?"

"You have to progress spiritually, otherwise you will drink
again."

"How on earth is a guy like me ever going to progress spiritually, I'd like to know?"

"By meeting with us several times each week, and helping
others to stay sober."

This happened pretty close to three years ago and I haven't had a drink since, simply because I like their way of life a lot better than I ever thought I liked to drink. Otherwise there would be absolutely no reason for living the way I am.

In my lengthy career of violence and fighting this was the first time I ever won by being counted out—by admitting to myself that I was powerless—for a change.

As I live my life from day to day as best I can, past character defects rise to the surface, and I am now able to understand and cope with them. And I find myself gradually joining up with society—something to which I never belonged in my past life.

People never even suggest that I have a drink like I imagined they would at one time; others seem to turn them down for me. Most of the places I go, without a word being spoken, my drink is the first served. Even the waiters and waitresses, though I am not conscious of it, seem to bring me a large pot of coffee before they serve my non-alcoholic friends their drinks.

With the weight of the obsession to drink removed I find that I have time now to appreciate some wonderful things I never thought about before. For an example, birds have always held my interest, but now, when I watch them fly, I think of the Infinite Wisdom telling the birds to fly south before the first snow appears. They know exactly the course to the best feeding, even if they have never been there. And they don't choose their leader; they take turns leading. One bird leads for a spell, then another takes his place; anybody who wants to can lead for a while.

Birds don't get caught in an early winter, because they aren't alcoholic, for one thing. One bird doesn't say to another: "I ain't gonna fly south with Joe this year, because I think he's a drunken bum."

I have learned that it is good for me to be criticized, right though I think I may be. Others have a right to their opinions. This is the only way any of us can progress.

Some are going to doubt the author's sanity. They shall be partially correct, for, God knows, I have practiced insanity on numerous occasions for twenty years. But the most beautiful part of it all—I am the guy who knows it.

But my past is not one of regret, for I can look back and chuckle at many things I wouldn't have done if I hadn't been a drunk. These memories come in mighty handy because it has been said: "Time doth make monks of us all."

If this story were to have a moral, then I would say: "Just name a hero and I'll prove he's a bum."